Motivating Students

25 Strategies to Light the Fire of Engagement

Solution Tree | Press

a division of

Solution Tree

Carolyn Chapman

Nicole Vagle

555 North Morton Street
Bloomington, IN 47404
800.733.6786 (toll free) / 812.336.7700
FAX: 812.336.7790

email: info@solution-tree.com
solution-tree.com

Visit **go.solution-tree.com/instruction** to download the reproducibles in this book.

Printed in the United States of America

14 13 12 11   3 4 5

FSC
Mixed Sources
Product group from well-managed
forests and other controlled sources
Cert no. SW-COC-002283
www.fsc.org
© 1996 Forest Stewardship Council

Library of Congress Cataloging-in-Publication Data

Chapman, Carolyn, 1945-
  Motivating students : 25 strategies to light the fire of engagement / Carolyn Chapman, Nicole Vagle.
    p. cm.
  Includes bibliographical references and index.
  ISBN 978-1-935249-78-8 (perfect bound) -- ISBN 978-1-935249-79-5 (library edition) 1.
Motivation in education. 2. Effective teaching. I. Vagle, Nicole. II. Title.
  LB1065.C43 2011
  370.15'4--dc22
                                        2010043824

Solution Tree
Jeffrey C. Jones, CEO & President

Solution Tree Press
President: Douglas M. Rife
Publisher: Robert D. Clouse
Vice President of Production: Gretchen Knapp
Managing Production Editor: Caroline Wise
Copy Editor: Sarah Payne-Mills
Proofreader: Elisabeth Abrams
Cover and Text Designer: Amy Shock

Education is not the filling of a pail,
but the lighting of a fire.

—William Butler Yeats

Acknowledgments

With immense gratitude we embarked on this journey involving the creation of a book to facilitate conversations about motivating and engaging students. The many amazing educators, authors, friends, and family who have believed in us, influenced our thinking, and supported us inspire the ideas offered in this practical resource.

We would like to thank our husbands, Jim and Mark, for their patience, grace, and loving advice throughout the process. This includes, but is not limited to, the many grueling conversations, the hours of reading drafts, and the much-needed words of encouragement.

Our thanks to Nicole's children, Maya, Rhys, and Chase, for their patience, understanding, and love during times when Mom was creating and writing. May you always be inspired and motivated to learn!

There are countless friends, family, and colleagues who have supported and inspired us in our work both separately and together. It goes without saying that we will miss naming very important people. It would be remiss not to mention a few people. Carolyn is grateful for her good friend and colleague, Rita King. Nicole shares credit for the successful completion of this project with Abby Attias; her parents, Tom and Judy Dimich; Laura Duffee; Cassandra Erkens; Kay Gregory; Vilma Guevara; Cyndie Hays; Tom Hierck; Tammy Heflebower; Elizabeth Palomino; and Yaquia Walker.

We would also like to extend our deepest thanks to Jeff Jones and the incredible staff at Solution Tree for facilitating the creation of this work. Thank you to Douglas Rife for believing in us and making the vision of this book a reality. Your unending support and friendship have made our first book with Solution Tree something to celebrate. We appreciate Claudia Wheatley for initiating the match made in heaven, this duo writing team. We extend immense gratitude to Gretchen Knapp and Sarah Payne-Mills for the hours of reading, revising, and editing to make this book a useful and inspiring contribution to the field.

Visit **go.solution-tree.com/instruction** to download the reproducibles in this book.

Table of Contents

6

Ensuring Learning

7

Keeping the Flame Burning!

About the Authors

Carolyn Chapman is an international education consultant, author, and teacher. She has taught in classrooms at all levels, from kindergarten to college. Her interactive, hands-on professional development sessions focus on many of the key components from her best-selling books. Carolyn works closely with educators throughout the country to ensure lifelong success in students of all ages and learning levels.

Carolyn has authored and coauthored many publications on differentiated instruction, literacy, multiple assessments, multiple intelligences, and the brain-compatible classroom. She is coauthor of the landmark book *Differentiated Instructional Strategies*.

Nicole Vagle is an educator, author, and consultant. Her passion for education and lifelong learning has led her to extensively explore and implement quality practices in school improvement, all in the spirit of facilitating student learning. As a middle and high school English teacher, Nicole worked to inspire and engage all students. As a high school reform specialist, she worked closely with school and district staff to support teacher collaboration and student learning. As a consultant, Nicole is working and learning with educators to facilitate and empower a school culture in which all students find success.

Nicole is the author of two chapters in assessment anthologies: "Inspiring and Requiring Learning" in *The Teacher as Assessment Leader* and "Finding Meaning in Numbers" in *The Principal as Assessment Leader*.

Introduction

Teachers already use innovative strategies to promote engagement. In fact, they work tirelessly to design new ways to increase learners' achievement and students *are* learning. Growth in the use of technology, standards, and quality instructional practices informed by assessment has made a big difference! Still, educators struggle daily with unmotivated students.

How do we motivate students who don't care? What do we do when a student refuses to participate or forgets to hand in homework? In our classrooms, we have all seen students who are daydreaming, doodling, fidgeting, staring blankly, tapping, humming, texting, or even resisting instruction. Sound familiar? This age-old scenario remains a critical issue for educators today. Disengaged students can zap the energy from teachers and throw a classroom into chaos. The focus of the classroom quickly shifts from igniting a love of learning to putting out the fires of misbehavior.

Successful educators use "the magical moments of best teaching practices" (Barkley, 2007, p. ix) to turn flickers of interest into a roaring desire to learn. Learning is contagious and spreads when motivated, passionate teachers engage students with relevant, interesting topics that are essential for student success. These teachers build relationships by getting to know their students' interests, strengths, learning tendencies, and prior knowledge. They create an engaging environment that is welcoming by offering diverse and challenging learning opportunities that foster a desire to learn. These magical moments occur in classroom communities that clearly define and describe the learning goals for students, make learning a fun adventure, promote student choice and control, and ensure success. This type of classroom builds trust and instills in students a sense of efficacy, or a belief in their own capacity to learn. Engaged learners link their acquired knowledge, backgrounds, and experiences to the concepts being taught. A teacher who fosters learning connections for students, bridging their interests, experiences, and prior knowledge will see this flame ignite and take hold. Clearly, motivation is a key component in meeting our ultimate goal of student success in schools today!

How to Use This Book

Many factors influence motivation, making engaging learners a profoundly complex task. Later, we articulate critical factors and describe what they look like and how they impact student motivation. However, what fuels student motivation—to learn, to try, to engage, to get excited—is different for each student.

What can teachers do when students are seemingly lazy, off task, volatile, or disinterested? Based on current research, years of experience, and conversations with educators, this resource is designed to provide teachers with twenty-five practical, effective strategies that can be adapted to motivate a whole class or an individual student. While we say and believe, "All students can learn!" *Motivating Students* offers tools that will help us *show* with evidence that all students really *are* learning. Figure I.1 illustrates our framework for motivating students and lighting the fire of engagement.

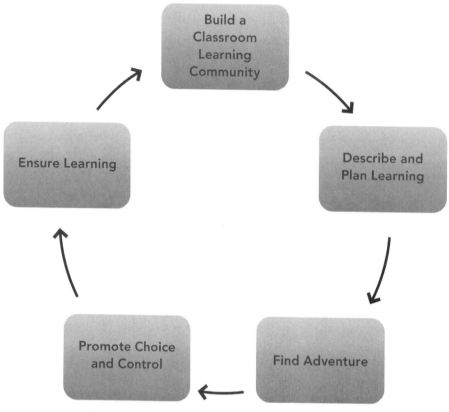

Figure I.1: The motivation framework.

Chapter 1 lays the groundwork by defining motivation, exploring the research, explaining influential factors, describing common unmotivated learners, and providing a self-assessment for teachers to reflect on their current motivational practice.

Chapters 2–6 discuss in detail each aspect of the motivation framework and outline twenty-five strategies to employ based on the root causes of particular unmotivated behaviors. In many cases, of course, these factors are interdependent. For each strategy, we describe its purpose and rationale, identify tips and traps for planning and implementation purposes, and finally provide detailed, specific activities to put the strategy into practice.

- Chapter 2 offers strategies for *building a classroom learning community*, including knowing your students' interests and learning styles, being culturally responsive, building relationships with and among students, and setting clear rules and expectations.

- Chapter 3 explains the power of *describing and planning learning* in order to hold high expectations for all students, make connections that provide relevance, and offer quality assignments and assessments.

- Chapter 4 identifies strategies for *finding adventure* by using irresistible hooks and clever closures, capitalizing on technology, playing games, spicing up activities, and celebrating success.

- Chapter 5 focuses on *promoting choice and control* for students, including providing quality choices, facilitating goal setting, and using the arts to engage learners.

- Chapter 6 is all about *ensuring learning* and provides strategies to engage students as partners in their learning through effective assessment practices, probing questions, descriptive feedback, and targeted interventions.

Finally, chapter 7 summarizes the big picture, explores how teachers, administrators, school staff, parents, and others contribute to student motivation, and provides suggestions for some of educators' most frequently asked questions about motivation and engagement.

Each of the seven chapters closes with a *campfire talk*, in which key questions guide teachers in professional learning conversations with colleagues. Research on professional development suggests that a focused study on motivation and engagement yields more effective facilitation of motivation and engagement in the classroom (Martin & Dowson, 2009, p. 331):

> Participants [in a study on professional development on motivation] increased their practical knowledge about student motivation, were better able to identify and consider motivational problems, and planned new instructional programs to sustain their students' motivation (see also Schorr, 2000). Similarly, Stipek et al. (1998) found that teachers participating in professional development focusing on student motivation were more likely to emphasize mastery and understanding in their teaching, to encourage student autonomy, and to create psychologically safer classroom environments. Participating teachers also made more accurate assessments of students' motivation—an important precursor to effective and targeted intervention (Martin, 2008a).

There is something magical and inspiring about the light from a campfire. These questions are intended to spark lively and engaging discussions that promote deep implementation of the research on best practice in motivation and engagement!

This book aims to provide innovative, research-based, classroom-proven strategies to engage learners. Read this book independently or with a team; focus on a section here or there to troubleshoot specific problems; or study it chapter by chapter to strategize how to create a culture primed for motivation. Our purpose is to inspire teachers, create an engaging classroom environment, and motivate students to become active, successful learners. Some ideas will be new and others familiar. Whatever the case, we hope you *use* these strategies to affect student motivation. Perhaps you have asked students about their interests in the past. But have you *used* their interests to plan instruction or make links and connections with their learning? We hope this book inspires not only fresh ideas but also new ways of using old ideas.

We all move in and out of being more or less motivating, and it is normal for some students to temporarily disengage now and then. But when students show a consistent lack of motivation, it is time to identify and address the root cause of their disengagement to create long-term changes in student behavior and motivation.

Give yourself a pat on the back each time a learner improves that internal desire of motivation. You are making a difference! We hope these enriching, high-energy ideas spark success and inspire educators to persevere to reach and teach every student.

Understanding Motivation

Motivation is an internal state or feeling that makes us want to act. Motivation is *intrinsic* when a person does something to gain a feeling of satisfaction, a sense of accomplishment, or deeper understanding. Motivation is *extrinsic* when a person does something to receive a specific reward such as money, a prize, food, a grade, or personal time.

Extrinsic motivation is often effective in the short term and can prompt students to comply or attend to a teacher's requests. A good grade, extra credit points, a favorite food, or an amusing toy creates positive feelings. Incentives like these propel students to acquiesce in the moment. In contrast, intrinsic motivation builds confidence and success that last beyond the moment. This intrinsic desire cultivates, ignites, and sustains lifelong learning. Daniel Pink (2009), in his book *Drive: The Surprising Truth About What Motivates Us*, describes studies across decades and disciplines that confirm the power of intrinsic motivation:

> In environments where extrinsic rewards are most salient, many people work only to the point that triggers the reward—and no further. So if students get a prize for reading three books, many won't pick up a fourth, let alone embark on a lifetime of reading—just as executives who hit their quarterly numbers often won't boost earnings a penny more, let alone contemplate the long-term health of their company. . . . However, when contingent rewards aren't involved, or when incentives are used with proper deftness, performance improves and understanding deepens. Greatness and nearsightedness are incompatible. Meaningful achievement depends on lifting one's sights and pushing toward the horizon. (p. 58)

Students are always motivated, but not necessarily toward what the teacher expects or wants. For example, some students may be more motivated to talk to a friend or walk about the room than follow directions, take copious notes, or participate in an activity.

Learners are inspired or discouraged for a variety of reasons. Consider when a teacher gives an assignment or a task; students who complete the assignment may:

- Understand the directions or the task
- Maintain confidence in their abilities
- Realize benefits of the activity
- Feel successful

- See personal relevance for future use
- Possess background knowledge to connect concepts
- Respect the teacher
- Want the grade

Students who do not complete the assignment may:

- Lack understanding of the directions or the task
- Have little or no confidence in their abilities
- Fear failure
- See no reason to complete the activity
- Lack background knowledge to connect concepts
- Have little or no respect for the teacher

For students, classroom appeal is a combination of what the teacher does, how the learning is framed, and how the student perceives the experience. Learners ask themselves: "Will the material be relevant, interesting, and important? Will I experience success?" Some students respond to an intriguing opening or a humorous story. Others need to see relevance or connections to the world or community before they will engage.

Suppose a group of adults decides to watch a serious documentary on television. Some people may have particular reasons to give their undivided attention to this program: perhaps they know the filmmaker personally. Others may have just found the title, the preview, or the topic intriguing. Ten or fifteen minutes into the program, only some viewers are still watching. For others, the documentary does not meet their expectations. Perhaps they feel it is a waste of time because the information is already familiar, too difficult to learn, presented in a boring way, or different from what was expected.

Consider your own classroom. Would students choose to stay through the lesson if they had a choice? While we can turn off the TV or go to another room if a program is no longer gripping, school is a different story. Students are not able to "turn off" the teacher, get up, and leave. Some students do, however, *flip the channel*. When learners become bored or frustrated, they are not motivated to continue with what the teacher expects. They turn their attention to their own worlds of daydreaming, talking to their neighbors, doodling on the desks, and so on.

According to Martin and Dowson (2009, p. 327), motivation is "a set of interrelated beliefs and emotions that influence and direct behavior" (Wentzel, 1999; see also Green, Martin, & Marsh, 2007; Martin, 2007, 2008a, 2008b). These beliefs and emotions are intensely personal. In our documentary example, some viewers felt positive and continued watching the program. For others, it produced a negative emotion, and they moved on to another activity. The same is true in the classroom. What influences one student to engage may cause another to shut down or tune out.

Given the complexity of motivating all learners, what are the causes of disengagement, and who is responsible for it? The student? The teacher? How many adults could attend to a lesson that did not hold their interest or seemed irrelevant to or disconnected from their world? A teacher must strive to make boring information interesting, challenging, and meaningful so learners yearn to listen, participate, and complete a task. Enticing content is only the beginning of the engagement issue. Let's face it—there are times when we have to do things we don't want to do. Learning to persevere through the mundane or the difficult is a valuable endeavor. Developing this perseverance is possible and probable when students learn through challenging, appealing, and rewarding experiences (Martin & Dowson, 2009). Learners keep on trying when they see where they are going and how they can get there.

When teachers effectively motivate students, they ignite an intrinsic desire to want to be in school and grow academically, cognitively, and emotionally.

How Does Motivation Affect Learning?

Motivation has been studied for decades. The research around it varies, depending on the focus of the study. For the purposes of this book, we explored the research on academic motivation and found both depth and breadth as it spans decades, cultures, age levels, and countries. As John Hattie (2009) notes in his synthesis of the research on motivation, "motivation is highest when students are competent, have sufficient autonomy, set worthwhile goals, get feedback, and are affirmed by others" (p. 48). Hattie's meta-analysis also notes the importance of exploring *demotivation*, or what shuts down a learner, such as "public humiliation, devastating test results, or conflicts with teachers or peers" (p. 48). We will address each of these findings with specific strategies in later chapters.

Clearly, relationships with teachers influence students' beliefs and values toward school and schoolwork. Motivation and engagement increase when teachers know their students and build trusting relationships. In addition, teachers who know their students develop interest and understanding of their cultures, beliefs, and values. Through these interactions, teachers build a community of learners and increases in motivation and engagement. Students with strong personal relationships with their teachers internalize the ways of being academically successful. Positive relationships with teachers and peers influence students' motivation to take on a task or activity. They also encourage students to achieve or learn something to gain satisfaction, such as fitting in with the group of peers, or to avoid something negative, like disappointing a parent or a teacher (Ryan & Deci, 2000; Barker et al., 2002; Dowson & McInerney, 2003).

This sense of belonging facilitates academic motivation. When students feel connected to the learning community, classroom, peers, school, or teachers, they are more likely to engage in schoolwork, try challenging tasks, engage in self-assessment, or analyze their understanding and mistakes (Meyer & Turner, 2002; Maslow, 1968; Glasser, 1999). Collaborative activities develop a positive learning community. Students who learn and work together feel more connected to their peers. Creating a classroom climate in which teacher-to-student and student-to-student relationships are fostered is integral to influencing academic motivation (Martin & Dowson, 2009; Martin, 2002, 2003).

When students experience quality relationships in school with both peers and adults, they not only perform better academically, their feelings of self-worth increase because they feel like valuable and contributing members of the community. Specific descriptions of students' progress also contribute to self-worth. The more students can identify their achievements in terms of learning, the greater their self-worth. This increase in self-worth helps students engage and try new and difficult challenges (Covington, 2002).

In fact, this sense of being self-directed, of working toward achievable goals, is critical. When students feel they have control over the outcome of any given situation, such as academic achievement, they seem to handle disappointment, demands, and fear of failure more productively (Martin, Marsh, & Debus, 2001). One way students begin to perceive a sense of control over their achievements is through positive reinforcement and feedback from the adults in their lives, such as parents, teachers, and other caregivers. In this scenario, students are receiving specific information describing their strengths. And motivating feedback also describes specific actions students can take to improve; this kind of success-oriented feedback facilitates positive emotions and a sense of hope. As a result, students are motivated because they know what to do and how to get there (Hattie & Timperley, 2007).

When students believe in themselves, expect success, and value their actions, motivation increases. Students' self-efficacy—belief in their own capacity to grow and positively affect their learning— *can* be nurtured through the actions of adults. When teachers believe in students and attribute their successes to effort, it fosters their abilities to achieve. On the flipside, when teachers attribute a lack of achievement to a lack of ability, students may perceive that nothing they do will make a difference, resulting in unmotivated behavior (Hareli & Weiner, 2000, 2002; Martin, 2005, 2008a). In these studies, when adults held positive expectations for students, motivation and engagement interventions were more successful.

Motivation and engagement research is similar for at-risk students. Strong relationships are important for all students, but essential to reach and motivate at-risk students (Martin 2006; Ladson-Billings, 1995). When teachers provide challenging opportunities and hold positive expectations for their students, motivation increases. When we believe that it is possible for our students to achieve, more students *will* achieve.

Why Are Some Students Unmotivated?

When students act unmotivated, their behaviors and attitudes are usually a smokescreen for other problems. If a student refuses to do an assignment, the teacher may enter a power struggle with the student to force him or her to complete it—thus missing the real issue. Perhaps the student doesn't understand what to do or doesn't see the work as relevant. Students only become motivated when educators identify and address those hidden issues. Table 1.1 describes possible *impactors* of motivated or unmotivated learners. In this context, impactors are personal views, feelings, and mind-sets of students that influence their motivation.

A teacher's response to unmotivated students must go beyond obtaining simple compliance and take into account and attend to the possible *reasons* for the disengagement. Long-term engagement occurs when educators address the underlying issue as well as the obvious behavior.

The following factors are significant influences on motivation. They are both the potential causes of unmotivated behavior as well as the key to engaging students in our classrooms. The subsequent chapters offer practical strategies to address these factors:

- Interests and passions
- Trust and belonging
- Strengths
- Efficacy and belief
- Adventure

- Challenge
- Connections
- Curiosity
- Choice and control
- Outside influences
- Past experiences

Table 1.1: Common Learner Impactors

A Motivated Learner . . .	An Unmotivated Learner . . .
Yearns or desires to learn—This student wants to be in school and looks forward to going.	Feels school is boring and offers nothing of interest—This learner does not like school, dreads going to class, and has lost any desire to learn.
Feels connected to the learning community in the school and classroom—This learner feels socially accepted with all his or her strengths, challenges, weaknesses, flaws, and quirks.	Feels isolated, disconnected, and rejected from the learning community—This learner may walk through an entire day and neither talk to nor be acknowledged by anyone. This learner has few friends and is just trying to get through the day.
Feels like a valuable and contributing member of the school and classroom community—This learner feels important in the eyes of his or her classmates and teachers.	
Feels school is a place that provides environmental comforts such as heat or coolness, food, and physical safety—This student feels his or her physical needs are met in a safe and inviting environment.	Feels like a failure with nothing to offer or contribute to the school and classroom community—This student lacks confidence and feels disconnected from the classroom or school.
Understands the access and power school has to help him or her be successful in the future—This student feels that school helps him or her achieve present and future goals.	Worries about physical and emotional safety—This student may fight, argue, and feel picked on. Most often, he or she feels more comfortable elsewhere.
Believes school is a helpful place that increases the learners' understanding—This student trusts that teachers and school resources will help him or her learn. Often, this student has the proper background and experience and so is ready to learn. This learner expects success and usually finds it.	Feels school is irrelevant—This student believes that success in school will not help him or her be successful in the future.
	Believes school is a place that doesn't help him or her—This learner doesn't feel he or she receives the assistance needed for success.

Interests and *passions* are personal to an individual. A student may disengage because he or she is not interested in the topic or does not see relevance. Passion is different for everyone, but how an educator frames the topic and connects to students can spark interest and foster motivation.

An atmosphere of *trust* and *belonging* creates the conditions for learning and engagement. When students feel safe, they become willing to take necessary risks that lead to deeper engagement and increased learning; they may even admit they care! In the absence of trust and belonging, some learners feel uncomfortable and disengage.

Operating from a place of *strength* builds confidence. Students often hear about what they can't do but little about what they can do. They feel empowered and see the potential for progress when teachers help them identify their strengths and show them what they already know and can do. In contrast, when students only see their weaknesses, they often lose hope and stop trying.

Students with a sense of *efficacy,* or a belief that the effort they put forth will result in success, achieve more. When students lack efficacy, they see little reason to try because they do not believe it will help them be successful.

A sense of *adventure* in learning is a great motivator. Laughter and excitement energize students and teachers, relieve tension and stress, and promote relaxation. In this relaxed state, learners take risks and see hope for the future.

Students also need *challenge.* Challenging situations stretch the mind and stimulate thinking. Students disengage when they feel bored or see the information at hand as redundant. There is intrigue and satisfaction in searching for a solution to a problem.

Students engage when their learning goals, community, and experiences *connect.* For many students, the school day is filled with isolated events. This fragmentation occurs in classrooms when students do not see the bridges among the learning goals, their home lives, their community, and their personal experiences. Some students have learned the role school plays in their lives and have accepted what it offers. For others, such fragmentation leads to confusion and withdrawal.

Curiosity is a natural motivator. From a very young age, children begin asking, "Why?" and wondering, "What if?" Discussions, debates, questions, and sharing times are essential parts of learning. Many times, schools give answers instead of providing opportunities for discovery, questioning, invention, exploration, and experimentation. When educators structure opportunities for students to wonder, motivation is sure to follow.

Choice sends the message that teachers recognize there are differences in how students learn, and those differences do not determine success or failure. In addition, when students have some *control* over how they demonstrate their learning or the path they take to understand, they become more independent learners who trust their own decisions and begin to rely on themselves. Without some choice and control, students lack ownership independently to recognize what is working and change what is not.

Outside influences—what students experience outside of school—are beyond the control of the teacher, yet they often dramatically influence the learning that occurs in the classroom. Some students go home to an empty house or an evening of babysitting younger siblings; families may have medical difficulties, personal struggles, or financial troubles. Students may walk into class after a big fight with a friend or an unpleasant incident on the playground. These stressful life situations influence motivation and engagement; identifying them will help teachers look at the whole picture and plan for what they control in the lives of their learners.

Past experiences can elicit positive or negative memories of school. Many students quickly identify reasons for not liking school. Previous teachers are often blamed for such negative attitudes and beliefs. To change this attitude toward school and motivate students, teachers must show them that learning is possible and they can do it.

The Effect of Standardized Testing and Accountability on Motivation

In this era of standardized testing and accountability, the goal in many schools has shifted from learning to achievement on a standardized test. While standardized testing plays a role in accountability and is one way to measure achievement, it is not the only measure of learning or success in schools. In the absence of an alternative efficient measure, educators often rely on a test. In turn, this single measure drives the educational work of classrooms, schools, districts, jurisdictions, and government. The level of stress increases monumentally on students and educators, negatively impacting achievement, confidence, and engagement (Chapman & King, 2009c).

Accountability measures and stress do not drive teachers or students to increased achievement. Some teachers replace valuable, intriguing content instruction with teaching testing strategies and basic facts a month prior to the standardized test. Still others align everything they do the entire year toward "the test." Once the week of testing arrives, students and teachers alike are tired and stressed. Test taking is not a motivating activity. Many students are so nervous during this assessment ordeal that it affects their ability to do well (Chapman & King, 2009c; Allensworth, Correa, & Ponisciak, 2008). Position the standardized test in context, and give it only the attention it deserves—as one snapshot of achievement at one moment in time—and use it in the way it was intended. Statisticians note that making profound decisions about students and their learning based on one measure is not an appropriate use of that information.

Many of the schools struggling to meet the accountability requirements eliminate "extras" like recess from the schedule. This is hurting our children. Every child needs free play or personal choice time built into the schedule of each day. In addition to the obvious benefits of free play and personal choice time—to get exercise, to grow socially—free time can actually make academic performance improve (Chapman & King, 2009b). The arts and other high-interest areas have suffered cuts in some schools. However, in other schools, teachers are finding natural connections to the arts, woodworking, and technology, providing meaningful opportunities to read, write, and problem solve. High-interest activities and high achievement are not an "either or" proposition. Educators can meet our students' academic needs *through* them.

W. James Popham (2001), in *The Truth About Testing*, describes the phenomenon of some schools inundating students with test-preparation items. The closer the item resembles a high-stakes test, the better—or so says the marketing from companies that promise student test scores will improve if their programs are implemented. Some schools and educators succumb to the tremendous pressure to improve their achievement on a single standardized test at one moment in time. Popham (2001) writes:

> But incessant "skill and drill" often turns into "drill and kill"—that is, such repetitious instructional activities tend to deaden students' genuine interest in learning. All excitement and intellectual vibrancy that students might encounter during a really interesting lesson are driven out by a tedious, test-fostered series of drills. In fact, one fairly certain way of telling whether a high-stakes test is a winner or loser is to see if unexciting drill activities can actually raise students' test scores. If so, the test is almost certainly inappropriate—measuring only low-level outcomes. . . . I have spoken with a number of teachers who admitted that pressures to boost test scores in their district are leading to a drill-focused form of schooling that inclines both disadvantaged students and second-language students to want to give up on school. If learning is no fun, and if all teachers do is drill, it's not surprising that some students seek a permanent recess. (pp. 21–22)

The stress educators feel about these tests is also felt by our students. In *Research-Based Strategies to Ignite Student Learning*, Judy Willis (2008) explores how stress and emotions affect learning. She states that schools must become a safe haven for students in this stressful world of today: "Enthusiastic learners retain more than a stressed learner" (p. 58). While inadvertent, the stress placed on students in high-stakes testing environments can have adverse effects on their achievement, their learning, and their motivation (Hattie, 2009; Ma, 1999). Instruction needs to be upbeat, interesting, and challenging for students. Instruction that solely emphasizes test preparation does students more harm than good.

Motivating the disengaged students requires educators to identify the factors that are getting in the way and plan our strategies in light of these factors. While teachers do not control every aspect of a student's life, they do have control over their teaching and classroom learning.

Types of Unmotivated Learners

Just like candy, students come in different wrappers that create expectations about who they are on the inside. Sometimes the wrapper is a label assigned explicitly or implicitly by previous teachers, schools, peers, or old report cards; sometimes the wrapper lingers because of a student's words, actions, facial expressions, or attitudes toward learning. But labels are deceiving. Each learner is unique despite a label that may, at first glance, look familiar. Educators must look beyond the wrappers that unmotivated learners wear. Table 1.2 describes seven wrappers unmotivated students often wear (you may know of others), using the three-step protocol for engagement: (1) describe the behaviors and attitudes that lead you to believe the student is unmotivated—the "wrapper," (2) determine the contributing factors or root causes—"What's inside the wrapper?," and (3) plan and employ strategies to intentionally address those factors—"How can we reach the learner?" Use the twenty-five strategies in this book to motivate all students!

There are many personal reasons why students are not motivated to do what we expect them to do, and of course, each student is unique. The wrappers described are just some of the ways we see disengagement expressed in our classrooms. Students may wear one wrapper one day or in one class, and another wrapper another day or in another class. The wrappers are tools to help us describe what we are seeing so that we can more intentionally plan for motivation and engagement. The solutions we have described here are general guidelines on how to address some common issues. There is a way to reach every student, and educators must find it!

Table 1.2: Seven Wrappers of Unmotivated Learners

What's Inside the Wrapper?	How Can We Reach the Learner?
"I Don't Care"	
On first glance, this student is:	Assign exciting tasks.
Lazy	Show that the material has personal benefit.
Disrespectful	Show connections to the student's world.
Unresponsive	Provide choice for her to show what she knows.
Rude	Ask for her input.
This student may:	Determine her level of proficiency and address her misunderstandings.
Not understand the material	
Feel like a failure	
Lack self-worth	
Feel disconnected from the school and peers	
Be bullied or bully others	
Be concerned about other things	

What's Inside the Wrapper?	How Can We Reach the Learner?
Stressed Out	

What's Inside the Wrapper?	How Can We Reach the Learner?
On first glance, this student is:	Get to know the student.
Worried	Listen to her thoughts and ask how she is feeling.
Flushed	Use questions to guide her to completing the task.
Concerned	Be explicit about the student's knowledge to provide her with a sense of accomplishment.
Overwhelmed	
Disruptive	Do something unexpected! Sing or dance to put a smile on her face.
Unwilling to participate	
This student may:	
Be confused about how to complete an assignment	
Be confused about how to participate	
Have problems at home or with peers	

Daydreaming	
On first glance, this student is:	Provide a new activity to get the daydreamer involved.
Doodling	Provide choice.
Staring out the window	Show the lesson's relevance and connection.
Looking through the teacher	Get him talking to peers.
This student may:	Talk to the student to get to the source of the off-task behavior.
Have his mind on other things	
Have anxiety about a peer, another teacher, or family member	Let him know you care.
Be anticipating an exciting event	Probe with specific questions.
Be bored or frustrated with the material	
Be confused and not understand the content	

"I Don't Know"	
On first glance, this student is:	Break the standards into parts, and share the learning goal with him.
Shrugging his shoulders	Tailor assessment and instruction, so he understands the steps toward success.
Giving you a blank look	
Looking at his shoes	Encourage him to participate in the lecturette.
This student may:	Provide guided practice.
Not have the proper background	Adjust assignments to give him another chance to prove his knowledge.
Lack prerequisite knowledge and skills	
Struggle to make connections	Provide choice for the learner to use a different modality to show what he knows.
Struggle with the content	
Remove himself from uncomfortable situations	Help the student analyze his mistakes and make adjustments.
Look physically present, but isn't there mentally or emotionally	Assure him that mistakes are OK.
Need more time to grasp the question or task	Provide think time.

continued →

What's Inside the Wrapper?	How Can We Reach the Learner?
Been There, Done That	
On first glance, this student is:	Scaffold activities to meet this learner's needs.
Capable of succeeding	Raise expectations by planning one step beyond the basic lesson.
Bored	
Rebellious	Provide an alternative independent assignment.
Careless	Provide choice.
Inattentive	Use the same standard or skill to create a more challenging assignment.
Off task	
Disruptive or distracting	Get to know her, and establish a relationship.
This student may:	Preassess to discover her understanding.
Not be challenged enough	Assure her that it is OK not to know.
Be working on tasks that are too easy	Establish a classroom culture that shows that mistakes are OK.
Feel responsible for "knowing everything"	
Not want others to know she doesn't know the material	
Defeatist	
On first glance, this student is:	Offer time for reflection after explaining a task or assignment.
Emotional	Plan specific strategies of how to cope with stress.
Failing	Build the student's confidence through teaching positive self-talk and giving effective feedback.
Making excuses	
Blaming someone else for his actions	Make success look possible.
Not participating	
This student may:	
Lack confidence	
Lack coping skills to counter his strong emotions and negative self-talk	
Think something is wrong with him because he doesn't understand	
Class Clown	
On first glance, this student is:	Seat this student so he doesn't have access to disrupt the whole class.
Disrupting the class	Determine his gaps in understanding.
Offering funny commentary	
Making silly gestures, faces, and sounds	Use the laughter to segue into an activity that allows students to talk to each other.
Amusing the class	Get students up and working at stations.
Pulling you into the fray	Pull him aside and provide specific reasons for why the behavior is not working.
This student may:	
Be bored	Call parents if the behavior gets too out of hand.
Struggle to sit still	
Be covering his misunderstanding of the content	

Who Is Responsible for Motivation?

While the decision resides in the student, the policies and practices of the school, teacher, and classroom influence that choice. We assert and firmly believe that there are many things an educator can do to support unmotivated learners and provide them with compelling and irresistible opportunities to engage. Jonathon Saphier (2005), in his chapter in *On Common Ground*, describes three messages teachers must send in order to motivate and engage students:

1 Learning is important and serious work.

2 I know you, the student, can do this.

3 I am not going to give up on you.

All students are motivated in some way—just not always in the way educators hope! Students may be more motivated to keep their heads down than to talk to a peer about the topic at hand. Unmotivated students may be exhausted from working, babysitting, homework, soccer practice, or simply the reality of life outside of school. These students are highly active but completely worn out by the time they settle down at desks for fifty minutes to listen to a teacher talk.

The most powerful motivation is intrinsic. It is inevitably up to an individual to decide whether to join in and participate in a class. So, if the decision to engage is left to the student, how does the teacher impact this choice? Some students yearn to learn something interesting, challenging, or inspiring. Some learners simply enjoy interacting and join in the activity or discussion to connect with their peers. In other cases, motivation comes from gaining approval from someone they respect and admire and want to make happy and proud.

With all of these possibilities, can a teacher really motivate students? Absolutely! We believe that students *want* to learn—even students who seemingly do not care. When they are invited, required, excited, pushed, safe, and interested, students *are* motivated to try, work hard, persevere, and eventually find success. Educators begin by exploring the disconnect students experience and intentionally building a bridge across that gap.

The three-step protocol for motivating students on page 20 provides concrete steps for teachers' individual or collaborative planning. Every student deserves to get fired up about his or her education. Learners need to experience school as profoundly valuable. There is no limit to the positive imprint a quality role model and an effective teacher have on the wellness, learning, and values of a student, often lasting beyond the scope of a school year or a course. Be the teacher who makes the difference.

Chapter 1 Campfire Talk

This chapter began the discussion of motivation, exploring what it is, how it is experienced, and what factors affect it. Discuss the following questions and activities in your professional learning community, department, grade-level team, or a staff meeting with colleagues.

1 What is motivation?

2 How does motivation occur?

3 Who is responsible for motivation, and how?

4 Review the research discussed in this chapter, and respond to the following questions:

- What is most compelling?

- What surprises you?

- In light of the research and your experience, what causes a lack of motivation?

- How could this research inform your practice?

5 Take the time to analyze your motivational practices, using the reproducible Self-Assessing Your Motivational Practice.

6 Plan how to address your focus areas. Your action plan may include reviewing the chapter of this book that is related to your area of focus. Consider sharing your strengths and personal best practices with your colleagues. If you are reading this book as part of a study group, consider sharing your goals and action plans with each other and checking in throughout the study.

7 Knowing your students is a prerequisite for intentional planning to increase their motivation and engagement. Spend a few days or class periods observing engaged and unmotivated students. Use the Three-Step Protocol for Motivating Students reproducible (page 20) to record your observations, then discuss with colleagues.

8 Review the wrappers of unmotivated learners, and identify possible root causes and strategies for each type of learner. Use the Understanding the Learners reproducible (page 22) to record your thoughts, then discuss with colleagues.

Self-Assessing Your Motivational Practice

Take inventory of your strategies for lighting the fire of engagement. The following statements list some of the most promising practices in motivating students, divided into sections for each element of our framework (page 2). Read each of the statements, then rate your understanding and implementation of the practice. After rating each statement, star your highest-rated section as your greatest strength. Circle your lowest-rated section as an area on which to focus your professional development and learning.

Rating Scale

4 = The fire is burning strongly! I do this frequently and with intention.

3 = The fire is lit! I sometimes do this.

2 = The wood is in place; fire is not yet lit! I know what this is, but I do not do it.

1 = There is no wood or fire! I do not know what this is or how to do it.

Building a Classroom Learning Community	1	2	3	4
1. I obtain knowledge of my students' interests and personalities.				
2. I assess my students' learning styles.				
3. I use what I know about students to plan instruction.				
4. I teach students how to pay attention to what helps them learn.				
5. I help students understand how I structure lessons and assignments to match their learning styles.				
6. I solicit student feedback on class activities and procedures.				
7. I gather knowledge of my students' cultural backgrounds and contexts.				
8. I create an environment and activities that reflect and respect the cultural backgrounds and contexts of my students.				
9. I build relationships with my students and help them build relationships with each other.				
10. I treat students with respect.				
11. I provide discipline and structure.				
12. I seek student input.				
13. I communicate clear expectations and directions.				
14. I quickly redirect disruptive behavior.				
15. I create a comfortable, clean, and welcoming classroom environment.				

Motivating Students © 2011 Solution Tree Press • solution-tree.com
Visit **go.solution-tree.com/instruction** to download this page.

Describing and Planning Learning	1	2	3	4
1. I prioritize the standards and learning objectives to emphasize the important content and throw out the garbage that wastes time.				
2. I write and share learning objectives in simple, easy-to-understand language for students.				
3. I create assignments with clear learning objectives that are aligned to the standards and assessments.				
4. I use formative assessment to measure students' progress toward the objectives.				
5. I make students think and problem solve.				
6. I ask students to brainstorm possible answers and defend their thinking instead of telling students the answer.				
7. I increase the level of complexity as students gain understanding.				
8. I create real-world connections with students' prior knowledge, experience, culture, and community.				
9. I co-create criteria and activities with students.				
10. I hold high and realistic expectations.				
Finding Adventure	1	2	3	4
1. I love teaching.				
2. I ooze with enthusiasm.				
3. I show passion for the content.				
4. I use irresistible hooks, clever closures, and humor to keep lessons fun.				
5. I use technology to engage learners.				
6. I use games to help students learn, review, and remember content.				
7. I create mystery and anticipation.				
8. I spice up the lesson. I go beyond direct instruction and worksheets.				
9. I celebrate successes, even the small ones.				
10. I plan for students to move around during instruction.				

Promoting Choice and Control	1	2	3	4
1. I provide quality choices in instructional activities, assessments, and tasks.				
2. I give students responsibility and make them feel important.				
3. I structure opportunities for students to set goals for progress on tasks or behaviors.				
4. I provide opportunities to celebrate student success, and I use rewards carefully.				
5. I integrate the arts into my lessons to engage students' different learning styles.				
Ensuring Learning	**1**	**2**	**3**	**4**
1. I use assessment before, during, and after instruction.				
2. I teach students to self-assess.				
3. I ask and elicit quality questions.				
4. I require students to analyze their mistakes and revise their work.				
5. I give specific feedback by describing what students know and what they need to do next to get better.				
6. I give specific praise that tells students what they have done well.				
7. I provide time for students to recognize quality and not quality work, review their work, recognize their own mistakes, and self-assess.				

Three-Step Protocol for Motivating Students

This template is designed to help you follow the three-step intentional planning process for increasing motivation and engagement: (1) describe the behaviors and attitudes that lead you to believe the student is unmotivated, (2) determine the contributing factors or root causes, and (3) plan and employ strategies to intentionally address those factors.

Student Name: _____

Step 1. Describe the behaviors and attitudes that lead you to believe the student is unmotivated. Check boxes that describe your general impressions, then detail what the student looks like, sounds like, acts like, and feels like.

- ○ lazy
- ○ bored
- ○ confused
- ○ giving up
- ○ frustrated

- ○ defiant
- ○ disrespectful
- ○ afraid of failure
- ○ angry
- ○ goofing off

- ○ underachieving
- ○ daydreaming
- ○ other _____

Looks Like	Sounds Like	Acts Like	Feels Like

How often does the disengaged behavior happen? Weekly, daily, hourly?

_____

_____

When does it occur?

_____

_____

What seems to trigger it?

_____

_____

When does it spread and escalate? What seems to escalate the behavior?

_____

_____

When does it slow down and de-escalate? What contributes to the de-escalation?

_____

_____

Step 2. Determine the contributing factors or root causes.

Possible Factors Influencing Behavior	Evidence

What other questions do you have about the root causes of the behavior?

_____

_____

What other evidence could you collect?

_____

_____

Who might have insight into the student's situation (the student, other teachers, parents, peers)?

_____

_____

Step 3. Plan and employ strategies to intentionally deal with the factors that are contributing to the behavior.

Describe your strategy:

Who's involved? What will each person do?

_____

_____

What materials or resources do you need?

_____

_____

When will you check in to see how it's going?

_____

_____

Understanding the Learners

Drawing on your reading and your experience, record the possible reasons students may wear the specific wrappers. Then, list your suggestions for improvement. Discuss your responses with colleagues.

The Wrappers	What are the possible factors at play with this particular learner?	What are possible strategies to reach this learner?
The "I Don't Care" Wrapper		
The Stressed-Out Wrapper		
The Daydreaming Wrapper		
The "I Don't Know" Wrapper		
The Been There, Done That Wrapper		
The Defeatist Wrapper		
The Class Clown Wrapper		

Building a Classroom Learning Community

Alex was a passionate and curious kindergartener. His first six weeks of school went just fine. He played with friends, listened to the stories, asked questions, and loved to make paper airplanes. But after those first six weeks, Alex started to act out during circle time. He seemed to have a hard time listening and transitioning to new activities. Though he had interacted well with his peers at the beginning of the school year, now he grabbed their toys and interrupted their play. His teacher tried talking to him, using nonverbal signals, giving consequences at home, communicating with his parents, and employing other strategies with short-lived success. After a few days, the behavior would reoccur.

After thinking about Alex's possible motivations for acting out, his teacher decided to try making a conscious point of positively connecting with Alex each morning as he walked in the door. She also spent time talking with him at certain times throughout the day. On the third day of his teacher actively checking in, Alex flung himself into her arms and gave her a great big hug. That night, he worked on a picture to give her the next day. Alex's teacher and parents saw the power of building a relationship after only three days! The positive relationship lasted throughout the year.

Even though this is a story about a kindergartener, it could happen with any student, at any age, with varying displays of emotion. Judy Willis (2008), who writes about educational neuroscience, challenges teachers to "build confidence by building community and connectedness" (p. 97). The relationships teachers have with their students significantly influence the culture of the classroom community and student motivation and engagement (Martin & Dowson, 2009; Ryan & Deci, 2000). This is true with learners of all ages. When learners feel connected to a community, a classroom, or a teacher, they have more confidence in their abilities, which increases their self-esteem and self-worth, traits linked to increased academic achievement (Ryan & Deci, 2000). When learners perceive that a teacher genuinely cares about, values, and accepts them, they begin to trust the teacher. Even when the teacher does something that frustrates or confuses a student, that student stays focused and persists longer, because he or she believes the teacher is acting with his or her best interests in mind. This sense of trust is part of building a strong community of learners.

The relationships among students are also important and integral to a thriving community. In *Visible Learning: A Synthesis of Over 800 Meta-Analyses Relating to Achievement*, John Hattie (2009) synthesizes an incredible number of studies incorporating millions of students. One of his findings notes, "A key factor in positive classroom climate is classroom cohesion—the sense that all (teachers and students) are working towards positive learning gains" (p. 103). When students and teachers are working together to learn and grow in a community of learners, this cohesion positively influences academic achievement.

In a classroom learning community, the teacher:

- Seeks to learn the interests, learning styles, beliefs, and strengths of each student
- Uses that knowledge to plan instruction, engage learning, and create relevance
- Fosters trust and belief in all students and their capacities to learn
- Builds quality relationships with and among students
- Makes students and their learning the center of classroom work
- Carefully chooses words and uses tone to instruct, redirect, and facilitate students

Teachers make a difference in the life of each student they teach every day. The five strategies in this chapter suggest ways to intentionally know students and build trust in the classroom community. When teachers capitalize on student interests, personalities, strengths, learning styles, and personal lives, the classroom learning community becomes a place where students are motivated to roll up their sleeves and engage in the work of learning.

Strategy 1:	Know Your Students' Interests, Personalities, and Beliefs
Strategy 2:	Discover How Your Students Learn Best
Strategy 3:	Be Culturally Responsive
Strategy 4:	Build Relationships With and Among Students
Strategy 5:	Set Clear Rules and Expectations

Strategy 1: Know Your Students' Interests, Personalities, and Beliefs

Building relationships with students is key in establishing a learning community that fosters motivation and engagement of all students (Martin, 2007). One important element of building these relationships is taking an interest in students. When teachers know students' interests, passions, pet peeves, and goals, they can begin to connect with them. All school personnel need to show that they care about each learner's successes and learning experiences. This support sends the message that what each student brings to the classroom community matters and is valued.

Knowing students and building quality relationships is an ongoing process. During the first few days of class, teachers ask questions and facilitate discussions to gain insight into the students' world. These insights inform instruction, lessons, and assessments by tapping students' personal passions and natural curiosity in the spirit of ensuring their learning. These initial information-gathering assignments also build a cohesive classroom community with a shared sense of purpose. When students see their responses integrated into lessons or instruction, learners know they are important and valuable contributors to the classroom community. Developing this type of student ownership is one way to create a motivating environment.

Educators seek student information to connect learners to the topic and learning goals, or to find new ways of engaging and motivating specific students who seem disengaged. When a teacher notices disengagement—either the passive, unresponsive learner or the visibly unmotivated student—informally soliciting the student's interests, passions, likes, or dislikes about learning and school can reveal the best way to re-engage him or her.

Good teachers plan with students' learning styles and intelligences in mind to increase the likelihood of reaching the intended learning goals. This planning also involves teachers facilitating student self-reflection on their own interests and learning tendencies, fostering a more self-directed stance.

Knowing your students takes time. As the pressure to "cover" everything increases, many educators rightfully struggle with spending time on relationships. The ramification of this time crunch is the feeling that this "getting to know you phase" is nice, but not necessary. In actuality, building these relationships in the beginning of the year ultimately *saves* time, because it establishes community and feeds into the instructional plan. In a strong classroom community with self-directed learners, the amount of time the teacher spends redirecting or offering feedback is slowly reduced because students own their learning and do more of the work to learn.

Tips and Traps

Be careful when asking personal questions. If students feel uncomfortable, offer an alternative assignment or explain the purpose. Offer choice in questions so students can choose the level of information they share. Until students feel safe, they may be more hesitant to reveal information about themselves, no matter what the topic.

For efficiency, design questionnaires and surveys online; if students have access to the Internet, their responses will be automatically stored and easier to manipulate. If you collect information, use it well. Questionnaires require time from both the teacher and the students. While they can be extremely valuable, questionnaires are only useful in the way they are applied, such as to understand our students, inform our planning, or make students cognizant of their own learning styles. When gathering information about students from other people (other teachers or parents, for example), be careful that their comments do not influence your judgments; avoid raising or lowering your expectations of a student according to what others say.

In addition, when making oral or written comments in reference to anything a student reveals about his or her interests, personality, or feelings about school, do not express judgment or evaluation. This strategy is designed for information collecting only, and you want the real story—the real thoughts and perceptions of your students. Communicate to students that there are no right or wrong answers. Even a well-intentioned comment can place value on an opinion or comment, making one student feel great and another belittled.

When using an idea from your students or building a lesson or activity based on the information gathered, be explicit about the connection as it builds trust and lends credibility to the "getting to know you" activity. In addition, recognizing the connection builds a bit of efficacy as students see and experience what it is like to contribute something in a community and have it directly influence their work.

Finally, involve students in the process and activities of building a learning community. Establish the expectation that everyone in our classroom will work together to support learning and achieve. Allow students time and opportunities to learn about each member of the classroom.

Putting It Into Practice

There are many ways to collect information about student interests, personalities, and beliefs. Following are some general tactics.

- **Surveys:** Provide students with a list of questions, and ask them to respond to each one or to write a letter to you answering a specific number of them. Use open-ended questions to encourage detailed answers. Alternatively, design a series of statements for students to rate their agreement on a Likert (graduated) scale.

- **Interviews:** Plan to interview each student intermittently during the year, and engage students in interviewing each other.

- **Informal conversations:** Talk to students before, after, and during class; during lunch; in the hall; while waiting for the bus; and in other informal interactions.

- **Parent or family conversations:** Ask parents or guardians to share reflections of their child with you or other appropriate school personnel.

Now let's examine some specific activities in more depth.

A Personal View of You

Use the following sample questions from various categories to gather information (vary the home and school focus of the inventories) throughout the year. Select the most appropriate questions for your students based on the occasion and the purpose. Personality questions are best suited for individual, open-ended responses. However, the interest and school-related questions can foster a classwide discussion.

Personality questions: What makes you tick?

1 What makes you happy? Why?

2 What makes you sad? Why?

3 What makes you angry? Why?

4 What is important to you? Why?

5 What is not important in your life? Why?

6 When do others make you happy? Why?

7 When do others make you angry? Why?

8 What are things you don't like? Why?

9 What are your favorite things to do? Why?

10 When are you most content? Why?

11 Who do you respect? Why?

12 Who is your role model? Why?

13 Who do you want to be like? Why?

14 When are you comfortable? Why?

15 If you had a dream, what would you wish for? Why do you want that?

16 If you could change one thing, what would you change? Why?

17 How would you change it?

Interest questions: What floats your boat?

1 What is your favorite thing to do? Why?

2 If you could be anywhere, where would you be? Why?

3 What do you do during your spare time? Why?

4 Who do you like to be with?

5 Who do you see as a role model?

6 Who can you talk to?

7 Who do you turn to in times of trouble?

8 Who helps you the most? How?

9 Who is your best friend(s)? Why do you like to be with him or her?

10 What do you like to do after school?

11 When are you the happiest?

12 When are you angriest?

13 Who are your heroes or people you look up to? Why?

14 What is your favorite thing to do at home?

15 What do you do on the weekends?

School, learning, and study habits questions: What builds your brain?

1 When are you happy at school or your job? Why?

2 When are you sad at school or your job? Why?

3 What is your favorite part of the academic day? Why?

4 Which class is the most difficult for you? Why?

5 Who is your best support at school or at work? Why?

6 What motivates you to want to be here? Why?

7 Do you concentrate best when it is noisy or quiet?

8 Who or what helps you learn the most?

9 What gets in the way of your learning?

10 Where is your favorite spot to study?

11 Do you have access to a computer at home? If not, where do you use a computer?

12 How do you feel about school? Why?

13 What do you want to be?

14 What would you rather be doing?

15 How do you feel about _____? Why?

16 What is your biggest fear in school?

17 What is your biggest hope in school?

Alternatively, you can distribute lists like these to students, and ask them to select questions to answer from each. Additionally, students can use an activity like A Personal View of You! found in figure 2.1 to gather their responses. This survey uses clever questions to engage students in a fun and lighthearted manner that reveals important information. Teachers may engage students in an informal discussion about the types of responses they might consider making to each of the three questions.

Community of Learners

Once a student enters the classroom conversation for the first time, he or she feels much more comfortable and is more likely to speak up again. This activity, which we observed in a sophomore English class, sets a welcoming tone and creates a classroom climate that accepts, expects, and values the active engagement of all students.

First, ask students to journal about a list of questions, similar to the sample questions on pages 26–28. Then, ask them to create, write, or produce something to introduce themselves to the classroom. Learners should know they are not required to reveal anything they do not want to share. Some students may write songs or stories, others may create posters, and still others may put together short video clips. In sharing their projects, students have the opportunity for their voices to be heard without anyone judging or evaluating, agreeing or disagreeing. This activity potentially encourages more class participation; once students' voices are in the room initially, they will more likely participate in the future.

Photo Memory Books

In elementary classrooms, students can work with their parents to put together photo memories of their favorite experiences, favorite pastimes, and the important people they love and respect. Students can share these memories with their classmates.

Of course, some parents take more photos than others, and some adults help students with homework or projects outside of the school day, while others do not or cannot assist. To avoid embarrassing or hurting students, the teacher can have students draw pictures or cut out images and words from magazines to introduce themselves to their classmates. If including the option for students to bring photos from home to add to the project, the teacher or other staff member may prepare to take pictures of those who do not bring personal photos.

A Personal View of You!

Directions: Draw or write something to describe you, using the question in the first column. There are no right or wrong answers.

Name: _____   Date: _____

What floats your boat?

What makes you tick?

What builds your brain?

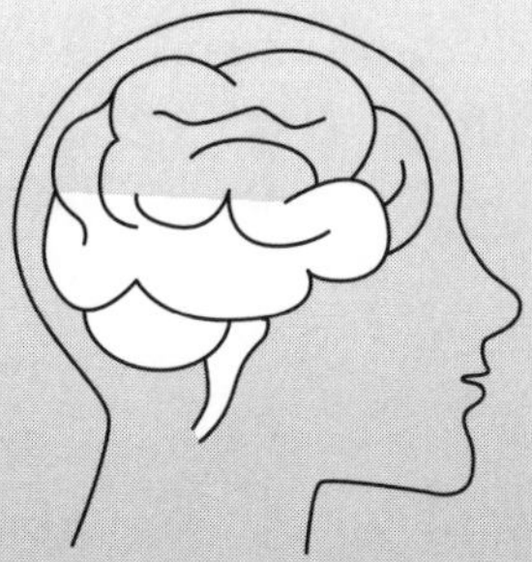

Figure 2.1: Sample student interest activity.

Life Map

Students can construct a life map as a way to both connect to each other and brainstorm possible writing topics. The steps are as follows:

1   Each student draws a graph and labels the *x*-axis to represent each year of his or her life.

2   On the *y*-axis, he or she numbers positive and negative numbers 1–5 to represent negative and positive life experiences.

3   Then, students brainstorm positive and negative experiences in their lives through words or pictures, plotting them on the graph according to the age at which each experience occurred. They rank the experiences (positive 5 being the most enjoyable and negative 5 being the most unpleasant), and connect the points. See figure 2.2 for an example. Sample life experiences students could plot are:

- I broke my leg on the playground at school.
- My baby sister was born.
- My family went to Disney World.
- Our class wrote and performed a play.
- My grandfather passed away.
- My mom got remarried.
- We moved to _____.
- I met my first friend.
- I made the soccer team.
- I got an A on my paper.
- I failed my biology test.

4   Students can share with each other or the whole class, or use these ideas to write a personal narrative.

Strategy 2: Discover How Your Students Learn Best

People bring their own styles to the table when learning and processing new ideas. Some students enjoy lectures, while others prefer dialogue with a partner or journaling. Still others learn best when the content is set to a rhythm or a tune. When working on a big project, some learners want to know and follow a clearly defined set of steps, while others want options and freedom in developing their own process; any single instructional style has the potential to succeed or fail in supporting students just by the nature of their diverse learning styles.

Part of facilitating students to become more independent learners is strategically helping them pay attention to their learning tendencies—how they remember, understand, apply, connect, and create. This metacognitive process is part of being self-directed learners (Zimmerman, 2008). When we ask students to reflect on how they learn best, what helps them learn, and what inhibits their learning, we promote self-awareness and support learners in planning their next steps to learn more.

As teachers, we mix and match instructional strategies in order to address the varying ways our students have identified the ways they learn best. Being transparent about how we design a lesson creates connections to students' learning, and it builds trust as teachers follow through with using information they have solicited. For example, when you give a lecture, mention that the student inventories for this class suggested some students learn best when the teacher explains things.

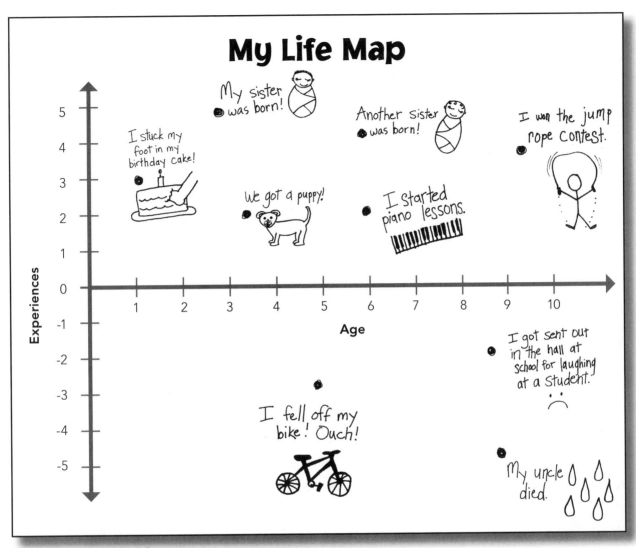

Figure 2.2: Sample life map.

Later, when you assign an activity for students to show what they learned from the lecture, mention that the inventories also showed that some students in the class learn best through talking to a partner or writing about what they do or do not understand. Making these connections for students not only meets their learning needs, but also builds trust and strengthens the community; you build credibility by showing that you are using information they have shared.

The research is mixed regarding the impact of students experiencing instruction in their identified "learning style" or "intelligence." Some researchers suggest that students learn best through their dominant learning styles (Dunn, Griggs, Olson, Beasley, & Gorman, 1995), while others find just the opposite—that teaching should focus on the styles students do not report as strengths (Apter, 2001). Hattie (2009) states:

> The emphasis should be on what students can do, and then on students knowing what they are aiming to do, having multiple strategies for learning to do, and knowing when they have done it. It is teachers having teaching strategies aimed at enhancing the learning that was identified as the outcomes for the lesson, and who provide appropriate feedback to reduce the gap between where the student is and where they need to be. (p. 199)

As students explore different strengths and ways of processing information, we facilitate their awareness of the extent to which that modality assists them in learning more. When learners begin to grapple with information on their own, they will have a wide repertoire of strategies from which to choose. Planning strategies in different intelligences or learning-style patterns benefits all students, not only those who have an increased propensity for that type of activity.

Tips and Traps

Clearly establish the learning goals for each lesson, and describe what success looks like so students will know when they have attained the goals. Keeping learning at the center focuses any instructional activity, no matter what the student's learning style.

In planning instruction and assessment, use a variety of strategies to accommodate different learning styles. Remember, variety and choice increase engagement. At the close of each activity, assess the impact of the strategy both in terms of the level of achievement (what did students learn or not learn?) and the sense of appreciation (did students enjoy or engage in the activity?).

Learning styles are not fixed characteristics. They are a description of how someone learns, not a measure of intelligence. With a variety of learning styles acknowledged in classroom instruction, assessment, and activities, students will view their learning preferences as traits that will grow and change, not as fixed characteristics that are hierarchical (that is, they understand it is not better to be linguistic than kinesthetic).

Again, when collecting information, explicitly use it in planning instruction and assessment. Not doing so creates more paperwork for teachers with little effect on learning or engagement. In general, students often feel like their participation in school is a series of disconnected events. They do not see linkages among their instructional activities, homework, assessments, grades, or marks. Nicole (September 5, 2008; November 6–7, 2008; February 4–5, 2009) interviewed a number of students to understand their perceptions of school. In response to the questions "What does a grade mean? If you get a B in science, does that mean you have a B understanding of science content?," most students chuckled and responded that a grade has nothing to do with how much someone knows. It has everything to do with how much effort the teacher perceives a student puts into the assignment and the amount of homework the student completes (not its quality).

Putting It Into Practice

Teachers plan learning activities for a variety of purposes: to introduce new content, to reinforce previously addressed concepts, or to attend to gaps in students' understanding. Knowing your students' preferences in terms of learning activities they enjoy and identify as aiding their understanding can further inform planning, create a sense of ownership in the classroom community, and spark engagement.

Rating Learning Activities

Learning activities are the creative ways teachers engage students in reflecting on the intended learning goals. For example, a teacher may provide a lecturette (short presentation) on how a bill becomes a law. The learning activity may involve students crafting their own proposal and argument in preparation for simulating the process in a classroom debate. Learning activities are the ways teachers structure opportunities for students to struggle and make meaning of the content of the class. A rubric like figure 2.3 (page 34, or see page 61 for a reproducible version) asks

Rating How You Learn

Directions: For each activity, rate how much you like the activity and how much the learning activity helps you understand.

How much do you like doing this activity?					How often does this learning activity help you understand something?				
I Love It	It's OK	Unsure	I Dislike It	I Strongly Dislike It	Always	Sometimes	Unsure	Rarely	Never
Taking notes									
5	4	3	2	1	5	4	3	2	1
Making outlines									
5	4	3	2	1	5	4	3	2	1
Reading about the topic in a textbook or article									
5	4	3	2	1	5	4	3	2	1
Playing academic games									
5	4	3	2	1	5	4	3	2	1
Talking with a friend or partner in class									
5	4	3	2	1	5	4	3	2	1
Working in a small group									
5	4	3	2	1	5	4	3	2	1
Writing about the topic in my own words									
5	4	3	2	1	5	4	3	2	1
Drawing a picture to help me remember									
5	4	3	2	1	5	4	3	2	1
Having one-on-one time or small-group time with the teacher to explain the concept									
5	4	3	2	1	5	4	3	2	1
Listening to teacher explanations to the whole class									
5	4	3	2	1	5	4	3	2	1
Other: _____									
5	4	3	2	1	5	4	3	2	1

Figure 2.3: Sample activity rating handout.

middle and high school students to rate both how much they like the activity as well as how much they feel the activity supports their learning. To adapt the activity for younger students, add pictures and reduce the number of words. Younger children benefit from a rating scale that includes pictures with big smiles, frowning faces, and confused expressions.

Explore Your Smarts

An inventory is a good way for students to examine how they process information and learn about their intelligences and preferred modalities. The survey in figure 2.4 (page 35, or see page 62 for a reproducible version) is based on the work of Howard Gardner as interpreted by Carolyn Chapman and Rita King (2009b) in *Differentiated Instructional Strategies for Reading in the Content Areas*.

It is important that students do not use their specific areas of strength or favorite ways to learn— "intelligences"—to define their self-worth. We all have weak learning styles that make it difficult to learn or make meaning of concepts. Our strengths and weaknesses are fluid and can change throughout life. In this activity, learners review the list of statements describing different types of intelligences or "smarts," checking the statements that represent their personal preferences. There is no right number or right placement of checks; it is up to the students to choose the items that best describe them. The results will show students' favorite ways to learn and can reveal information about the personality of the class as a whole. In addition, this conversation opens the door for the teacher to support students' feelings of discomfort as some learners participate in activities that are not identified as strengths. Most importantly, encourage students to be comfortable with struggle or unease—through struggle, new understandings and talents can be discovered. Reflecting on the weak areas may be just as beneficial as a focus on strengths.

One way to follow up on this activity is to place signs for each "smart" around the room and have students move to the area that they identified as their strength. Together, the students in each area then brainstorm answers to one or more of the following questions to share with the class:

- "What kind of activities do you like to do in class to help you learn?"
- "What do you dislike doing in class?"
- "Which smart areas make you most uncomfortable?"
- "Why is your smart important to the classroom?"
- "How can your smarts help students who have different smarts?"
- "What could you teach others? How?"
- "Which smart do you want to learn more about? Why?"

As a whole class, be sure to debrief and talk about the purpose of the activity. Gather responses from students to the following questions:

- "What did we learn from doing this activity?"
- "Why did we complete it?"
- "Why is this activity important?"
- "How could we use what we learned to make the classroom more effective?"

Exploring Your Smarts

Directions: Read each item, and check all statements that apply to you to determine your preference.

Verbal/Linguistic: I am all about words!

☐ I am a comprehending, fluent reader and writer.

☐ I like to write or dream up stories.

☐ I enjoy reading.

☐ Words come easy to me when I talk to people.

☐ Words come easy to me when I write.

☐ I spell well.

☐ I often join in discussions and conversations.

☐ I often volunteer to present my group's ideas to the class.

Logical/Mathematical: Give me numbers!

☐ I enjoy solving problems with numbers.

☐ Math classes are often my favorite part of the day.

☐ I am a logical thinker.

☐ I enjoy puzzles and games that strain my brain.

☐ I search for patterns.

☐ I sequence. I need steps to solve problems.

☐ I like to read directions to put things together.

☐ I want to know what we're going to do next in class.

Interpersonal: I am all about people!

☐ I learn while working in groups.

☐ I get ideas by brainstorming with others.

☐ I turn to friends, family, or trusted adults when I have a problem to solve.

☐ I enjoy cooperative learning activities.

☐ I learn when I study with a partner or study group.

☐ I like being a team member.

☐ I empathize with others.

Musical/Rhythmic: I like to sing and dance!

☐ I learn when I put difficult content to a beat.

☐ I participate in musical activities, such as listening to music, playing an instrument, or singing in the choir.

☐ Noises and sounds help me identify places I have been. For example, when a bell rings, I think of a game at the fair.

☐ I know a lot of songs.

Figure 2.4: Exploring Your Smarts handout.

continued →

- ☐ I hum or sing a lot.
- ☐ I study better with background noise.
- ☐ I have a favorite type of music.
- ☐ I remember information by listening to the teacher explain the topic.

Intrapersonal: I enjoy working independently.

- ☐ I need to work alone.
- ☐ I enjoy personal journals, keeping a daily log, or writing diary entries.
- ☐ I need time to think before I speak aloud.
- ☐ I enjoy personal time.
- ☐ I can easily explain to you what I do well and what I need to work on.
- ☐ I like independent assignments.
- ☐ I use organizers.
- ☐ I make personal decisions on my own.

Visual/Spatial: Show me a picture!

- ☐ I need to see the information.
- ☐ I visualize pictures in my head.
- ☐ I study graphics and pictures to better understand the written information.
- ☐ I can recall an experience visually.
- ☐ I like graphic organizers.
- ☐ I doodle.
- ☐ I match colors well.
- ☐ I like art and exploring different media.

Bodily/Kinesthetic: I like to move it, move it!

- ☐ I need to vary my movement: sitting, standing, and jumping.
- ☐ Manipulatives help me learn.
- ☐ I enjoy role-playing and acting out activities.
- ☐ I like to dance.
- ☐ I participate in sports.
- ☐ I learn during active activities.
- ☐ If I sit still too much, I can't pay attention to what the teacher is saying or doing.
- ☐ I like to draw, sculpt, or create to express myself.

Naturalist: Let's work with the environment!

- ☐ I enjoy learning science, especially about the earth.
- ☐ I know what I need to survive in the wilderness.
- ☐ I adjust to different environments and situations.
- ☐ I take care of a pet and enjoy being with it.
- ☐ I like to grow things.
- ☐ I enjoy working outside.
- ☐ I like to explore things.
- ☐ I enjoy studying other cultures.

Student Feedback on Class Activities and Procedures

Effective teachers constantly ask for feedback from students after activities, assessments, and lessons to learn how to make instruction more engaging and effective. Consider adding student reflection time after administering tests or introducing particularly difficult materials. Use exit slips with scaled surveys (figures 2.5 and 2.6) to collect student feedback.

Class Activity: _____ **Date:** _____

Name: _____

The best part of this activity was _____ because _____.

The most challenging part of the activity was _____.

   1.   From this activity, I learned _____.

   2.   If I had to do one thing over again, it would be to _____.

   3.   The next time we do this activity, let's change it by _____.

Figure 2.5: Sample exit slip for secondary students.

Class Activity: _____ **Date:** _____

Name: _____

Rate this activity by shading in the number of stars that describes your feelings. Then draw a picture or use a few words to describe your thinking.

5 stars—It was the best! It was fantastic! It made me think!

4 stars—I learned and enjoyed most of it.

3 stars—I learned, but I have some questions.

2 stars—I liked some of it. I learned a little bit.

1 star—It wasn't fun, and I didn't learn. I was bored or confused.

☆   ☆   ☆   ☆   ☆

Figure 2.6: Sample exit slip for elementary students.

For figure 2.6, locate five places in the classroom to display words associated with each rating. Visually showing the connection between the evaluation (number of stars) and the words describing these ratings can be a stepping stone to written expression. As an instructional tool, learners indicate their evaluation by drawing or coloring in the number of stars, drawing a picture that supports their rating, and finally copying a word or two posted on the visuals around the room. This activity shows students the connection between pictures and words.

Strategy 3: Be Culturally Responsive

It's crucial to believe in every student—to know, value, and respect every learner. Teachers boost morale, create hope, and inspire motivation through culturally responsive teaching. Teachers who are culturally responsive send the following message to each student: "Come in my classroom, and you will learn. I will challenge your mind, and you will grow as a problem solver, thinker, communicator, and self-directed learner!" Send this message at the beginning of the class, through words, smiles, and encouragement, to every student. Actions speak loudly. Establish the expectation that your classroom is a place where learning is not only possible, but a sure thing for all students, no matter their ethnicity, culture, background, or prior experience.

Being responsive requires more than just accepting or tolerating differences. It requires taking action to learn and build on the diverse life experiences, prior knowledge, interests, and communication methods that students bring. Culturally responsive teachers help students connect to the world of academics so they begin to see achievement within their grasp. Geneva Gay (2002) defines the practice well:

> Culturally responsive teaching is defined as using the cultural characteristics, experiences, and perspectives of ethnically diverse students as conduits for teaching them more effectively. It is based on the assumption that when academic knowledge and skills are situated within the lived experiences and frames of reference of students, they are more personally meaningful, have higher interest appeal and are learned more easily and thoroughly. (p. 106)

This definition of culturally responsive teaching is key to reaching all students. By tapping into students' current realities, we can find ways to light the fire of engagement, positively affect their motivation, and increase their achievement.

According to Gay (2002), there are five elements to culturally responsive teaching.

1 **Learn about cultural diversity:** Know characteristics of different cultures and ethnic groups. Know the significant contributions made to the content by culturally diverse people in the field (Latino sociologists and doctors, African American scientists and artists). Learn about the different ethnicities within a culture. For example, Latino families from El Salvador are different than families from Cuba or Mexico. Read the research on multicultural education.

   Learning about cultural diversity provides teachers a lens with which to review their instructional plans, assessments, and classroom policies and their potential impact on motivating and engaging culturally diverse students. These insights may provide unique insight into the barriers learners sometimes face in the current educational setting, and, in turn, promote more effective instructional approaches.

2 **Design culturally relevant curriculum:** When educators learn about cultural diversity, it enables them to plan curriculum that explores and incorporates multiple perspectives and makes cultural connections through texts, facts, images, and situations. Incorporate multicultural examples, people, and resources. Represent expectations, values, and hopes for all students through words and images. In this spirit, culturally diverse examples and people go beyond just well-recognized celebrities and include everyday citizens, who characterize the majority of Americans.

Designing a culturally relevant curriculum develops and promotes a strength-based view of culture, or one that perpetuates the assets of multiple perspectives and differing points of view. By incorporating materials, examples, and people that reflect the strengths diverse cultures bring to a community, we offer a more balanced perspective than just polarized issues such as racism or the rare examples of a rise to fame and fortune. As teachers, we may encounter negative stereotypes or perceptions of culturally diverse students in the classroom that majority groups sometimes have of minority groups. Preparing curriculum that addresses cultural diversity from the point of strength dispels the negative stereotypes while at the same time opens doors for culturally diverse students to imagine different positive paths for their lives by depicting various examples of success.

3 **Enact culturally diverse curriculum flexibly and responsively:** The first two elements create the foundation of a culturally responsive classroom and positive classroom environment. Learning about the cultural characteristics of students and intentionally planning to incorporate these ideas into our content, instruction, and assessment set up the conditions for all students to achieve. The actual enactment of the curriculum, instruction, and assessment determines the impact on student learning, perceptions, and confidence. The art of teaching comes into play when acting out curriculum. As instructional strategies are employed, culturally responsive teachers observe and check the engagement of students and modify and adjust their teaching to positively influence learning. This is, again, where the complexity of teaching, learning, and motivation collide. We have all probably had the experience of an activity used successfully in one class producing the opposite effect in another class. Different personalities, learning preferences, and background experiences can construct a unique classroom that responds differently than the next. Effective teachers are reflective about these dynamics and gather student insight to fully assess the impact of their lessons, instructional strategies, and teaching on learning and engagement. As a result, they are flexible and responsive to students and their needs both in terms of classroom environment and successful learning experiences.

When you make instruction reflect the best interests of the learners who populate the classroom, students feel, experience, see, and hear the spirit of care and community.

4 **Learn about cultural communication patterns:** Know culturally diverse students' communication patterns, including informal and formal language and interactions. Different cultures value and employ varying communication elements: context, intonation, gestures, vocabulary, speaker roles, listener roles, silence, eye contact, and more. Bridge to students' most comfortable communication styles when defining expectations, offering feedback, and requiring participation. For example, teacher-directed dialogue can be restrictive for some cultures. Students may struggle to sit passively, listen, and respond only when invited or required by the teacher. In some nonwhite cultures in the United States, "speakers . . . expect listeners to engage with them . . . by providing prompts, feedback, and commentary" (Gay, 2002, p. 111). The confusion and frustration students feel may stem from this gap between their familiar communication patterns and what is occurring or expected in the classroom. Gay (2002) states, "Uninformed and unappreciative teachers consider them [students] rude, distractive, and inappropriate and take actions to squelch them. Students who are told not to use their specific communication style can be, in effect, intellectually silenced. Because they are denied use of their natural way of talking, their thinking, intellectual engagement, and academic efforts are diminished as well" (p.

111). Understanding these communication patterns can make the difference in a student's motivation.

Knowing cultural communication patterns is critical to effectively reach and teach all students and will help reframe "interruptions" or "disruptions" as students' attempts to engage.

5 **Align your new cultural understandings with your classroom practice:** Use what you know about each student's culture, its characteristics, and his or her communication style to design instructional strategies. Learning and trying new ideas that attend to the needs of your students is simply good practice. Gay (2002) likens this element to the practice of matching learning styles to individual student needs.

Aligning your cultural understanding with classroom planning and practice may eliminate disruptions and proactively avoid disengagement just by bridging the personal experiences of students with their academic experiences. One student shared the contradictory words and actions experienced in her school. Every day, morning announcements exclaimed excitement and passion for learning; the announcer promised students a day of active and engaged learning. Minutes after one such announcement, however, her boyfriend was kicked out of class for wearing the wrong shirt. He really needed to be there to understand what was happening, she explained; the twenty minutes he missed because of a shirt set the course for further confusion in class and, ultimately, his disengagement in school.

Expecting achievement from *all* learners is an important component of being culturally responsive. Effective teachers care deeply about students "and their achievement that they accept nothing less than high-level success from them and work diligently to accomplish it" (Foster, 1997; Kleinfeld, 1975, as cited in Gay, 2002, p. 109). As classroom practice is aligned with cultural understanding, messages of high expectations translate into actions and improved achievement for culturally diverse students.

To summarize, to motivate the culturally diverse students in your classroom: get to know them personally (see strategy 1, page 24), learn about their cultures, and include diverse instructional strategies and activities that meet their unique learning and communication styles.

Examining our learning goals, standards, and curriculum documents and infusing them with culturally diverse examples and learning styles is a great first step in practicing cultural responsiveness.

Tips and Traps

Set high expectations for every student. Ask a colleague to observe the classroom and teacher interactions with all learners. He or she can specifically look for signs of high expectations being set—or not set—for all students. For example, the types of questions asked and the response patterns can be an important indicator of engagement. Observing a classroom and writing down every question asked and who responds can provide important feedback to the teacher regarding communication patterns and the level of expectation.

Ask students how they expect to perform. Their answers will provide insight into perceptions of their own academic work. If they do not predict success, they need encouragement and confidence. Operate from a place of strength. Each student brings cultural capital to the classroom;

find those strengths! View differences in tradition, communication, experience, and knowledge as possibilities—places to bridge from students' prior experience to the world of the classroom.

When students interrupt or act inappropriately, ask questions or build on their enthusiasm before jumping to conclusions. For example, when a student shouts out an answer without raising a hand or waiting for the appropriate moment, the teacher makes a choice in his or her response. The teacher can scold the student, unintentionally embarrassing the student, or he or she can ask everyone to write a possible response and continue the conversation, reminding students to take turns.

Better yet, ask questions before behavior becomes an issue. Ask students how they communicate, learn, and interact. Gather their perceptions and ideas, and use them to make the classroom comfortable.

Avoid joining the negative teacher talk that may exist regarding students. Negative talk spirals and can easily lead to inadvertent actions that negatively impact students. Try this: go ahead and gripe a bit, because it can air the problem and our frustrations. However, immediately turn the discussion to brainstorming actions that may solve the problem or alleviate the frustrations.

Mainstream media offers stereotypes of many cultures. Be careful not to perpetuate these ideas through newspaper articles, magazines, and TV bits used in class. If you find media excerpts that provide information relevant to the lesson, be sure to explore multiple perspectives. Using media stories of high-profile ethnically diverse people can stimulate discussion, but it can also promote stereotypes. For example, while many powerful athletes are African American, the probability that the students in your classrooms will follow their path is quite low. Find the lower-profile successful people—the scientists, medical doctors, archeologists, and writers—and showcase them instead.

Talk directly about controversy, but limit the controversial topics. If discussions about racism are the only way students hear, discuss, or view issues related to their culture, it perpetuates negative and tense feelings. Offer these topics and discussions, but also infuse noncontroversial stories of success and achievement.

Hold all students to high expectations, despite the hardships they may experience. Many students enter our classrooms with significant life challenges that range from unmet basic needs to various forms of abuse, neglect, or financial hardship. We care about these issues, for personal and academic reasons. However, Gay (2002) states that this type of concern or attention can lead to "benign neglect under the guise of letting students of color make their own way and move at their own pace" (p. 109). For example, in a high school social studies classroom we observed, the higher-level thinking questions were extra credit. When asking an African American student if she was going to attempt the extra-credit questions, she paused, as if she had never even considered trying "those" questions. She slowly shook her head, and Nicole promptly responded, "Let's try it together." The look in the student's eyes at the end of those brief eight minutes was of pure joy and immense pride.

Culturally responsive teaching is not reserved for culturally diverse classrooms. Whether our communities are diverse or not, the world in which our students are living and will soon enter as adults is global and profoundly varied. Thanks to technology, our students can be connected to students around the world and other countries we are studying. Curriculum can be richly infused with examples and discussions that open up new ways of viewing our world.

Putting It Into Practice

A culturally relevant curriculum connects students to the increasingly diverse world. A plan for success, a visible picture of success, and different communication methods will infuse cultural learning into the classroom to engage all students.

Collaborate for Success

Many minority students experience their cultural community as valuing the interests of the group over the individual (Gay, 2002; Ladson-Billings, 1995). Individuals lend their assets to the community to problem solve and share so it functions well. As a result, the individuals feel collective responsibility and commitment to the success of the group.

In our schools, by contrast, the individual is valued over the group. If an individual student does not learn something, it is up to him or her to figure out how to proceed. In a culturally responsive classroom, the classroom as a whole acts as a cultural group, capitalizing on the strengths of its members to achieve a group outcome. For example, a science class embarks on a mission to use lovely plants, flowers, and sitting areas to make the courtyard an inviting yet eco-friendly place to study. In the process of designing the layout, studying the environment, and executing the plan, individual members of the class reflect on their potential contributions to the project. While all students will have an understanding of certain environmental concepts, the individuals in the class will contribute in their unique ways to create a successful, collaborative courtyard.

Make Success Visible Using Words and Pictures

When the words and pictures posted in our classrooms and hallways show culturally diverse boys and girls actively engaged in science experiments, reading books, and talking with each other, the visuals create an expectation that students will "be" and "act" smart. This begins to counteract opposite messages that sometimes infiltrate the beliefs and climate of our schools in subtle but highly influential ways.

Using examples of the positive contributions made by culturally diverse scientists, authors, engineers, mathematicians, teachers, and doctors gives students a sense of possibility and expands their worldviews. Learners are able to bridge what they know about their present to what is possible in their future.

Using a chart like table 2.1 (see page 64 for a reproducible version), take pictures of your students engaged in academic work, quality conversations, or quality work showing their insights. Paste their pictures in the boxes at various times throughout the year to acknowledge and celebrate their academic successes.

Table 2.1: Celebrating the Accomplishments of Our Students!

Student Accomplishments	Classroom Examples
Our students talk smart!	
Our students produce important work!	
Our students love to learn!	
Our students believe in each other!	

Vary Your Communication Methods

Knowing the varying cultural communication cues and ways of talking and thinking about our students is pivotal in creating a classroom where all students can learn. Consider engaging students in a conversation about various ways to talk and express excitement, frustration, anger, understanding, questions, and confusion in the classroom. One example of what this might look like in practice could entail splitting students into groups of three or four and giving them a form such as table 2.2. The intent of this table is to facilitate conversations that open the door to students' comfortable communication methods, illustrate how they compare to current communication styles in school, and help the class define how to communicate together. This conversation has potential to bridge the gap between learners' communication styles outside of school and teachers' and the school's communication styles. The result might be something in between that propels both groups forward in achieving learning for all students.

Table 2.2: Understanding Students' Communication Styles

	Happy	Confused	Proud	Angry	Determined	Hurt	Sad
How do you respond at home? List words and actions you might use.							
How do you respond when you are with friends? List words and actions you might use.							
How do you respond in class? List words and actions you might use.							
How do you respond in school (such as in the hallways and cafeteria)? List words and actions you might use.							

Another possible instructional application is integrating a call-and-response protocol. In this scenario, teachers plan questions to trigger a response that students call out in unison. The response can be something students practice and repeat throughout a lesson. It can also be something the teacher asks in the moment and then repeats so students respond. Both the repetition and the calling out can lift the energy and re-engage students. Another version of this may involve students reading a poem, a quote, or an excerpt in unison, and then turning and talking to a partner to make meaning of the information or connect the text to the concept being addressed.

Strategy 4: Build Relationships With and Among Students

Relationships are built through interactions with and among students. Teachers and students are building relationships on a daily basis as they interact with each other and engage in the work of learning and teaching. However, *intentionally* building relationships is so critical to motivation and engagement that we are treating it as a separate strategy.

Martin and Dowson (2009) explored the impact of interpersonal relationships on motivation and engagement by reviewing studies on various theories of motivation. In every study, relationships students had with teachers, peers, parents, guardians, and other adults affected their academic motivation, engagement, self-worth, and self-esteem, as well as their academic achievement. The quality of relationships among students in a classroom is also essential to a sense of community, as we learned earlier. Nancy Frey, Douglas Fisher, and Sandi Everlove (2009) state, "The best opportunity students have for learning to learn and solve problems with others is in the classroom" (p. 38). When students work with peers, they are better able to solve problems and learn deeply. Working with others requires trust. Otherwise, peer interactions will be surface level at best, and learners will hold back. A learner is more apt to commit to complete assigned tasks and join in discussions when there is no feeling of threat. A safe classroom atmosphere provides the conditions for students to take risks and make mistakes, without fear of humiliation, and without fear that a teacher or classmates will think less of them for doing so.

Overcoming Fear

Fear is vicious. The unfamiliar and the unknown can cause fear, and so can the familiar and the known; our memories of an unpleasant event make us unwilling to go through it again. Students feel fear in all kinds of learning situations, such as learning new information or tackling new activities, encountering content or situations that have been difficult, struggling to master challenging material, and performing or answering questions in front of peers.

For some students, change is exciting, and they meet new lessons and tasks with great anticipation. For others, change creates fear. Explain the what, when, and how in directions and instructions. Details inform students about what to expect and provide them with opportunities to feel in control. Reacting with empathy to these concerns is of utmost importance. Teachers may feel the student has nothing to worry about, but we are adults—in control and in power. Students need to have complete trust to plunge forward and take risks in learning. Affirming learners' fears is important, but only the beginning. Fear needs to be assuaged by guiding students through the new experience and providing support when needed. These actions build genuine trust and create a safe place for students.

Some learners' fears come from feelings of inadequacy. Their self-talk may be something like: Why can't I do this like the others? Some students try as hard as they can and still cannot pass the test. For students who don't feel competent, it is important to show what success looks like and the precise steps they need to take to achieve the learning goal. It's also critical that teachers model the struggle it takes to learn something. Often, if the answer doesn't come within moments of being asked, students feel the material is too hard for them. Communicate that true learning often comes after a struggle with the content. By modeling the struggle, you affirm that learning does not mean always knowing the right answer immediately.

The adage "Once burned, twice shy" is very true in the classroom. As teachers, when we see unmotivated students, we need to consider whether prior experience has left them "once burned, twice shy." These students may need to take small steps toward re-engagement, with plenty of reassurance that trying again will not produce another humiliating experience. For example, if in the past classmates ridiculed a student making a presentation or sharing a piece of writing, consider allowing the student to share it in a one-on-one situation. Offering students praise and encouragement for the small steps they achieve along the way can start to replace fear with feelings of confidence.

You could also take steps to make sure the problem is not repeated by creating firm guidelines about students' responses to each other's work.

As teachers, we must plan to ensure that students believe that each activity or task is worth their time and effort, and that the classroom atmosphere is safe enough for students to take risks. If students fear being humiliated or being ridiculed in public, they will shut down. Relationships built on fear or shame will not increase motivation.

When teachers and students honor everyone's strengths, the classroom becomes a safe place to reveal confusion, concerns, and authentic hopes. Making the classroom a safe place where there is respect for everyone—where each student and adult in the classroom is an important and valued part of the community—is the foundation of motivation.

Tips and Traps

Encourage students to express themselves with words. Ask questions or probe with lead-in statements to get the student to talk. Actions speak louder than words. Be consciously aware of your body language and nonverbal expressions, which can unintentionally give negative feedback or contradictory messages.

Stay neutral during disputes or brainstorming sessions. Have reflective times about negative events that have occurred to discuss what happened, why, and what should take place next time. These strategically planned sessions assist students in voicing feelings, understanding diverse points of view, setting productive goals, and making future decisions. Remember you set the tone of the classroom and build safety nets for each learner according to his or her needs. When you make mistakes, acknowledge them and apologize. Students will take their leads from you. Model and demand respect from and among learners.

Be careful not to show favoritism. Students know if you like some learners better than others. Find likable traits in each learner. Negativity spreads and can impact the way peers treat each other.

Be open to discussions and suggestions from students, and build appropriate teacher-student relationships. Students are not peers. Teachers' authority and power in the relationship must be used appropriately with respect and care. The teacher is always the responsible party. All happenings must get your approval or not be acceptable parts of the classroom.

Do not let outside forces and pressures, such as higher test scores or new mandates, consume you. In addition, do not pass stress on to students. The learners will be much more likely to succeed in a safe, positive classroom community.

When you are having a bad day, remember not to take it out on the students. Avoid sarcasm and put-downs. They are demeaning. Open a two-way street of communication between you and your students so they express themselves honestly. Learn from negative student feedback; this is an indication that students feel safe enough to express their feelings and attitudes and provide the real story. When learners give constructive feedback, analyze it carefully, and use the feedback for growth. Do not take it out on learners. If you react negatively to the feedback, students will stop providing their honest comments.

Putting It Into Practice

Teachers can use a number of strategies to build relationships with and among students. Creating open lines of communication, sharing personal information, and creating a welcoming environment are a few ways to encourage classroom bonds and engage learners.

Get Students Talking to Each Other

Many times during peer-to-peer tutoring, the assisting student simply provides the answers. Students do not know how to ask probing questions to let their classmate arrive at his or her own answers (Frey, Fisher, & Everlove, 2009). Why is this? In the hurried teacher's world, answers are provided without having learners work or investigate their own solutions or responses. Students see very few models of struggling or searching for solutions to problems. When learners search for their own answers and meanings, they gain better understanding. In this case, the process of questioning leads to new understanding. Consider teaching students how to use questions to probe and allow others to generate their own thinking. This practice will result in a win-win situation. Not only will students become better thinkers while solving a problem, but they will also see models of students probing and may, in turn, use these techniques when assisting another student. Effective questioning strategies need to be taught and modeled on a regular basis for them to become routine in classrooms. Consider using the following tactics, *group sharing* and *cubing*, to facilitate this practice.

Group sharing is a time for the unmotivated student to express ideas and feel heard. This activity builds respect while eliminating barriers and labels. Provide time for individual students to share something they can do or know, an exciting adventure or trip they experienced, or an unexpected accomplishment. Often learners reveal talents and experiences that others would not expect. Students need to get to know personal information about peers to build friendships and mutual respect. Have students share:

- Ideas
- Adventures, hobbies, and experiences
- Links and connections with the content information
- Work and the way they solved and processed the problem
- Struggles
- Successes and accomplishments
- Goals, hopes, and dreams
- Feelings and emotions
- Celebrations of learning and life

In *cubing*, the teacher identifies a topic, event, person, or concept. Then students use questions to talk about the idea. The questions can vary but essentially have the following pattern:

- "Can you describe it?"
- "Can you analyze it?"
- "Can it be reinvented?"
- "What does it remind you of?"

- "What are its uses?"
- "What do you think will happen to it?"

Use a handout like the one in table 2.3 to facilitate this activity. You can also accompany the table with the questions on a folded paper cube. (See page 65 for a reproducible of table 2.3 and page 67 for a blank foldout to create your own cube.) The left column identifies different questions members of the group will answer. Group members fill in their answers in the right column. The number of questions discussed will parallel the number of group members. For example, if there are four group members, only four questions would surface in discussion. In turn, learners share their responses to their assigned question. The teacher may vary the protocol. In one scenario, students share their assigned question and then others in the group contribute their thinking. Group members may share their answers with the whole class or just with partners.

Table 2.3: Sample Event Cube

Questions	Student Answers
What happened?	
When did it happen?	
Who was there?	
Why is it important?	
How did it affect the people living at that time?	
What impact does it have on us today?	

Following are some sample questions to create a cubing activity about an artifact.

1 What are three adjectives that describe the artifact?

2 What does the text say about it?

3 What does it remind you of?

4 What is its impact on the world?

5 What are its uses?

6 What do you think will happen to it?

Following are some sample questions to create a cubing activity about a real person or a fictional character.

1 What are his or her biggest accomplishments?

2 When and where did he or she live?

3 How did others feel about him or her? How do you know?

4 What would be the neighbors' reactions if he or she lived next door to you? Why?

5 What was his or her role?

6 What are his or her strengths and weaknesses?

Make It Personal

Share appropriate personal stories from your life that link with content information. When teachers tell short stories with a point that connects to the intended learning, relationships are built. Revealing aspects of your life offers students a glimpse of your life, experiences, values, and perspectives. As a result, learners may feel more comfortable being honest and open in the classroom. The modeling we do for our students often translates into more learning for our learners. Plan time for students to connect new information to their experience and apply the ideas to their personal lives.

Remember the Little Things

People of all ages like to know they are welcomed, honored, accepted, and recognized for who they are. This sense of belonging is an integral part of a positive classroom culture that fosters relationships. Small gestures create a welcoming environment that builds relationships with and among students. Consider using the following small gestures in your practices.

- Welcome students when they enter the school or classroom. If possible, stand at the door. A hello or smile can make a student's day.

- Take photos or videos of students and their work.

- Recognize birthdays and celebrate significant personal events.

- Schedule conferences or make home visits to keep communication open with parents.

- Plan specific times to be in the classroom or available to support students.

- Increase your proximity to students: move around the classroom while students are working. This shows you care and gives time for personal assistance while keeping students on task.

- Accept, do not judge, what the students know or do not know; build opportunities to grow and learn.

Check the Mailbox

Set up a mailbox or suggestion box for student comments or notes to the teacher. Even if you do not take and implement their suggestions, simply acknowledging their ideas sends important messages to the students. Summarize all comments even if they are not something the class will change immediately. It could be something to continue working on together. At the very least, honor student comments by posting them or reading them aloud. This act builds stronger relationships between students and teachers.

Strategy 5: Set Clear Rules and Expectations

Clear rules and expectations create an environment in which students know what will happen, what they are supposed to do, and how they are expected to act. Marzano (2007) found that teachers who provided this type of structure and clarity positively affected student motivation and engagement. Hattie (2009) cites various research studies that indicate these attributes in teachers and classrooms are linked to higher achievement.

Clear rules and expectations impact the flow and transitioning in a classroom. They help students know what to do, when to do it, how to do it, and why to do it, while reassuring students that they are safe, respected, and protected. In classrooms where rules, directions, and expectations are clear and clearly communicated, students:

- Know places in the school or classroom they can explore and areas that are off limits
- Understand the rationale of the rules and regulations
- Know the routines
- Understand how to complete tasks and assignments
- Know their roles in working with others
- Are able to stay on task
- Move in an orderly fashion, at the right time
- Feel comfortable in their work areas
- Feel accepted by peers and the teacher

Unclear procedures and rules lead to confusion, frustration, and giving up. There is a higher probability the environment will be chaotic, with the teacher constantly having to deal with misbehavior, lack of engagement, and energy-zapping questions and comments. Behaviors in chaotic classroom environments escalate, and students feed off this negative energy when there is no other model or clear expectation.

When students break rules or refuse to follow directions, they can react physically or emotionally. Review the expectations, and be sure that guidelines are not only set but also enforced and understood. Consider the following common classroom scenarios:

- Learners sometimes move about the classroom to sharpen a pencil, throw away a piece of paper, or toss a crumpled piece of paper to a friend. Consider the real motivation for this movement. Students might be:
  - Frustrated about a task and need to clear their heads
  - Confused about the directions and therefore employing procrastination techniques
  - Tired of sitting down and need to stretch their legs and awaken their brains
- Students are sometimes given the consequence of going out in the hall. Consider the purpose of this move and the impact on the learner. Is that really something they want to avoid? Some students:
  - Like the hall because it is more interesting
  - Want to avoid the classroom because they are confused, frustrated, or bored
  - Want to connect with their peers outside the classroom

If a teacher tells a student to go to the board and the student angrily refuses, this emotional response signals any number of possibilities. Perhaps the student had a negative experience in the past, and the thought of replaying that scene was just too much. Sometimes the response is because of a lack of preparedness, uncertainty of the task, or a desire to save face or avoid feeling or looking "stupid" in front of peers. Other students may not want to look "smart" in front of their classmates. Knowing students personally and academically will help you to not take these emotional outbursts personally. It would be easy to respond to the student by reflecting the same anger and using a tone of impatience, but this reaction often does more harm than good. The goal is to motivate this student to participate, and it will do no good to humiliate or embarrass him or her any further. When learners feel put down with a look or comment, it has an emotional impact on their engagement and motivation. Although it is important to establish a rule to show respect, the steps taken after that rule is set make it concrete versus just a symbolic part of the classroom community. These expectations must be applied in every aspect of the classroom. Students need to be taught how to show respect for the ideas and feelings of other individuals. This begins with the teacher, who models respect in all interactions.

More often than not, there is an underlying cause for a student's emotional reaction. Speaking to the student privately can build trust and reassure him or her that the goal is for each student to learn without power struggles. Consider the following questions when thinking about the emotional safety in the classroom:

- Do students feel safe emotionally?
- When they are frustrated, do they verbalize their concerns?
- When students make a comment or suggest an idea, what happens?

If classmates laugh or the teacher dismisses the comment, a student may shut down and refuse to take any more risks. When the rules of productive discussions have not been established or upheld, classroom discussions are shallow, and only a handful of students dare to speak.

In fact, when we consider the amount of negative feedback and comments learners receive in the course of their lives, it becomes urgent that we set, model, and uphold positive expectations and rules. Disrespectful commentary and responses are modeled everywhere. Television, video games, media, social networking sites, and other sources constantly expose students to sarcasm, pessimistic outlooks, and negative responses. Many kids experience evaluative and critical reactions and feedback at home and in the media. In fact, the majority of feedback students receive is negative, and often it goes in one ear and out the other.

Intentionally plan what to do when these expectations are not met or rules are broken, and plan to give more than negative feedback. In fact, students who are accustomed to negative feedback are surprised when they receive specific feedback that leads them to take positive action. Descriptive feedback does not back students into a corner or make them guess their next step. Effective feedback provides descriptive statements to help students learn more or engage appropriately in the situation. Help students develop coping skills by providing positive redirection, specific feedback, and strategies they can use throughout life to deal with social, emotional, and academic situations.

Clear rules and expectations motivate students to engage in classroom activities. If students do not know how to participate appropriately, they disengage. Defining acceptable classroom behavior and etiquette, planning responses, establishing procedure, and giving clear directions are a few ways to set classroom guidelines.

Define Acceptable Classroom Behavior and Etiquette

Students need to be taught how to act in an academic setting and should be held accountable for the rules with consistency and persistency (Chapman & King, 2005). Set aside some time to thoroughly explain classroom rules and expectations. Enlist students in brainstorming the established rules and routines of the classroom to instill a feeling of involvement and belonging. Establish a small number of rules initially so students don't feel overwhelmed.

Plan Your Response to Broken Rules or Expectations

Once the expectations are set, the first few days are important and send influential signals to students about the way the classroom will run and how safe it will be to try, be their real selves, and learn (Hattie, 2009). Students wonder: how serious is this teacher about the rules, the expectations, and my learning? If a rule is broken, nip it in the bud. This is a crucial step in establishing trust and a feeling of safety with students.

When you respond, consider taking the following steps.

- **Describe the action or behavior you are observing:** If the rule is clear, students will be able to self-correct. When you tell students what you want them to do, their natural reaction is often the opposite. This response eliminates that possibility.

- **Describe the behavior you want to see.**

- **Stay neutral in tone and the words you choose:** Anger, sarcasm, and impatience can create negative reactions. Condescending tones shut students down.

- **Predict student questions, frustrations, or confusion:** Present students with procedures for dealing with common situations. Consider the following student questions:

  - "What if I missed the directions and don't know what to do?"

  - "What if I am confused about what we are learning?"

  - "What if I have to go to the bathroom?"

  - "What if I forget my homework?"

  - "What if I am frustrated with the teacher?"

  - "What if a classmate's comment offended me?"

  - "What if someone asks me for help? When is it *helping*, and when is it *cheating*?"

Ineffective responses to contrary behavior usually involve engaging in a power struggle. When teachers perceive a negative comment or rude behavior as intentional disrespect, their reaction is usually to punish the student. An effective response re-engages, redirects, or corrects the behavior to help students understand what is appropriate. Effective responses are focused on keeping the student present emotionally and ready to learn. Punishment and power struggles usually make the student feel just as devalued or offended as the teacher! Reactions should model the way students should behave. You may be the only positive role model in the student's life. This interaction is a learning process. Remember, too, that when a student displays appropriate engagement or behavior, specific feedback is also needed then to reinforce expectations (Ryan & Deci, 2000). Be positive whenever you can.

Establish Instructional Procedures and Expectations

Clear procedures and expectations set up the ways students will interact with each other and you, the teacher. Create rules and roles for working in small groups, and revisit them each time you ask students to work in small groups. Establish expectations and ways of working with partners so students understand how appropriate learning dialogue sounds. The conversations students have with peers are powerful learning opportunities. If students have not been shown how to have good conversations, they can be a waste of time. Hattie (2009) found that other students tend to be the primary source of feedback students receive. Unfortunately, the majority of peer feedback is inaccurate. Teaching students explicitly how to ask questions, stay on track, and focus their words on the academic content sets these interactions up for success.

Give Clear Directions

Consider this frustrating scenario: a teacher works hard to give directions for an upcoming assignment. The moment the teacher utters the last words, students begin asking, "What am I supposed to do?" or exclaiming, "I don't understand!" In this situation, the teacher often shows verbal and nonverbal frustration—understandably! Here are some suggestions to avoid some all-too-common communication errors.

- **Give directions right before work time:** Develop the habit of finding the best place in the timeline to give directions. For example, if there is student movement during the activity, get students settled, distribute the materials needed, and *then* give the directions—just in time, right before they are to perform the task. If you give directions too far ahead of the work time, students will forget what they are supposed to do.

- **Provide written directions:** Not all students are auditory learners! Written directions provide a visual to follow during the oral explanation and to refer to throughout the activity. In addition, written directions allow students to self-check at the close of the activity whether they have completed the assignment. Directions may be passed out on a separate sheet of paper, posted in the room, or written on the board.

- **After giving directions, have learners explain to each other what they are expected to do:** Students often understand directions and explanations better when they explain the guidelines or hear a peer reiterate the details.

- **Display task openers and key words:** Examine the tasks you are asking students to perform. Identify confusing terminology. Be clear about the academic vocabulary used to explain the task. For example, the word *plot* in literature means the main story line, but in mathematics or science, it can pertain to graphing. Designate a space in the room as a data board of directions and key terms with their meanings. Use age-appropriate, student-friendly definitions and terminology. Students can refer to the data board when they come across unfamiliar terms in the directions (Chapman & King, 2005).

Tips and Traps

Sometimes student engagement can be as easy or as difficult as changing directions or setting up a structure so learners have a clearer idea of what they are supposed to do.

Spoon-feed long directions that have many procedural steps. Too many directions overwhelm students because they cannot remember each step. Try the following procedure: give one part of the direction, and have the students complete that step. Then explain and give the directions for the next segment, and continue step by step until the end of the activity.

Do not depend on students to always grasp meaning from textbook directions. Often, the text does not provide clear directions that students can understand. When the terms are difficult to read and the learner feels too embarrassed to ask a question before the work has even started, the learner may quit. Read directions together, explain the expectations of the assignment, and ask students to share their interpretations to clarify misunderstanding.

Avoid asking "Do you have any questions?" immediately following directions. Many learners either do not know they have a question until they start working, or they are too confused to even know what to ask. Circulate the room to address questions, make observations, and provide assistance as needed.

At the same time, be aware of time wasters. Do not let useless questioning and discussions about directions consume vital work time. Some students make teachers explain too much even after they understand the directions. Many students are pros at using this delay as a procrastination tactic.

A trial run can give all learners a common and clear understanding of the task. When setting up an activity that requires movement or sharing, demonstrate it with an individual or a small group to show the expected actions. Next, walk the entire group through the task, reflecting on what the students just observed. Instruct and explain through each step in the procedure. Then, the students can try the task themselves. Recognize success with a celebration clap, noting how everyone followed directions and completed the task.

When behavioral problems arise, make students a significant part of the solution. If an entire class seems to be struggling with rules, engage students in a conversation about why the rule is not being followed and why it is important. Create a plan to revise or modify it. Include descriptions of the student and teacher actions when the rule is broken. Establishing guidelines with students creates more trust and buy-in. Students can then start to hold each other accountable for the mutually agreed-on expectation.

Use laughter, not sarcasm, to distract, break silence, and relieve stress or uncomfortable moments. When tense situations happen, use specific, observable comments on the behavior, and omit adjectives and adverbs, which can make feedback subjective and evaluative. Do not make the situation feel personal by reacting with demeaning comments. Respond to the negative behavior by redirecting it rather than mirroring the student's negative energy.

Some students are motivated to do things their way and are resistant simply because a teacher or other adult wants them to do something. To counteract this resistance, try the following:

- Involve students in daily decision making.
- Explain what students have to do and why it is important.
- Have a reason and a purpose that appeal to and fit the learner.
- Be goal specific; set tasks and small goals that are attainable.
- Understand that the misbehavior or refusal to follow directions may be the student's need for power or control in his or her world.

Putting It Into Practice

To build a classroom learning community, it is important for the teacher to set clear rules and expectations. Establish classroom guidelines and engage learners by asking them to describe best and worst outcomes and ineffective and effective responses to classroom disruptions.

Describe Best and Worst Outcomes

When students enter a new classroom, whether they are in elementary, middle, or high school, they come with existing feelings and experiences. The best-and-worst outcome letter is based on

Bob Chadwick's (1999) conflict and consensus work. First, have students identify their worst possible outcomes in taking this course or grade. By doing this, we bring any fears or negatively preconceived ideas out in the open, where we can deal with them in a proactive manner. These fears can take over and cause stress before the class even begins. With this information in hand, the teacher can plan ways to alleviate some of those fears.

Next, identify the best possible outcomes. This is when we explicitly state those expectations and hopes to plant success in the minds of our learners. Then we identify actions that will make the best possible outcomes a reality. This activity builds relationships and sets up a culture for learning.

Students can answer a sequence of best-and-worst outcomes questions on note cards or in the form of a letter. Note cards make it easy for students to jot down their ideas and then share them in small groups (see figure 2.7). (See page 68 for a reproducible version.)

1. What is the worst possible outcome of taking _____ ?

2. What is the best possible outcome of taking _____ ?

3. For the best to happen, what are some things you can do to plan for the best?

4. For the best to happen, what are some things your classmates can do?

5. For the best to happen, what are some things your teacher can do?

6. Given this information, what are some expectations or rules we should set up for our classroom community?

Figure 2.7: Sample best-and-worst outcomes questioning sequence.

Deal With Frequent Disruptions

Disruptions to the classroom environment occur unexpectedly. Effective teachers recognize and respond to these moments as quickly as possible, to keep students motivated to engage in the work of the class (Marzano, 2007). Table 2.4 displays ineffective and effective teacher responses when students disobey established rules and exhibit inappropriate classroom behavior. Reflect on the ineffective and effective responses and positive reinforcement. Consider the actions and strategies you would take to address the misbehavior.

Table 2.4: Ineffective and Effective Teacher Responses to Student Misbehavior

Example of Misbehavior	Ineffective Teacher Response	Effective Teacher Response	Positive Reinforcement
A student runs down the hall.	"You know better than that! Stop running!" *Outcome:* Student feels put down and ashamed.	"Remember, walk down the hall!" "I see students running down the hall." *Outcome:* Students are reminded of the rule and know what to do, especially after the teacher models the appropriate behavior.	When the student walks in the hall, celebrate in the classroom: "I was so proud of you for walking!"

Example of Misbehavior	Ineffective Teacher Response	Effective Teacher Response	Positive Reinforcement
Students are too noisy.	"Stop talking so loud!" *Outcome:* Students receive the message "Do as I say, not as I do."	"Remember, use your inside voice." "How quiet should our voices be when we are inside?" "I hear really loud voices." *Outcome:* Student is reminded of the rule and knows what to do.	When students talk at an appropriate volume level, celebrate and acknowledge with specific praise: "You certainly know how to use your inside voices. It sure makes learning fun and possible."
A student leaves a book or other materials in his or her locker.	"Go back to your locker and get it." *Outcome:* The student misses part of the instruction and context of the class. (Students often use this excuse to get out of class.)	"You may borrow our classroom copy or share with a peer until next time." *Outcome:* The focus remains on learning, not being distracted by details or excuses that just waste time and energy.	Affirm students the next time they bring materials to class: "I'm so proud that you remembered all your materials!"
Students are having sidebar conversations at inappropriate times, such as during a lecturette, teacher-focused demonstration, or activity.	"Be quiet!" *Outcome:* The whole class is pulled off task and off topic. Energy and flow of the classroom focus to the negative behavior instead of the expected behavior.	"Summarize what I just said." "Come up with an example of the learning being addressed." "Write two questions on a sticky note and share them with the class." *Outcome:* Students often try to make connections with sidebar conversations because they feel lost or confused. Involve all students in the content, and turn the side conversation into an opportunity to reflect.	Teach students to honor responses from their peers even if they say something with which they disagree: "Share a comment you heard from your classmate." This reflection from a peer reinforces the important contribution made to the classroom.
Students have a strong emotional reaction to an event (for example, a pep rally, holiday, bad news, or a fight) that has potential to derail the class.	Ignore the reaction. *Outcome:* Students have the event on their minds and are distracted throughout class. "Look, you're in my class now. That was before class, straighten up." *Outcome:* The teacher tells the student to stop feeling sad, angry, or hurt, and the student feels uncomfortable and remains unengaged in class.	"Are you all right?" *Outcome:* Students are able to decompress and connect with the teacher. "What emotion are you feeling? Share your thoughts with a peer." *Outcome:* Even seemingly insignificant issues can consume students' minds. Honoring students' feelings upfront ensures the problem does not escalate and allows them to move on instead of remaining off task.	Allow students to talk about the situation to show empathy, build trust, and open the door of communication. Show students that whatever they are experiencing is OK. Reinforce students' comfort levels through talking to them and allowing them to tell the real story.

continued →

Example of Misbehavior	Ineffective Teacher Response	Effective Teacher Response	Positive Reinforcement
After the teacher calls on a student, the student shrugs his or her shoulders and says, "I don't know."	"Well, you know the rule! Call on someone." *Outcome:* The teacher's demeaning and impatient tone offends the student. Demanding an answer right away, moving to another student, or answering yourself encourages a "faster is better" mode of thinking. Thinking deeply takes time.	"You may answer, partially answer, or pass the question to another student." *Outcome:* The teacher's calm restatement of the established procedure or rule encourages the student. "If you did know, what might you say?" *Outcome:* The additional question allows the student to think through a response.	Affirm that it is acceptable to take the time to formulate thoughts, because it is an opportunity to learn: "Write down how you might answer the question. Then, turn and talk to a peer and share your possible answers." Then, call on students again. Ask students to reflect on why they say "I don't know." Celebrate when "I don't know" moments turn into learning moments.
Students give partial answers to a question.	"You know you know more than that. You have got to explain that better." *Outcome:* The teacher's frustrated and impatient tone offends students.	"Turn to a partner and write down your thoughts about this question." *Outcome:* The classroom works together to construct an appropriate response. Ask probing questions or remind students of certain events to help trigger the correct response.	Model answers and offer specific comments on student responses that are effective.

*Visit **go.solution-tree.com/instruction** for a reproducible of this table.*

Chapter 2 Campfire Talk

This chapter described strategies to build a classroom community. Consider your own understanding, perceptions, and experiences about what works to create a supporting learning environment. Discuss the following questions and activities in your professional learning community, department, grade-level team, or a staff meeting.

1   Capitalize on the ideas and experiences of your colleagues. Discuss your current practice regarding the following questions:

— What strategies and activities do you currently use to learn about your students?

— What are effective ways to provide student choice?

— What works with learners at this age to build better teacher-student relationships?

— What are your best tips and ideas to handle cooperative learning and other group assignments?

— What goals can we set to improve the school culture of acceptance and respect?

2   Work with other faculty team members to create interest surveys or journal topics to administer to students.

3   Brainstorm possible cultural contributions to make your curriculum more culturally relevant:

— Identify the learning goals or objectives for your unit of study.

— Decide on the focus or topic of your unit of study.

— Research the contributions of culturally diverse people in your current topic of study.

— Infuse those examples into the appropriate unit of study.

4   Use the Plan for Student Motivation reproducible (page 58) to discover, diagnose, and plan to address the needs of individual unmotivated students in building a classroom learning community.

5   Discuss strategies and techniques to build relationships among staff and faculty. Become acquainted with staff members through well-planned personal sharing sessions. Getting to know each other brings the staff closer and bonds the team with mutual respect. Consider using the following questions to guide this conversation:

— Who or what got you into education?

— What is a successful moment you have had with students?

— What is your biggest pet peeve in working with colleagues? Dealing with students? In general?

— Have you had an embarrassing or memorable moment in your classroom?

— How was your experience while in school?

Plan for Student Motivation

Strategy	Name the Unmotivated Student(s) in Need of the Strategy	Identify the Wrapper the Student Is Wearing	List Observable Evidence, Behavior, Habits, or Traits	Develop an Action to Address the Need	Assess and Reflect on Implementation	Additional Comments
1. Know Your Students' Interests, Personalities, and Beliefs (page 24)						
2. Discover How Your Students Learn Best (page 30)						
3. Be Culturally Responsive (page 38)						
4. Build Relationships With and Among Students (page 43)						
5. Set Clear Rules and Expectations (page 48)						

Personal View of You Questions

Directions: Answer the following questions about your personality, interests, and school habits.

Personality questions: What makes you tick?

1. What makes you happy? Why?

2. What makes you sad? Why?

3. What makes you angry? Why?

4. What is important to you? Why?

5. What is not important in your life? Why?

6. When do others make you happy? Why?

7. When do others make you angry? Why?

8. What are things you don't like? Why?

9. What are your favorite things to do? Why?

10. When are you most content? Why?

11. Who do you respect? Why?

12. Who is your role model? Why?

13. Who do you want to be like? Why?

14. When are you comfortable? Why?

15. If you had a dream, what would you wish for? Why do you want that?

16. If you could change one thing, what would you change? Why?

17. How would you change it?

Interest questions: What floats your boat?

1. What is your favorite thing to do? Why?

2. If you could be anywhere, where would you be? Why?

3. What do you do during your spare time? Why?

4. Who do you like to be with?

5. Who do you see as a role model?

6. Who can you talk to?

7. Who do you turn to in times of trouble?

8. Who helps you the most? How?

9. Who is your best friend(s)? Why do you like to be with him or her?

10. What do you like to do after school?

11. When are you the happiest?

12. When are you angriest?

page 1 of 2

13. Who are your heroes or people you look up to? Why?

14. What is your favorite thing to do at home?

15. What do you do on the weekends?

School, learning, and study habits questions: What builds your brain?

1. When are you happy at school or your job? Why?

2. When are you sad at school or your job? Why?

3. What is your favorite part of the academic day? Why?

4. Which class is the most difficult for you? Why?

5. Who is your best support at school or at work? Why?

6. What motivates you to want to be here? Why?

7. Do you concentrate best when it is noisy or quiet?

8. Who or what helps you learn the most?

9. What gets in the way of your learning?

10. Where is your favorite spot to study?

11. Do you have access to a computer at home? If not, where do you use a computer?

12. How do you feel about school? Why?

13. What do you want to be?

14. What would you rather be doing?

15. How do you feel about _____? Why?

16. What is your biggest fear in school?

17. What is your biggest hope in school?

Rating How You Learn

Directions: For each activity, rate how much you like the activity and how much the learning activity helps you understand.

How much do you like doing this activity?					How often does this learning activity help you understand something?				
I Love It	It's OK	Unsure	I Dislike It	I Strongly Dislike It	Always	Sometimes	Unsure	Rarely	Never
Taking notes									
5	4	3	2	1	5	4	3	2	1
Making outlines									
5	4	3	2	1	5	4	3	2	1
Reading about the topic in a textbook or article									
5	4	3	2	1	5	4	3	2	1
Playing academic games									
5	4	3	2	1	5	4	3	2	1
Talking with a friend or partner in class									
5	4	3	2	1	5	4	3	2	1
Working in a small group									
5	4	3	2	1	5	4	3	2	1
Writing about the topic in my own words									
5	4	3	2	1	5	4	3	2	1
Drawing a picture to help me remember									
5	4	3	2	1	5	4	3	2	1
Having one-on-one time or small-group time with the teacher to explain the concept									
5	4	3	2	1	5	4	3	2	1
Listening to teacher explanations to the whole class									
5	4	3	2	1	5	4	3	2	1
Other: _____									
5	4	3	2	1	5	4	3	2	1

Exploring Your Smarts

Directions: Read each item, and check all statements that apply to you to determine your preference.

Verbal/Linguistic: I am all about words!

☐ I am a comprehending, fluent reader and writer.

☐ I like to write or dream up stories.

☐ I enjoy reading.

☐ Words come easy to me when I talk to people.

☐ Words come easy to me when I write.

☐ I spell well.

☐ I often join in discussions and conversations.

☐ I often volunteer to present my group's ideas to the class.

Logical/Mathematical: Give me numbers!

☐ I enjoy solving problems with numbers.

☐ Math classes are often my favorite part of the day.

☐ I am a logical thinker.

☐ I enjoy puzzles and games that strain my brain.

☐ I search for patterns.

☐ I sequence. I need steps to solve problems.

☐ I like to read directions to put things together.

☐ I want to know what we're going to do next in class.

Interpersonal: I am all about people!

☐ I learn while working in groups.

☐ I get ideas by brainstorming with others.

☐ I turn to friends, family, or trusted adults when I have a problem to solve.

☐ I enjoy cooperative learning activities.

☐ I learn when I study with a partner or study group.

☐ I like being a team member.

☐ I empathize with others.

Musical/Rhythmic: I like to sing and dance!

☐ I learn when I put difficult content to a beat.

☐ I participate in musical activities, such as listening to music, playing an instrument, or singing in the choir.

☐ I hum or sing a lot.

☐ Noises and sounds help me identify places I have been. For example, when a bell rings, I think of a game at the fair.

☐ I know a lot of songs.

☐ I have a favorite type of music.

Motivating Students © 2011 Solution Tree Press • solution-tree.com
Visit **go.solution-tree.com/instruction** to download this page.

☐ I remember information by listening to the teacher explain the topic.

☐ I study better with background noise.

Intrapersonal: I enjoy working independently.

☐ I can easily explain to you what I do well and what I need to work on.

☐ I like independent assignments.

☐ I use organizers.

☐ I make personal decisions on my own.

☐ I need to work alone.

☐ I enjoy personal journals, keeping a daily log, or writing diary entries.

☐ I need time to think before I speak aloud.

☐ I enjoy personal time.

Visual/Spatial: Show me a picture!

☐ I like graphic organizers.

☐ I doodle.

☐ I match colors well.

☐ I like art and exploring different media.

☐ I need to see the information.

☐ I visualize pictures in my head.

☐ I study graphics and pictures to better understand the written information.

☐ I can recall an experience visually.

Bodily/Kinesthetic: I like to move it, move it!

☐ I participate in sports.

☐ I learn during active activities.

☐ If I sit still too much, I can't pay attention to what the teacher is saying or doing.

☐ I like to draw, sculpt, or create to express myself.

☐ I need to vary my movement: sitting, standing, and jumping.

☐ Manipulatives help me learn.

☐ I enjoy role-playing and acting out activities.

☐ I like to dance.

Naturalist: Let's work with the environment!

☐ I like to grow things.

☐ I enjoy working outside.

☐ I like to explore things.

☐ I enjoy studying other cultures.

☐ I enjoy learning science, especially about the earth.

☐ I know what I need to survive in the wilderness.

☐ I adjust to different environments and situations.

☐ I take care of a pet and enjoy being with it.

Celebrating the Accomplishments of Our Students!

Take pictures of your students engaged in academic work, quality conversations, or quality work showing their insights. Paste their pictures in the boxes at various times throughout the year to acknowledge and celebrate their academic successes.

Our students talk smart!

Our students produce important work!

Our students love to learn!

Our students believe in each other!

Cube Activity

Identify a topic, event, person, or concept and use the following table and accompanying foldout for a questioning activity with your students.

Topic: _____

Questions	Student Answers
What happened?	
When did it happen?	
Who was there?	
Why is it important?	
How did it affect the people living at that time?	
What impact does it have on us today?	

page 1 of 2

Directions: Cut out foldout, fold on lines, and glue together.

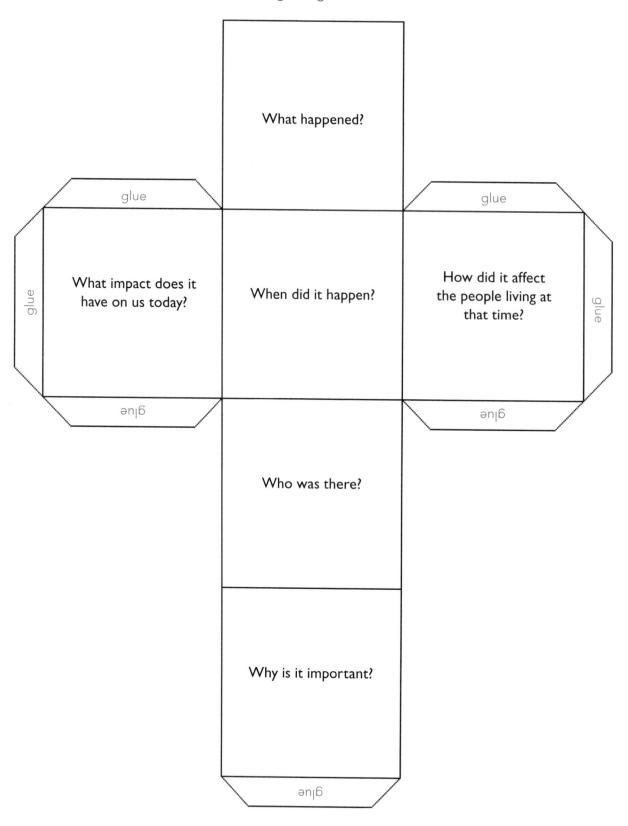

Blank Cube

Directions: Write your own questions for a cube activity. Use the blank cube to create a folded paper cube. Write questions in the six boxes. Cut out foldout, fold on lines, and glue together.

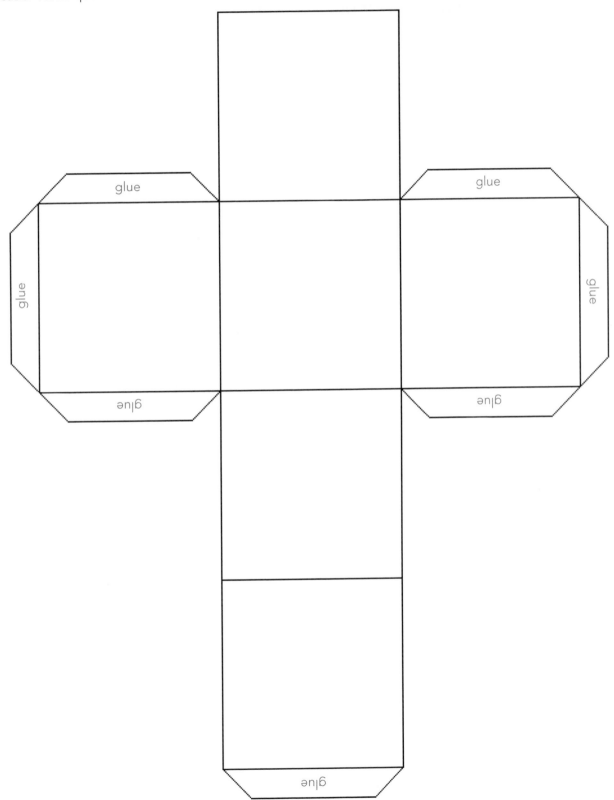

Best-and-Worst Outcomes
Questioning Sequence

Directions: Identify the worst possible outcomes in taking this course or grade. Next, identify the best possible outcomes. Lastly, identify actions that will make the best possible outcomes a reality.

1. What is the worst possible outcome of taking _____ ?

2. What is the best possible outcome of taking _____ ?

3. For the best to happen, what are some things you can do to plan for the best?

4. For the best to happen, what are some things your classmates can do?

5. For the best to happen, what are some things your teacher can do?

6. Given this information, what are some expectations or rules we should set up for our classroom community?

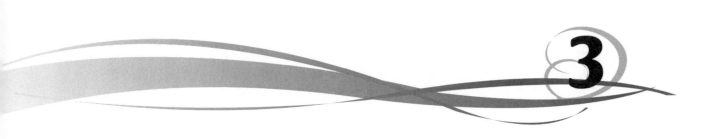

Describing and Planning Learning

Frustrated with the results of his summative assessment on the Revolutionary War, Mr. Creighton was looking for new ways to help his students learn. Under immense pressure to meet adequate yearly progress, Mr. Creighton and his colleagues were working tremendously hard. When so many of his students failed the unit test, he was quite discouraged, as were his students.

After examining the assessment, it became clear that the majority of the items on the test were at a knowledge or recall level in which students were asked to identify the causes of the Revolutionary War and explain how and why the colonies fought for their independence. Each of these topics was discussed at length during class, and the test asked students to recall those discussions in multiple-choice and short-answer questions. The test should have been a slam-dunk for students as the instruction—lectures and discussions—all addressed these concepts.

In response to a professional development training focused on defining learning with a focus on high expectations, Mr. Creighton constructed the next test at a much higher level, with questions that asked students to contemplate specific situations and consider how the law might be applied in response. While some items were simple, such as identifying the branches of government and their functions, the majority of the test incorporated more complex tasks that required students to discuss the role each branch might play in authentic scenarios.

Given students' lack of success in the past, Mr. Creighton also realized this higher-level thinking would require practice. As a result, he planned *check-ins* along the way to see what was sticking with students (understanding), and what was fuzzy (misunderstanding). Mr. Creighton used more frequent formative assessments that allowed students to practice the skills and reasoning they were to demonstrate on the assessment.

The test day came. The results were exciting and motivating. The students had achieved at higher levels. They had experienced more success on this higher-level, complex assessment than on any previous test. The pride and excitement among his students created momentum that launched his students into thinking much deeper.

The research is compelling and unmistakably consistent; high expectations for all students yield increased academic achievement (Reeves, 2007; Weinstein, 2002). While it is difficult work to hold all students to high expectations, research and practitioner experiences show such high expectations are an imperative if educators want all students, without exception, to achieve more.

While it may seem counterintuitive, students who are struggling often do not make connections in their learning, experiences, or classroom activities. If they consistently work on discrete skills, they may be missing how those skills connect to a bigger idea. Students wonder, for example, "Why do I need to know how to add fractions?" The purpose is not solely computation; acquiring this discrete skill leads to students solving problems and making connections. In the opening vignette of Mr. Creighton's social studies class, the real-life situations provided students context that contributed to student understanding. For his students, the branches of government made sense when students applied them in scenarios.

In their book *Deeper Learning*, Jensen and Nickelsen (2008) describe learning as "a process of acquiring knowledge, skills, attitudes, [and] mental connections in the brain memory" (p. 7). This process is the focus of instruction, assessments, and learning in the classroom. When teachers describe knowledge, skills, and attitudes, and use them as the basis for planning, students make connections and learn more.

There is passion, excitement, and relevance in the big ideas. If not, we should not be teaching them! Keep the big ideas and the relevance in front of learners so they can see how each part fits into the whole picture.

Sometimes students disengage and take themselves out of this learning process, because they do not see or understand what they are learning, or they have no idea why it is important. Generally speaking, two common situations can lead to "learner shut down"—when students are not challenged enough, and when they find the work too difficult. When learners perceive they know the information being taught or that they have done the same assignment before, boredom and unmotivated behavior often occur. They need to be challenged. Accordingly, it's essential to check with students before and during learning to determine their individual progress. Challenging assignments can be planned for students who already know the learning objectives based on the formative assessment data.

If the work is too difficult, some students become frustrated. For them, it is easier to stop working than be embarrassed because of not knowing. Frustration can cause anger, nervousness, defeat, or a loss of confidence, and therefore the learner does not complete the task. Again, a preassessment or formative assessment provides information about what students know and what they need to work on. A student who is overwhelmed or confused may need the task broken down into manageable chunks that build on his or her knowledge and interest.

Creating a culture of learning can be a difficult process that involves many moving parts. Chapter 2 described key aspects of setting a foundation for the classroom learning community by getting to know your students' interests, exploring learning styles and strategies, being culturally responsive, building relationships, and setting clear expectations and directions. A learning community is sustained through these actions. This chapter builds on that foundation and provides strategies and activities that help create the conditions for students to engage and learn more in their classroom learning community.

Educators use various methods to obtain clear learning goals. These objectives often come from standards. Using a process to guide the work, teachers break down the standards to find learning objectives. There are various protocols to do this work. Strategy 6 describes one such process influenced by Ainsworth's (2003a; 2003b) unwrapping process and the work of Stiggins et al. (2005) on deconstructing standards and writing student-friendly learning goals.

This chapter provides strategies to guide teachers in describing simple and complex learning objectives. Teachers first examine the complex learning objectives to find the big ideas that are most engaging. When this is clear, teachers help students practice and prepare (formative), and teachers plan assessments that represent students' achievement (summative). Clear descriptions of learning and well-planned assessments provide a foundation for motivating students to learn.

Strategy 6:	Clarify Learning
Strategy 7:	Drive Instruction With Assessments
Strategy 8:	Provide Challenging Learning Opportunities
Strategy 9:	Make Connections
Strategy 10:	Co-Create Criteria and Activities

Strategy 6: Clarify Learning

Jay McTighe writes, "Research and experience underscore a truism in our profession: learners of all ages are more likely to focus their efforts when they can see a clear and worthwhile learning goal. Conversely, when the goal is unclear or irrelevant to the students, it is less likely they will try their best" (2010, p. 283). When students clearly see what they are expected to accomplish, the path to success is paved! Teachers plan instruction and assessment to light their way. Motivating students to learn begins with paving the way.

Describing Learning: A Three-Part Process

Marzano (2003) reported findings from a study examining the amount of time it would take for students to master all standards given the average school day and the average set of standards. At the end of the study, the researchers estimated that mastery of the average set of standards would make education a K–22 experience. There is an overwhelming amount to teach and too much for students to master in K–12. The first step in clarifying the learning for our students, therefore, is prioritizing our standards. Many experts have offered processes to do this work. Doug Reeves (2001) describes three criteria for establishing which standards are most essential: readiness, endurance, and leverage. Grant Wiggins and Jay McTighe (1998) advocate for teachers to categorize their standards as *most essential*, *important to know*, or *nice to know*. The following three steps provide teachers—individually or in collaboration—a simple and meaningful process for paving the way: (1) prioritize your standards, (2) unpack the standards to identify learning objectives, and (3) write student-friendly learning objectives.

Prioritize Your Standards

We have adapted these criteria based on the work of Reeves (2001) and Ainsworth (2003b) to define priority standards. A priority standard has the following:

➤ **Readiness**—Critical to student success in future coursework and life. In reviewing standards, teachers look for knowledge and skills needed to be successful in students' next grades or courses.

➤ **Endurance**—Value beyond a single assessment. These standards reflect enduring knowledge and skills intended to last beyond a test. For example, students may not remember certain facts, but we want them to know how to think about facts in history, data collected in an experiment, or cause and effect in a nonfiction text.

➤ **Leverage**—Used throughout a course, a grade, or across content areas. These are powerful standards reflected in multiple content areas. For example, making a claim and supporting it is a learning goal in language arts when studying texts, in science when drawing conclusions from data, in social studies when discussing the impact of historical events on other factors, and in mathematics when planning to solve a problem and justifying our process and solution.

➤ **Repetition**—Addressed in an ongoing way. This is knowledge that spirals through units. As students write throughout the school year, organization and coherence appear in assignments within individual units of study and are assessed over time to ensure students are improving. In reading, students identify main ideas, specific details, inferences, and predictions throughout different texts over the course of different units.

➤ **Test priority**—Heavily assessed on high-stakes tests. One factor among many is the weight a standard has on an annual standardized test. This information is often found in the test specification chart on your state department website.

➤ **Identified area of growth**—Revealed by previous data on a standardized test. Teachers identify areas to emphasize based on the previous year's standardized test data. Because the results come too late, the information cannot be used to inform instruction the same year, but it is an indicator that reflects some of the effectiveness of curriculum.

Departments or grade levels follow this protocol for prioritizing standards as *most essential, important to know*, or *nice to know* (Wiggins & McTighe, 1998).

1 Review the checklist of criteria for prioritizing the standards. Discuss any clarifications or other considerations to add to the list.

2 Identify fewer than ten standards that you feel are most essential and meet the established criteria. Use pacing guides, frameworks, or other documents that describe the learning for students in your grade or course.

3 Share your lists, and record them on chart paper or a whiteboard. Place tally marks next to big ideas that reoccur across individual lists.

4 Examine the commonalities. Come to consensus on whether each standard is most essential, important to know, or nice to know. Use the criteria to debate your differences and make decisions.

5 Categorize the remainder of the standards as *important to know* and *nice to know*.

Unpack the Standards to Identify Learning Objectives

The next step is to define the individual learning objectives that students must achieve to successfully master the standard. Again, experts provide many different processes to do this work.

Larry Ainsworth (2003b) advocates unwrapping standards, while Rick Stiggins et al. (2005) promote deconstructing the standards. The overall purpose of doing this step is to offer teachers a process to interpret standards and identify simple and complex learning objectives. Keep in mind that the standard is the minimum goal for all students. These learning objectives become the focus of lessons and the basis for assessments.

Use the following steps to break down standards:

1 Using the criteria and protocol described earlier, decide on the priority standard or standards for the unit or intended time frame.

2 Circle the verbs. The verbs are the actions and types of thinking that the standard expects. They lead to the learning objectives required to achieve the standard. (See table 3.1.)

3 Identify the knowledge students must know or be able to locate to achieve the standard, including the required vocabulary.

4 Describe the reasoning or the thinking required in the standard. These learning goals become more complex, depending on the type of reasoning. For example, *apply* might mean students will identify literary elements in a text and explain why, while *analyze* might mean students will describe the different events that led to a certain conflict.

5 Name anything the standard requires students to produce or create. The standard does not always explicitly ask for a product. Teachers may construct an assessment that asks students to create something in order to demonstrate understanding.

Table 3.1: Skills and Knowledge Implied in Verbs in the Standards

Verbs That Often Signal Recall or Simpler Thinking	Verbs That Often Signal Reasoning or More Complex Thinking
Verbs define, describe, explain, identify, label, match, measure, memorize, move, name, read, recall, recognize, relate, review, move, state, summarize	**Verbs** analyze, apply, appraise, categorize, choose, classify, compare, compose, consider, contrast, construct, create, criticize, defend, design, develop, differentiate, distinguish, draw conclusions, evaluate, examine, explain, formulate, infer, interpret, investigate, judge, operate, predict, present, produce, recommend, show, support, write
Examples Define terms related to _____ Identify the steps in the writing process. Describe the characters in a story. State the variables from a graph or a table. Label the lakes, rivers, and major cities. Recall the steps in the water cycle. Read fluently. Move from left to right while reading.	**Examples** Analyze how different civilizations respond in economic crises. Formulate a strategy for solving a problem. Compare and contrast various civilizations' religious beliefs. Interpret events in a text. Present using effective public-speaking techniques. Design a sculpture. Produce a PowerPoint presentation. Write persuasively using convincing evidence.

As stated, verbs are an important part of this work. This process is designed to assist teachers in interpreting the standards to better plan engaging activities and quality assessments. Table 3.1 lists various verbs that are often associated with learning objectives that represent simpler concepts and those that describe more complex concepts. When breaking down the standard, you will have some simple learning objectives and some more complex learning objectives. Depending on how you phrase or interpret the standard, these verbs may be more or less complex and may cross the categories displayed in table 3.1. For example, let's take the learning objective, "I can explain the theme in a literary text." If the class has discussed the theme in the text they read together and the assessment asks students to write an essay describing this same theme, the learning objective is on the simpler side as students need to recall the theme from a prior discussion. In contrast, if students independently identify a theme and support it with evidence from the text in their explanation, the learning objective is represented in much more complex terms. This is the very reason groups of teachers need to meet and discuss their interpretations of these standards and learning objectives. Consider the verbs in table 3.1 and the accompanying examples when writing your own statements of learning goals.

Write Student-Friendly Learning Objectives

Once individual learning objectives are identified and clearly represent the standard or the intended learning, use them to craft student-friendly statements.

Some educators turn learning goals into "I can" statements in order to make them more student friendly (Stiggins et al., 2005), such as "I can identify the parts of a cell." The verb is important in this step, as it is in the standards, because it describes the type of thinking or action required. These statements are then posted in the classroom alongside the activities or agenda for the day so students begin to connect what they are *doing* in the classroom with what they are *learning*.

These statements also appear on assessments such as quizzes, tests, and projects. Students begin to connect their work to what is being assessed to their progress on the learning objectives. Some assessments separately indicate each "I can" statement and the items associated with that learning objective.

Tips and Traps

For younger children, write the student-friendly statement of the learning objective, and have students draw or write pictures representing the learning objective.

When identifying the simple and complex learning goals through breaking apart standards, discuss what student work could show achievement. This can aid in clarifying any possible tension in the interpretation of the standard. For example, *identify* is different than *produce*. If the standard says students will use what they know about grammar to write effectively, our lessons, activities, and assessments must go beyond just a multiple-choice test asking students to identify parts of speech. Clearly, the verb *produce* means that students will need to create their own writing and use what they know about grammar to do it.

Reflect on the process of prioritizing standards and finding learning objectives. Collaborative teams can easily become bogged down in the language and the sheer number of standards. Remember the purpose of doing this is to be clear on what you want students to learn and then to tie that to your lesson, activity, and assessment planning. Use questions such as, What parts of the process worked well? What was most frustrating? How could we change the process in the future? This debrief helps sharpen the process and makes it more productive in the future.

Be sure there are simple and complex learning objectives when breaking down standard parts. It is sometimes easier to identify basic knowledge and understanding. Some teachers have found the image of a ladder useful, where the lower rungs are the simple learning objectives, the middle the somewhat complex learning objectives, and the top rungs the most complex learning objectives. Posting them in this fashion, when appropriate, can help students see the big picture and the parts.

Make sure assessments reflect the reasoning in the standard and the verb that describes what students should be able to know and do.

Putting It Into Practice

Use "I can" statements to plan instruction with the standards. They can be used in multiple subjects to engage learners and describe planning and learning. Here we discuss their use in language arts and math.

"I Can" Statements in Language Arts

Language arts teachers can create "I can" statements for writing assignments and have students track their own progress over the course of multiple writing assignments. Table 3.2 (page 76) is a sample sheet students can use to track their progress on learning goals. (See page 102 for a reproducible version.)

Students record each writing assignment on a chart like table 3.2. After they have self-assessed their writing assignment using a rubric, they record their scores in the column marked *self-assessment*. The actual rubric should sketch out various proficiency levels from the beginning stages, perhaps a 1, to the more sophisticated levels, often a 4. The rubric would contain descriptions of each of the learning goals outlined in the first column of table 3.2. Then, after making a plan to revise their writing, students complete the revision and write the revised score in the second column. There are many options for "making a plan." In some cases, the teacher may offer students options for their plan such as *review your writing and look for words you can change to be more descriptive* or *edit your writing for correct punctuation*. In other cases, students would choose their plan based on the learning goal that needs the most work (consulting their scores recorded on a form such as table 3.2). In this case, the teacher might offer minilessons to support these different learning goals. The key here is to have students choose an area and actually make revisions. They only write a revised score for the areas on which they worked. Focusing on one or two areas makes revisions more manageable. For students who struggle, this tracking can be motivational as the table visually shows their growth and progress, breaking down what they know and what they really need to work on.

This tracking also becomes a form of data for teachers to review. If students are not focusing on an area of need, then the teacher helps direct or creates a classroom activity to prompt this focus. An individual conference is also appropriate. Students don't work on areas they have mastered. All writing assessments could be kept in a folder with this tracking sheet, which could then be used to calculate part of the language arts grade, using the students' most recent writing scores.

Table 3.2: Sample Student Tracking Sheet for Language Arts

Learning Goals	Writing Assignment 1		Writing Assignment 2		Writing Assignment 3	
	Self-Assessment	Revised Score	Self-Assessment	Revised Score	Self-Assessment	Revised Score
Content						
I can write an effective topic sentence.						
I can write effective supporting details.						
I can explain how my supporting details connect to the main idea.						
I can use words that pop. This means that the vocabulary I use is specific and descriptive.						
Mechanics						
I can accurately apply the rules of capitalization to my writing.						
I can spell accurately in my writing.						
I can apply the rules of punctuation in my writing.						

"I Can" Statements in Math

Math teachers can also use "I can" statements on their assessments. This connects what students are learning to how they are being assessed. The learning objectives, phrased as "I can" statements, come directly from the process of unpacking a standard. Clearly connect learning targets to the assessment task. Figure 3.1 is a sample assessment with student-friendly statements tied specifically to an assessment (J. Whitehead, personal communication, September 23, 2010).

Strategy 7: Drive Instruction With Assessments

Assignments, assessments, and activities serve different purposes during the learning process. Some are designed to introduce concepts; others facilitate practice or alternative explanations; others provide evidence of proficiency. The purpose drives the timing. The learning objectives drive the content. The assessment results drive future instruction or the next assignment.

Learning Targets

- I can create a survey question.
- I can organize data collected from a survey question into a chart.
- I can calculate measures of central tendency from a data set.
- I can represent data by creating graphs.
- I can interpret my data.
- I can draw conclusions from my data.

1. Select a question to investigate. It should be a question that can be easily surveyed by fifty people. (We will do some surveying here at school.)

   My question is: _____

2. Create a chart on which to collect your survey responses. (Please put on notebook paper.)

3. Once all of your data has been collected, calculate the mean, median, mode, and range on notebook paper. Your work must be shown. (It is OK to use a calculator to CHECK your work!)

   Mean _____

   Median _____

   Mode _____

   Range _____

4. Choose two types of graphs to represent your data. Create the graphs on graph paper or note-book paper. (No computer-generated graphs!) If you need graph paper, please ask!

5. Make three statements that interpret your data. Interpret, in this case, means make statements about what is represented in your graph: "When surveying people about their favorite ice cream, chocolate was by far the favorite flavor, beating vanilla by fifteen votes. Strawberry was the second most favorite flavor with twenty-one votes."

6. Draw some conclusions about the data. These are statements describing why the data may have come out the way they did or their implications. For example, you might write, "Chocolate is the most popular ice cream flavor, so this means that when the cafeteria serves ice cream and gives students a choice, they will need to order more chocolate than vanilla or strawberry."

Scoring Checklist

Data Table

- Data table is organized.
- Data table has labels, including headings.
- Data table is easy to read.

Figure 3.1: Sample graphing project assessment.

continued →

Mean, Median, Mode, and Range

- Given the data in the data table, measures are set up accurately.

    + If not, which ones are inaccurate? _____

- Calculations of all measures are accurate.

    + If not, which ones are inaccurate? _____

	Achieved at Basic Level	Achieved at Standard Level	Achieved Beyond Standard Level
Interpreting Data and Drawing Conclusions	Statements of interpretation describe the data at face value. For example: "Twenty-five students chose soccer as their favorite sport."	Statements depict relationships among data collected. For example: "Soccer was the most favored sport with twenty-five people choosing it. Football came in a close second with twenty-two votes." Conclusion statements reflect potential reasons why the data came out the way they did.	Conclusion statements make predictions about what these data mean for future events or circumstances. For example: "Given how popular soccer is in our class, many students will probably watch the World Cup this weekend."
Graphs	Both graphs have: • An appropriate scale • Consistent intervals • Clear labels • Clear headings	Both graphs are appropriate to display the data table. Both graphs accurately reflect the data in the data table.	Color enhances meaning of the data (versus just making it look nice).

This rubric is proficiency based and builds on each column. A score of "Achieved at Standard Level" means the student work reflects the statements in "Achieved at Basic Level" and "Achieved at Standard Level."

Adapted with permission. © 2010 Jolaine Whitehead. Oconee County Schools, Bishop, Georgia.

Formative assessments are checkpoints along the learning journey to determine what progress students are making toward the intended learning goal. Formative assessments can be informal, such as classroom observations, student discussions, exit slips, or conversations with students. They can also be more formal, such as quizzes or rough drafts of writing projects. Whether formal or informal, teachers use the data to plan instruction and interventions to reteach the unknown material and develop opportunities to challenge the learners who demonstrated mastery. Students also use the information to identify their strengths and challenges, and to plan actions to move their learning forward.

The ultimate level of understanding or proficiency students achieve toward the learning goal is measured by a *summative* assessment. A summative assessment is an evaluation of learning at a particular moment in time. A quiz, test, project, or paper can be summative when assigned to capture the learning that occurred during a unit, a semester, or year. When teachers assign a summative assessment, students are expected to know and be able to reach the learning goals measured on the assessment. Formative assessment practices reveal understanding throughout the unit, which in turn directs instruction to help students understand. For example, performance on a quiz indicated two-thirds of students struggled to include transitions in their writing, so the teacher planned a minilesson on transitions with accompanying homework. If assignments are given at the right time for the right purpose, there will be no surprises.

The difference between formative and summative assessment is in how we use the information, not in the testing method. For instance, a summative assessment might be when homework is assigned and students receive scores with no opportunity to fix mistakes or reflect on their misunderstanding. However, this assessment becomes formative when students examine that homework assignment, correct mistakes, reflect on what they understand, and decide what they need to do next. The actions the student and teacher take based on the information from an assessment make it formative or summative, not the activity or method itself (Stiggins et al., 2005; Wiliam, 2007; Chapman & King, 2005).

Consider this analogy: when a chef tastes her soup, it is comparable to formative assessment; she adds spices, adjusting the flavor to achieve the desired taste. When the customer tastes the soup, however, he makes an evaluative judgment about its quality. This is a summative assessment. If the soup is not to the customer's satisfaction, it fails the test. Most likely he will not return, or at the least will not order that soup again. Similarly, when all classroom assessment is summative and students are frequently failing, they may check out by skipping class, forgetting or not doing assignments, or just simply putting forth little effort. When a student experiences no success and has no way to fix it, a lack of motivation will surely follow. Students need opportunities to "taste the soup" and adjust it before they are evaluated.

In essence, formative assessment is descriptive and summative assessment is evaluative. Formative assessment, when used well, has great power to influence both student learning and the extent to which students are self-directed. The evidence that intentional formative assessment practice dramatically increases student achievement is convincing (Black & Wiliam, 1998; Wiliam, 2007).

Homework as formative assessment has received mixed reviews, especially when we consider not only how often students hand it in but also whether it supports their individual learning needs. High school students gain the most from homework, followed by junior high students, and then elementary students (Marzano, 2003; Hattie, 2009).

Interestingly enough, homework is not as effective for students who are struggling:

> For too many students, homework reinforces that they cannot learn by themselves, and that they cannot do the schoolwork. For these students, homework can undermine motivation, internalize incorrect routines and strategies, and reinforce less effective study habits, especially for elementary students. (Hattie, 2009, p. 235)

Grading formative assessment also receives mixed and contradictory reviews from the experts. At its best, formative assessment is designed to support learning, not evaluate it. As a result, when used well, it does not need a grade. In fact, some of the research indicates that putting a grade or a mark on an assessment detracts from any learning that might occur as a result of the assessment itself or the feedback provided (Butler, 1988; Hattie, 2007; O'Connor, 2002).

A grade is often acceptable *if* students receive another opportunity to fix their mistakes or revise their work, and any growth is reflected in the final grade without penalty or reduced score.

When students show evidence of understanding, the most recent scores should be used to calculate a grade (O'Connor, 2002).

A learner's negative self-perception can influence learning and engagement in profound ways. These hidden realities often have significant consequences on the effectiveness or lack of it as teachers employ different strategies. For example, if students receive an F or a 60 percent on an assignment, do they know what that grade means in terms of their learning? Do they know how to improve the score or learn more? If the answer to either or both of these questions is no, students may interpret the F in terms of their own self-worth and may define themselves as dumb, a "bad" math student, or someone who doesn't like to read.

This lack of self-worth can manifest itself in many ways. Students often get the assignment and say to themselves:

- "The teacher thinks he can make me do this."
- "It would not be cool for me to do this. The others will laugh at me."
- "I'm angry, and I am not going to work today."
- "I am so bored, and this is stupid."
- "I am frustrated, and I don't understand."
- "She does not expect me to do this, so I won't."

A student who feels like a failure will not engage in most activities and assignments. No one wants to fail again or disappoint others. In this case, a failing grade does not provide hope or describe an action to move a student to finding success. Quality formative assessment offers students hope. Teachers and students spend time reviewing mistakes and addressing misunderstandings. When students make mistakes or are not yet proficient, they have another opportunity to learn without being penalized or receive a lower grade. See strategy 21 (page 172) for more on analyzing mistakes to fire up understanding.

Constructing the Right Assignments

The relationship between learning objectives, formative assessment, instruction, and summative assessment is at the heart of the right assignment at the right time. Learning objectives must drive assessment and inform instruction. Let's say teachers are planning by unit. The unit summative assessment reflects the essence of the prioritized standards addressed in this unit. The summative assessment is the student work that reflects achievement of the standard.

If students are to be successful on a summative assessment, teachers strategically plan practice or check-ins along the way. These check-ins are planned as formative assessments. When the standard is broken down, learning objectives—the smaller parts of the standard—are identified. These learning objectives are turned into student-friendly statements, as described in strategy 6 (page 71). Formative assessments are based on the learning objectives. Usually, they are smaller assessments intended to plan instruction. For example, students may take a formative quiz on Wednesday covering the learning objectives "I can identify the five themes of geography" and "I can apply the five themes of geography to various locations." On Thursday, students are broken into groups based on which items they got wrong. The groups work to fix their mistakes and then write a short paragraph describing what they now understand. This quiz is formative because students and teachers use the data to learn more. Instruction was planned based on how students performed on the quiz.

The *right* assignments share several characteristics:

- A clear learning objective
- A clear alignment to learning goals derived from standards
- A clear purpose, such as the following—
  - The assignment is designed for students to practice a skill, to check understanding, or to build skills for an activity the next day. This is a formative assessment.
  - The assignment or assessment is designed to evaluate or quantify the amount of learning that has occurred at a certain point in time using a rubric score, percentage, or grade. This is a summative assessment.
- A doable amount of work with objectives that are designed for a specific purpose
- Work that is broken down into parts enabling students to see the whole, while at the same time working on the parts
- Work that is purposeful, meaningful, and challenging; not busy work
- Work that teaches responsibility by being meaningful, challenging, and responsive to students' learning needs
- Work that is worth the effort, helps students learn, or identifies what students know or do not know to plan how to improve
- Work that stretches students' understanding to reach the more complex part of the big idea
- More time and support for students who legitimately need it

When possible, plan assessments prior to beginning the unit, the quarter, or year in order to ensure that the intended learning is clear both in description and end product. Follow these three steps:

1 Identify or create the summative assessment that shows evidence students have achieved the intended learning. Does the summative assessment measure students' understanding and mastery of the standard? Does the summative assessment reflect the essence of the big idea—not every individual part?

2 Plan formative assessments. If students are going to be successful on the summative assessment and achieve, what will they need to practice along the way? These formative assessments should strategically check for understanding on the most important learning goals required for success on the standard and be administered in a timely fashion. Leave enough time in the instructional calendar for students to address the results, identify their strengths and areas of need, and achieve mastery.

3 In designing plans for formative assessments, check in with students on learning goals represented on the summative test. Instruction should facilitate practice on the thinking and reasoning required on the summative assessment. If the standard requires a product, the criteria should reflect the relevant learning goal, and formative assessments should include revisions to improve the final product. In this case, the revision process or feedback directs the revision process and is considered formative.

Tips and Traps

Design formative assessments that include items at the simple, medium, and complex learning-goal levels. Interpreting the results and planning to adjust instruction will be much more efficient to help individual students receive the instruction needed at the level of proficiency.

Gareis and Grant (2008) recommend constructing four to six items per learning goal to ensure teachers have a better sense of students' proficiency on an individual learning objective.

Pay attention to students' self-talk and nonverbal actions. These indicate students' levels of confidence, which drastically impact their motivation to try, fix mistakes, and become more independent learners.

Make mistakes low risk. If students never made mistakes, they wouldn't need to come to school. These "glitches" are rich sources of reflection and discussion. Analyze mistakes and a student's reasons for struggling or misunderstanding. Use them to inform your instructional planning. When students are practicing, their mistakes help teachers and learners figure out learning problems and identify next steps. (See strategy 21, page 172.)

Do not give assignments to fill time. Quality, *planned* academic choices provide ways for students to demonstrate what they know and need. Critically assess each possible assignment; analyze the learner's purpose, interests, engagement, and motivation to complete the task as well as the assignment's ability to teach the needed information. If the assignment does not meet the criteria, throw it out and replace it with one that will. There are too many boring assignments that are busywork with little value in engaging or inspiring student learning. These useless time fillers create the conditions for uninterested, turned-off students.

Putting It Into Practice

Use learning objectives to plan formative and summative assessments. When students have an opportunity to practice, fix their mistakes, and try again, their confidence increases, and so does their achievement (Guskey, 2009; Wiliam, 2007; Hattie & Timperley, 2007).

In this example, a group of middle school language arts teachers identified the learning objectives from the standard they wanted to focus on in an upcoming unit. From those learning objectives, the team planned two formative assessments and one summative assessment. Their intent was to use the formative assessments in their instruction to help students practice. The summative assessment's purpose was to reflect the students' progress that occurred as a result of the formative assessment and instruction. Follow their framework to create assessments for your classroom. (Thanks to Molly Miller, Carrie Hogue, and Shannen Rey at Thomas Jefferson Middle School, Decatur, Illinois, for permission to share the example we co-created during a collaborative meeting on September 29, 2009.)

First, the team identified the learning objectives for the unit. After consulting the Illinois Assessment Framework and their school pacing guide, the teachers identified and wrote the following learning objectives in student-friendly terms, or "I can" statements:

- I can identify the events in a text.
- I can identify relationships among events using cause and effect.
- I can draw conclusions based on the events in a text.

These learning goals were intended to increase in complexity. For example, the first statement uses the verb *identify*, which signals a simpler objective, and in this case it means to literally pick out the events in the text. Reading comprehension is required in this situation. The second learning goal also uses *identify*, but this time it holds a medium complexity as students are to look at the relationships among events and understand cause and effect. The third is the most complex in this example as the verb *draw* is coupled with *conclusions*, meaning learners are going to need to use what they know about the text and the relationships among events to make sense of the reading. While there might be clues to potential conclusions in the text, students can display some original thinking.

Next, the team discussed what the assessment or student work would look like when students had achieved these learning goals. It was decided students would read a short text and then take a formative assessment made up of the three learning goals. First, three multiple-choice questions were constructed to see if students could identify the events in the text. Then, students answered three true/false statements and explained their selection by describing why they thought each statement was true or false and how it reflected cause and effect. If the statement was false, they explained how to revise the statement to make it true. Finally, a short essay question would ask learners to draw conclusions based on the context of the text.

The team, after deciding the format of the assessments, chose three texts. The first text was about physical force, the second was about squirrels, and the third reading focused on grief. Figure 3.2 illustrates the format of the was formative assessment.

Name: _____

Learning Objective 1: I can identify the events in a text. (____ /3)

1. What should you do before you use any of the self-defense tips?

   A. Use physical force.

   B. Determine if fighting is your only option.

   C. Use your natural weapon.

   D. Determine if your path to safety is blocked.

2. What should you do if you are attacked from behind?

   A. Stomp the attacker's foot with your heel.

   B. Kick the attacker in the shins or jab the face.

   C. Use your legs to resist.

   D. Use your voice.

3. What should you do if you are picked up?

   A. Stomp the attacker's foot with your heel.

   B. Kick the attacker in the shins or jab the face.

   C. Use your legs to resist.

   D. Use your voice.

Figure 3.2: Sample formative assessment on physical force.

continued →

Learning Objective 2: I can identify relationships among events using cause and effect. (_____ /3)

4.   True or false: If you are attacked from the front, kick the attacker in the shins. Explain how this statement is an example of cause and effect.

5.   True or false: According to the passage, you should try and get away from the dangerous situation to a safe location. What does the passage suggest is the effect of getting away from the dangerous situation?

6.   True or false: The article suggests at least two causes for using physical force in self-defense. If so, name these two causes.

   1.   _____

   2.   _____

Learning Objective 3: I can draw conclusions based on the events in a text. (_____ /3)

The article describes certain causes for using physical force. Based on these causes and the possible positive or negative effects of using physical force, read the following scenario:

You have taken the bus to the mall to hang out with some friends. As you round the corner, just about to the place you planned to meet, there are a few older kids coming toward you. Your intuition or gut tells you they intend to mess with you (or cause a bit of trouble).

Given the information in the article, how would you respond if you were in this situation? Consider the following bullets in writing your response.

Possible score of 3:

•   Clearly state how you would respond (conclusion).

•   Clearly explain why you would respond in this way.

•   Use evidence from the text to show why.

Questions adapted from Study Island (www.studyisland.com).

Using the learning goals in figure 3.2, the team created a data table listing individual students' scores based on the learning goals for the two formative assessments and the summative assessment. (See table 3.3) Based on student performance on the multiple-choice questions for the first learning goal, "I can identify the events in a text," the teachers recorded the number each student got correct out of three. Then, they recorded the scores for the second learning goal, "I can identify relationships among events using cause and effect." Finally, they recorded the rubric score students received on the third learning goal, "I can draw conclusions based on the events in a text." (The second formative assessment was identical to the first in terms of learning objectives and format. However, the questions reflected an article about squirrels. Again, teachers recorded individual scores on the data table, inserting their scores for each learning goal.)

After analyzing the data from the first formative assessment, teachers decided which students needed more work on identifying events from the text, identifying cause and effect, and drawing conclusions. For a couple days, instruction focused on responding to the misunderstandings reflected in this formative assessment. Table 3.4 is a planning template used to identify three learning stations for instructional purposes. The first row contains the "I can" statements measured on the assessments. In the second row, teachers listed the individual students who needed

Table 3.3: Sample Data-Tracking Sheet on Learning Goals

Students	Formative Assessment on Physical Activity Reading			Formative Assessment on Squirrels Reading			Summative Assessment on Grief Reading
	Learning Goal 1	Learning Goal 2	Learning Goal 3	Learning Goal 1	Learning Goal 2	Learning Goal 3	

Table 3.4: Sample Classroom Intervention-Planning Template

I Can Identify the Events in a Text	I Can Identify Relationships Among Events Using Cause and Effect	I Can Draw Conclusions Based on the Events in a Text
Students	Students	Students
Activity	Activity	Activity

to work on that particular learning objective. Students were placed into groups accordingly. If students had more than one area that needed work, the teacher chose the objective that needed work first. The third row is a space where individual teachers or collaborative groups can write the instructional plans for each group. This is to address the gaps in understanding. Students may also use a table like this to analyze their mistakes and what they will do to fix them. After administering the second formative assessment, teachers could see any change in performance between the two. They planned instruction to reflect the data; students worked on the learning objective they most needed to address. Those who mastered it worked on an enrichment activity such as writing their own article or finding an article of interest. (Strategy 25, page 188, provides more examples of effective responses to assessment information.)

During this process, disengaged students benefited, especially those wearing "I don't know," "I don't care," defeatist, and been there, done that wrappers. In a student-centered activity like this, students work on specific areas of need rather than participating in general activities or whole-class activities that may or may not meet their needs. When a lack of motivation comes from being confused or not knowing the content well, this type of structure can reach and teach those students!

Finally, after administering and planning instruction based on the results of the two formative assessments, the summative assessment was given. The scores were recorded on the data-tracking sheet in the "Summative Assessment" column. By specifically describing and planning learning and using assessments to drive instruction, students and teachers had a clear idea of the impact of their instruction and assessment on student learning. If the formative assessments and the instruction are effective, students should experience success on the summative assessment. This success is motivating!

Strategy 8: Provide Challenging Learning Opportunities

B-O-R-I-N-G! This word rolls all too easily off the tongues of children of every age. While some are quick to use it for any activity, in general, students describe activities and content as boring for reasons such as the following:

- Low interest
- Lack of excitement
- Perceived lack of relevance
- Lack of understanding in how or where to begin (it is easier to say the task is boring than admit confusion, especially for high achievers)
- Repetitive work or something they already did last year or something they already know

Ask individual students or the whole class questions to assess the level of challenge in their school lives:

- "Are you challenged in school?"
- "Do you understand why you need to know the information you are studying?"
- "Are you bored? When? Describe a specific example."
- "Are you frustrated? Explain."
- "Do you feel you know everything? Are you always getting things right with little or no studying or struggle?"
- "How is what you are learning in school going to help you in the future? Are there content or activities you feel will not help you in the future?"

Student responses to these questions may help teachers determine if challenging tasks are needed to re-engage students. Certain characteristics define challenging work. Learners engage, are energized, and just can't help themselves when teachers hit the right challenge that is relevant and connected to big ideas. Challenging work takes more time, requires determination, and builds high expectations (Ames & Archer, 1988). The following sections build on these characteristics of challenging tasks.

Challenging Work Is Energizing

Avoid burnout, boredom, and bad attitudes by offering challenging activities, assignments, and assessments. When lessons and assignments are challenging, students get enthusiastic. Some students may not jump for joy right away, especially if they aren't used to challenging activities. Challenging activities require thinking, and the answers do not always come within a split second. Remember that challenging tasks require that students try over and over again. When something does not work, the answer is not a lower grade, but another opportunity to find an effective solution. When challenging tasks are effective, students are energized and excited about their work and engaged in the process of doing it.

Challenging Work Is Relevant

Design curriculum around real problems embedded in the content to make learning meaningful and interesting to each learner. Students learn by making links to their world, so provide time for them to ponder and build these personal connections through student-focused activities.

Authentic learning is applying what is learned in the world outside of school. Schools must prepare learners for the world of tomorrow. Students need to be prepared to live and work in a world that is fast paced and constantly changing. Keep current and use new sources of information. This future-thinking connection is challenging and stimulates students' interests (Strong, Silver, & Perini, 2001).

Challenging Work Takes Time

Learners need time to solve, develop, create, probe, try, problem solve, and decide. Time is a very precious resource these days. In an already crowded curriculum, spending time with challenging activities may seem like a luxury. In some cases, teachers feel pressure to cover material at the expense of students really understanding or attacking learning objectives that are relevant and important. Doug Reeves (2001) discusses the power of prioritizing what we spend time teaching by prioritizing our standards. One of the criteria he uses in determining what gets priority over something else is endurance: what is the learning that will last beyond the test? When students spend more time with concepts and think through them at a deeper, more challenging level, they tend to get more enthusiastic and retain the learning after any test.

The other fear that is a reality in our climate today is accountability on a standardized test measure. Wiliam (2007) notes that "in a variety of settings teachers have found that teaching for deep understanding has resulted in an increase in student performance on externally set tests and examinations" (p. 20). While educators are held responsible for these measures, that does not mean that teachers cannot introduce challenging assignments and concepts into the curriculum. In fact, by doing so, teachers create enthusiasm and relevance for students and increase their success!

Challenging Work Requires Determination

Determination plays a major role in meeting a challenge—as long as it is not too frustrating. For example, a gardener can be determined to turn a blighted area of the yard into a beautiful eye-catching spot. After trying many types of plants and watching them die, some gardeners will keep trying different plants, improving the soil, or seeking expert advice until they find the hardy, beautiful plants that can withstand the conditions. Others get frustrated and decide to forget it and cover the area with stone and cement.

To plan for implementation of challenging learning opportunities, consider the following steps:

1 Identify the learning goal or focus of your lesson, assessment, or activity.

2 Determine a task or project. Use the verbs in the more complex learning goals to find or design tasks.

3 Engage learners in activities and discussions to help define high quality. If it is a discussion, describe and give examples of questions that inspire conversations and quality responses. If it is something students need to produce, offer them examples or descriptions of quality products.

4 Implement the challenging tasks with students. Debrief the activity or experience. This is an important opportunity to highlight that challenging thinking takes time and the right answer does not always emerge immediately. The best solutions surface from persevering and trying new things. Have students ask themselves the following questions:

- "What went well?"
- "What was challenging?"
- "What was surprising?"
- "What was exciting?"
- "Were there times I wanted to give up? When? How did I make it through?"

Tips and Traps

Deep thinking and challenging assignments take time, so be sure to include ample time to explain the purpose, process, and outcome as well as time to think, struggle, and complete the challenging task.

Model the struggle that deep thinking requires, as students often want the answers immediately, and challenging problems and experiences frequently require some confusion before coming to an understanding of how to proceed.

Beware of planning too little time or not being flexible when you recognize students are engaged and really working. If they are learning, working, and incredibly excited about the task at hand, moving on to the next agenda item just because it is in the plan squashes excitement and sends negative messages about classroom work.

Keep a set of ready-to-go challenges in your toolbox to pull out at any moment to occupy the minds of your students. For example, design a problem or a scenario for the class to solve or address.

Do not make the challenging questions extra credit. Focus on what students need to be doing and thinking about in their learning. Be sure the challenging problem is aligned to the action or type of thinking required in the standard. For example, identifying the scientific process is different than executing the scientific process. Analyzing literature differs from writing in different genres.

Do not use the parts of the textbooks that are boring. Find exciting, stimulating, and challenging resources.

Consult information on authentic intellectual work for more examples of challenging tasks and rubrics, such as Newmann, King, and Carmichael's (2007) "Authentic Instruction and Assessment: Common Standards for Rigor and Relevance in Teaching Academic Subjects."

Solicit folks who work in careers that deal with challenging topics. Ask them to describe some of the challenges they encounter, and use those real-life examples in activities. For example, suppose an engineer had to design a cell-phone lightbulb that used less energy and lasted a long time. He found a solution, but customers are unhappy because the light is too dim. Students could brainstorm possible solutions to this dilemma.

Asking students to solve more challenging problems requires that they have an understanding of where to find needed information and the process for attacking the problem. Jumping too soon to the real-world problem without walking students through the process or modeling it leaves these types of projects open to surface-level responses.

Do not mistake difficult for challenging or complex. Reading multiple stories and identifying the main characters, theme, and literary elements may initially seem challenging. However, if we stop at identifying, the challenge is lost. Move on! Consider assignments like changing the ending of the story or discussing the implications of the theme in a current event.

Putting It Into Practice

In thinking about disengaged or unmotivated students, ask yourself how a challenging task could change the direction of their energy. For example, consider the reasons for a particular student's disengagement; ask questions about his interests, passions, and outside-of-school activities. If cars intrigue the student, an interest discovered because of the magazine he was reading during a lecture, have him write a letter to an auto company recommending a certain change in fuel. Tap into student interests, and then match a challenging task to those interests and the learning objective.

The following section examines two math learning goals and makes them more challenging and engaging for students.

Go Beyond Worksheets

For the learning goal "I can identify and represent slope and y-intercept," students can choose from many options that are more challenging and fun than simply working through a list of equations:

- Devise a series of equations that create a design when plotted.
- Write equations for some plotted points from a design already printed on graph paper.
- After completing the design or the equations, exchange designs with a peer and challenge each other to figure out each other's problems.
- Search for examples of the importance of slope in architecture or other disciplines.

Connect Goals to Interests

For the learning goal "I can interpret, describe, and create graphs in various situations," try the following activity to make the lesson personally relevant to students:

1 Brainstorm with students a list of possible topics that are of interest to them, for example, cell phones, video games, movies, driving, playing outside, and so on.

2 Brainstorm a list of questions that they want to learn about the topic, such as:

- What percentage of students our age have cell phones?
- About how much time do we spend on our cell phones each day?
- What are uses for students' cell phones?

3 Have individuals or groups of students search to find the answers to the topic questions. Students could design their own surveys and administer them to peers in their school, or research the questions online and in their media centers.

4 Ask students to prepare graphs or other visual representations of their findings, using techniques discussed in the math lessons leading up to the activity.

5 Instruct them to draw conclusions about their findings. Use a lead-in such as, "What do these results say about cell-phone usage?"

6 Direct students to make predictions and design new questions such as the following:

- How does cell-phone usage impact our grades?
- How much time do we spend arguing with our parents over cell phones?
- What would happen if I didn't have my cell phone for a week?
- How do kids who don't have cell phones feel? Do they want one? Why or why not?
- Are there differences in how or how often kids with and without cell phones communicate with their friends?

If multiple classrooms participate in a project like this, students could trade their questions with another class or group, and then embark on a second round of research and graph making.

Strategy 9: Make Connections

Our brains look for ways to connect what we have experienced and learned to new information. When we find these connections and make meaning of the new concepts or instructional activities, we learn more and remember (Wolfe, 2001; Jensen, 2001; Sousa, 2006).

Everyone's experiences and backgrounds are different, and when we learn a new piece of information, our brains sift through the internal filing cabinet to find a match so the learning is in the memory bank. The brain wants to find a place for that new chunk of information to fit. If no connection between the new information and existing knowledge is made, the new information remains in short-term memory and does not move to long-term memory. A *schema* is essentially a print of the brain much like a fingerprint or blueprint. Everyone's schema and fingerprints are different, and so connections are personal and individual. The reason so much information gets quickly forgotten is because it doesn't move to long-term memory—there is no connection to our personal schema (Sousa, 2006). Learning is a natural fit when it builds on prior knowledge, connects to already-understood material, and links to relevant and interesting experiences.

Learning is thus a very personal and individual experience. A connection to new content can create a lightbulb moment. The learner grasps the concept, understands the skills, and realizes:

- "I got it!"
- "I see the need!"
- "I see the relevance!"
- "I see the connection!"
- "I see how I can use it!"

Allow time for students to ponder, talk, or process. Demonstrate how and provide time to make personal connections. When connections are lacking, steer students to new ways of thinking about learning so it connects. Have you ever watched a video clip or read a novel in which the message or story did not make sense? Most often, one stops playing the video or reading the book. Similarly, if students do not make connections, they may shut down, give up, or even act out in a disruptive manner.

Content must be relevant. Learners need an important personal reason to learn the information. Students ask themselves, "What will I gain from this? How is this going to help me in the future? How does this fit into my previous understandings or experiences?" If the answers are negative or not clear to teachers or students, there is little hope for students to engage or retain the learning to use in the future. If students see a personal use and connections, they are more apt to participate and engage in learning.

Connections can occur in various contexts. Teachers can create connections to support learning in many ways, such as the following.

1 Use personal experiences to explain a concept:

- Personal stories can help provide relevance or explain a phenomenon.
- "Have you ever . . . ?" statements can help students tap into their own experiences in relation to the topic.

2 Make connections to students' interests:

- Offer students a scenario (such as going to the grocery store), a movie, or a song that has a similar theme or an application of the concept. Students can then work individually or in a group to compare and contrast the concept against the scenario, movie, or song.
- After reading a fiction or nonfiction piece, ask students to find a song that would make a great opening to the text.

3 Create analogies, or ask students to think of an analogy to help them remember an idea.

4 Create connections to other mediums, people, places, and times by asking:

- "What does this music make you think of?"
- "Why do you think the producers used this song for this movie?"
- "What places have you visited?"
- "Who would the characters be in a different time period?"
- "If this character had to choose a favorite TV show, what would it be and why?"
- "If this historical figure lived today, what job would he or she hold?"

Students can also connect new content and concepts to previously learned skills, themselves, or their communities. Consider the following strategies when helping students make connections.

- **Connecting to self:** When you offer students new learning opportunities, ask the following questions, and embed the answers into instruction and assessment to structure the connection.
    - "Why is this important?"
    - "How does this topic affect the work, our community, and ourselves?"
    - "Have you experienced this concept before or in similar ways? Describe and explain."
- **Connecting to the community:** Relevant ideas influence schools, communities, and the world. Ask students to reflect on the following.

~ "What are the implications of these ideas and learning goals on other countries? On our relationship with other countries? On our role in the world? On our science and mathematics research?"

~ "How do these ideas affect our community? How do they support and contribute to our community? Why would these ideas be important for someone to understand?"

~ "Are there ways that our school community uses these concepts or ideas?" For example, environmental research has prompted some schools to compost in their cafeterias.

Tips and Traps

Especially with difficult material that might turn off or overwhelm students, a link or a connection to today's world may draw students in or help them make meaning. Use connections to help students avoid frustration and giving up. Be sure to repeat the information or spiral it through multiple lessons: the learning may initially connect, but if students do not use it, they will lose it.

At the same time, avoid redundancy. Ruts cause learners to turn off and shut down. When students get it, teachers sometimes keep making connections in the same way at the same level. It can go something like this: as a result of instruction or some type of connection, learning occurs. Then, teachers keep instruction and activities at the same level—essentially the same old, same old—by using the same worksheet, homework, activity, or tutoring. Students get bored and turned off when there is nothing new. Keep challenging them and pushing understanding.

Be sure that *all* students make the connection. Sometimes, when a few students get it, the teacher moves on instead of differentiating by helping those who get it go deeper and trying new strategies with those who haven't made the connection. With so much to teach, educators often feel pressed to move on. Choose the most essential skills, and take time to differentiate.

Connect vocabulary. When we introduce new academic vocabulary without using familiar information or experiences to explain the concept, students remain lost and confused. Help students relate to new language. When you are talking or introducing something, use definitions, examples, synonyms, and antonyms to help students gain deeper understanding of a term or concept (Chapman & King, 2009b).

Understand the age of your students, what they think, and what they know. The connection must match the age, experience, and prior knowledge of the students you are teaching. If students are using a song from the 1950s that is not familiar to them, the connection is lost and becomes another term or concept that is sitting in their short-term memory without a home. An effective teacher knows when to make connections to himself or herself and when to provide students time to make their own connections.

Interdisciplinary units provide great opportunities for connections across topics. When possible, arrange different courses or content so the topics and concepts are addressed at the same time. Look at the complex learning goals across disciplines to find natural connections. For example, drawing conclusions occurs in science, math, social studies, and reading.

Putting It Into Practice

Movies and novels, children's stories, and interdisciplinary units are helpful ways to describe and plan learning to guide students to connect to the content and remain engaged.

Movies and Novels

Current movies and novels provide lessons and connections to the past. Classic stories have themes that show up in movies or novels today. For example, *West Side Story* and Shakespeare's *Romeo and Juliet* share similar characteristics and themes. Select a segment of a movie or a novel as hooks or links for students to obtain a better understanding of the content through an inviting medium. Also, take time to read a chapter a day of a novel that relates to the topic being studied.

Children's Stories

Children's stories offer perspective and connections. *Math Curse* (1995) by Jon Scieszka and Lane Smith is a funny story describing how math appears or haunts people in everyday life. We just cannot escape math! Students can write their own examples of math "hauntings" and compile them in a classroom edition of *Math Curse*.

Teachers can use many other children's stories to make connections or offer new perspectives on familiar stories or difficult content, including:

- *Science Verse* by Jon Scieszka and Lane Smith
- *The Grapes of Math* by Gregory Tang and Harry Briggs

Interdisciplinary Units

Interdisciplinary units also offer rich connections, relevance, authenticity, and challenge. The following scenario illustrates the use of an interdisciplinary project. Consider designing a similar one for your school.

In a secondary setting, students studied water quality. In science, they performed nine water-quality tests on various rivers and streams, analyzing the results and drawing conclusions about the impact on the community (on golf courses or on drinking water, for example). In math, they graphed the river bottom and used those sections to select soil samples and "creature" samples, which also provided evidence of water quality. In language arts, students wrote persuasive letters to the city, businesses, and nonprofit organizations, describing the results and posing possible actions that could improve the quality of the water in the community.

Create links across subject areas in an elementary school or self-contained classrooms at any grade level. Sometimes this requires looking at the order of units and realigning them to make natural connections, which results in not following the textbook sequentially. When organized around standards and learning objectives, various subjects can link content so students learn the complementary information across the content. For example, when learning about the Civil War in history, students can read a short story set during that time frame.

Another way to integrate curriculum is to target a skill and thread it across the curriculum. For example, use cause and effect in each subject area. Design a persuasive essay–writing rubric, and use it across courses and content areas.

Strategy 10: Co-Create Criteria and Activities

The previously described strategies in this chapter show how essential clear learning goals are to the work of motivating and engaging students. Stating the learning goal verbally to students and posting it in our classrooms and on handouts and assessments are fabulous first steps and one factor in making expectations clear. How students interpret these goals is another matter, however. Students make their own meaning regardless of whether or not we ask them to. By constructing together, with students, what quality and success look like, we give students a clear picture of the learning goal and how they might get there. And in brainstorming and constructing activities together, students practice thinking about their own learning (see strategy 24 on student involvement, page 183).

Whenever we help brainstorm, plan, build, organize, or create something, we have much more investment in the product's care and future. This type of partnership with students makes responsibility for teaching and learning a shared endeavor rather than a relationship wherein the teacher plans something and the learning is left up to students. This section suggests ideas and strategies to help students own and engage in the process of their learning. Students will be motivated to learn and engage when teachers include them in constructing classroom activities and criteria.

Co-Constructing Activities

Students are often an untapped source of creativity and energy. Learners have unique interests and experiences that can inform the activities of a classroom. Draw students in and engage them in constructing activities and instruction to address specific learning objectives. Not only will learners engage more fully, but they will also learn more during the process of planning an activity.

Before collaboration, teachers should identify a learning objective and create a time frame for the activity. Consider the following steps to co-construct activities with students.

1 Ask students to describe the intended learning in their own words. Come to a consensus on a common definition or description of the learning.

2 Brainstorm topics for students to study in order to learn the objective (in particular when the objective focuses on a process or skill such as reading and comprehending text, solving problems, or writing persuasively).

3 Brainstorm activities or tasks that may help students learn this objective.

4 Use the ideas generated by the student discussion, and further direct the activities and learning. Alternatively, divide the activities among small groups or individuals, and ask students to begin planning and constructing these learning activities. In this role, the teacher facilitates the learning and organizes a structure for learning through the co-constructed activities.

Co-Constructing Criteria

When students know and understand the success criteria of an assessment, project, or activity, they are much more likely to succeed (Hattie, 2009). While giving students a rubric or a list of scoring criteria is one way to begin informing them of the expectations, co-constructing the criteria with students helps them own the criteria, develop a deeper understanding of the parts in the process, and visualize what success will look like. Consider the following steps to co-construct criteria in your classroom.

1   Choose the standard or learning goals that are the focus of the project, writing assignment, presentation, or target assessment.

2   If you have examples from a previous class, choose six to eight pieces of student work.

3   Ask students to individually read or review the examples and score them according to the continuum in figure 3.3. Have each student write a brief explanation of his or her ranking.

4   Ask the students to share their rankings, and present the findings to the class:

   — Place signs that display the rubric choices *amazing*, *good*, *OK*, and *needs work* along one wall of the classroom. Call out the student examples one at a time. Students move to the area in the room where their scores are displayed.

   — Lead a classroom discussion in which students defend their responses. You may have students first talk in small groups to determine their reasons for their scores before discussing as a whole class.

   — Collect scores on each piece of student work. A graph could easily display the results to the class. Students can sketch one on the board or chart paper.

5   Set three to four criteria based on the discussion. Students may first brainstorm individually and then move to small groups to try to come to consensus on the criteria. Writing criteria might include organization, conventions, or support.

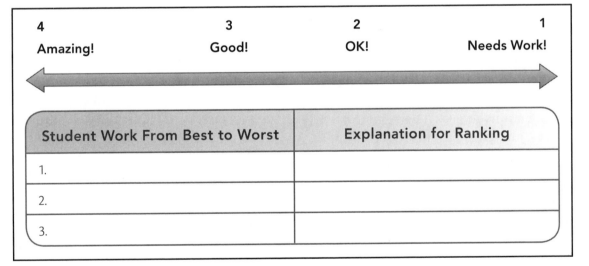

Directions: Provide students with three to eight examples of student work (problem-solving examples, explanations, essays, papers, and so on). Have students rank each piece of student work on the following scale.

4	3	2	1
Amazing!	Good!	OK!	Needs Work!

Student Work From Best to Worst	Explanation for Ranking
1.	
2.	
3.	

Direct students to meet in small groups to discuss and come to a consensus on their rankings. The whole class may engage in the consensus process.

*Visit **go.solution-tree.com/instruction** for a reproducible of this figure.*

Figure 3.3: Sample worksheet for co-constructing criteria activity.

6 Have the class describe what each criterion means and looks like. The students may search the student work for examples of the criteria at every proficiency level. The rubric may contain a few phrases to describe the criteria as well as examples from actual student work.

Have students use table 3.5 to chart their progress on the co-created criteria of an assignment. In response to the question, "What is quality writing?," students generated a list of criteria. Then, they began to describe varying stages of each criterion.

Table 3.5: Student Co-Created Rubric Template

Criteria	Amazing!	Got It!	Making Progress!	Got a Start!
Organized	My writing has a beginning that makes the reader excited. The middle builds on the beginning. The end leaves the reader thinking.	My writing has a beginning, middle, and end the reader can understand.	My writing may have a beginning, but is missing details in the middle and end that make it hard to see how the parts connect.	My writing has ideas that need to be organized to help the reader understand.
Descriptive and Interesting	My writing uses lots of adjectives that clearly help the reader picture my meaning.	My writing has adjectives and descriptions that add to the text.	My writing has some adjectives that distract from my message instead of add to it.	The words used in my writing are simple vocabulary.

*Visit **go.solution-tree.com/instruction** for a reproducible of this table.*

Tips and Traps

Increase engagement by making students part of the learning process, not just passive participants. Use the co-constructing process and engage students in planning for priority standards (strategy 10, page 94). Start small, and create learning goals that have gradations of proficiency rather than right and wrong answers.

When brainstorming with students, differentiate between sessions when you are collecting all ideas and when you are trying to make a decision. When we collect all ideas without judgment, students feel free to respond without worrying about saying the "right thing" or what they think the teacher wants to hear. Ideas—no matter how feasible, interesting, or relevant—often lead to more ideas, and great insights. In brainstorming, it is the process that counts.

When students are planning activities, it is important to make observations about quality work. Students must do a significant amount of research, brainstorming, and drafting to arrive at quality ideas. In the absence of this depth, these activities become surface level, deep learning does not occur, and students may remain confused—more potential for unmotivated students to disengage and give up. Keep samples of student work from prior years to have plenty of examples of strong and weak work to use in instruction.

Putting It Into Practice

In the following examples, we discuss co-constructing activities and criteria in a middle school and a preschool. In the middle school example, we illustrate how to build criteria for a persuasive topic. In the preschool example, we demonstrate that learning goals can be used to co-construct activities at a young age. In each case, students and teachers are using these processes together to describe and plan for learning.

Choose a Persuasive Topic and Build Criteria

At Stephen Decatur Middle School in Decatur, Illinois, an eighth-grade language arts team discussed how to help students review the important components of writing a persuasive essay. The team designed a series of questions to help students determine a persuasive topic that would interest them and be suitable for the writing assignment (Eldon Conn, Tasia Spencer-Burks, Crystal Eilers, Leslie Johnson, and Sandra Bell, personal communication, September 29, 2009). Here we use their plan to construct an activity you can use in your classroom for the learning goal "I can identify the characteristics of a persuasive composition."

1   Ask, "What is persuasive writing?" Students write what they know and what they want to know.

2   Give students three sample persuasive pieces. Individually, students identify the pros and cons of each piece. Then, working in pairs, students do the following.

- Discuss what makes a quality persuasive essay.

- Score each piece using a rubric. Place the rubric scores on the wall, and ask students to move to their respective scores. After each sample work, discuss and come to a consensus about the pieces.

3   Ask, "What are the parts of a quality essay?" Use the idea of a three-legged stool to describe them.

- **Take a stand:** Make a statement of position (the seat).

- **Give it three legs:** Briefly explain three reasons for the position. For each leg, develop specific details.

- **Review the details:**

  - Straw details are weak examples, and the stool will not stand.

  - Pipe-cleaner details are a little stronger, but any wind (any counter argument) will tip over the stool.

  - Dowel-rod details are strong explanations that clearly support the argument.

- Explain how the details support the seat (the stand or statement of position), using the mechanics of writing.

4   Brainstorm topics to defend or write about.

5   Discuss and establish an audience. Ask students, "Whom are you writing for or to? What is the purpose? What do you want them to do with information? What do you hope your writing will make happen?"

6   At the close of this activity, describe the most important parts of a persuasive essay.

Co-Construct Activities Tied to Learning Goals

Co-planning activities and learning goals produces intrinsic motivation and engagement. Younger children can also play an active role in their learning. At the University of Georgia's Child

Development Lab, Phillip Baumgarner listened carefully to his three- and four-year-olds at play. Noticing their conversation centered on castles, pirates, space, and nature, he decided to engage the students in a dialogue around these topics. The students created a graph indicating their topic choice for the following week. Pirates received the most votes. After engaging the students in a dialogue about all the things they could do to learn about pirates, Baumgarner sketched out the topics, activities, and learning goals for the week. In a curriculum map (table 3.6) sent out to parents, he described the activities and noted which student had conceived each. He included a list of intended learning outcomes and linked each to an activity.

The Creative Curriculum for Early Childhood (Dodge & Colker, 2001) identifies the following goals and objectives for early childhood development, which Baumgarner used to co-construct his curriculum.

- **Social/emotional development:** Illustrates a sense of self, responsibility for self and others, and prosocial behavior

- **Physical development:** Exhibits both gross and fine motor skills

- **Cognitive development:** Demonstrates learning and problem solving, logical thinking, and representation and symbolic thinking

- **Language development:** Can effectively listen, speak, read, and write

In reflecting on this co-construction process, Baumgarner realized that some students might prefer to offer their thoughts on an individual basis and decided that he would take some of them aside the next time (P. Baumgarner, personal communication, January 5, 2009).

Table 3.6: Sample Co-Constructed Preschool Curriculum Map on Pirates

Theme: Pirates   **Classroom:** Preschool 2   **Week:** September 15

Activities	Monday	Tuesday	Wednesday	Thursday	Friday
Morning	Build a pirate ship from hollow blocks. Ask children to draw pictures of ship and keep an inventory of blocks used for building (Peyton). These activities promote representation and symbolic thinking, fine motor, and reading and writing skills.	Create pirate maps (Alex). This activity promotes representation and symbolic thinking and reading and writing skills.	Play with ships in the water tubs (Joshua). This activity promotes responsibility for self and others.	Discuss hiding and finding treasure. These activities promote learning and problem-solving skills.	Make pirate shakes (Andrew). This activity promotes logical-thinking skills.
Afternoon	Design and make pirate flags (Jeanne). These activities promote logical-thinking skills.	Make and decorate pirate hats (Noah). These activities promote fine motor skills.	Make telescopes (Sally). This activity promotes logical-thinking skills.	Use index cubes. This activity promotes logical-thinking skills.	Make pirate collages. This activity promotes fine motor skills.

Activities	Monday	Tuesday	Wednesday	Thursday	Friday
Group Time	Tell me about pirates! Write responses down on paper. Search for letter. These activities promote fine motor and reading and writing skills.	Make pirate maracas (playing gourds) (Sam), and dance to pirate music. These activities promote gross and fine motor skills.	What is scurvy? We will chart our likes and dislikes after a citrus tasting (George). These activities promote logical-thinking skills.	Taste seaweed—Nori (Jose). Discuss how Nori is made. These activities promote learning and problem solving and logical-thinking skills.	Using a pirate map, we shall find a treasure somewhere in our school (Gerry). This activity promotes reading and writing skills.
Story Time	*Shiver Me Letters* This activity promotes reading and writing skills.	*Rupert the Wrong-Word Pirate* This activity promotes reading and writing skills.	*Pirates Don't Change Diapers* This activity promotes reading and writing skills.	List how to become a pirate. This activity promotes reading and writing skills.	Selection of book will be made after next week's theme study has been determined (used as intro). This activity promotes reading and writing skills.
Outside	Dig for treasure (John). This activity promotes responsibility for self and others, prosocial behavior, and gross and fine motor skills.	Dig for treasure. This activity promotes responsibility for self and others, prosocial behavior, and gross and fine motor skills.	Walk the plank (Ian). This activity promotes prosocial behavior, gross motor skills, and representation and symbolic thinking.	Put on a pirate ship dramatic play. This activity promotes representation and symbolic thinking.	Put on a parachute play. This activity promotes responsibility for self and others.

Adapted with permission. © 2009 Phillip Baumgarner. University of Georgia, Child Development Lab.

Chapter 3 Campfire Talk

This chapter described strategies to describe and plan for learning. Consider your own understanding, perceptions, and experiences about what works to help students understand the goals and own their learning. Discuss the following questions and activities in your professional learning community, department, grade-level team, or a staff meeting.

1 How clear are your learning objectives? Do they reflect the most important ideas in the standards?

2 How do you communicate these learning objectives to students? Do they appear on activities, worksheets, homework, and assessments? Are they posted in the classroom alongside agendas?

3 What could you do to help students understand what they are learning?

4 How do students know the expectations for their assessments? Their writing projects? Solving problems? What other ways could you use to show them what you expect?

5 How aligned are your assessments with your learning goals? Are you confident that what you are assessing represents the standards you taught?

6 How much practice do students get before the test, project, or summative assessment? Is the practice focused on the learning goals that students need to be successful on the summative assessment? Is the practice low risk?

7 Do students approach the summative assessment with confidence? How do you know?

8 Ask students what they think they are learning about. Their responses will give you great information about the perceptions of students.

9 Use the Plan for Student Motivation reproducible to discover, diagnose, and plan to address the needs of individual unmotivated students in order to describe and plan for their learning.

Plan for Student Motivation

Strategy	Name the Unmotivated Student(s) in Need of the Strategy	Identify the Wrapper the Student Is Wearing	List Observable Evidence, Behavior, Habits, or Traits	Develop an Action to Address the Need	Assess and Reflect on Implementation	Additional Comments
6. Clarify Learning (page 71)						
7. Drive Instruction With Assessments (page 76)						
8. Provide Challenging Learning Opportunities (page 86)						
9. Make Connections (page 90)						
10. Co-Create Criteria and Activities (page 94)						

Student Tracking Sheet for Language Arts

Learning Goals	Writing Assignment 1		Writing Assignment 2		Writing Assignment 3	
	Self-Assessment	Revised Score	Self-Assessment	Revised Score	Self-Assessment	Revised Score
Content						
I can write an effective topic sentence.						
I can write effective supporting details.						
I can explain how my supporting details connect to the main idea.						
I can use words that pop. This means that the vocabulary I use is specific and descriptive.						
Mechanics						
I can accurately apply the rules of capitalization to my writing.						
I can spell accurately in my writing.						
I can apply the rules of punctuation in my writing.						

Finding Adventure

Alisa was a creative and active fourth grader. For the most part, Alisa enjoyed school, but she was particularly captivated by the more innovative projects. This proved true during a Native American unit in her social studies class. Students were asked to explore a tribe of their choice and present it in some way. Alisa worked tirelessly to gather information and prepare a PowerPoint presentation to include just the right colors, pictures, and message. In awe, her parents observed her engagement with and ownership of the project. Each word was carefully composed. While Alisa cared about school, they had never seen this type of focus on her learning before. In the past, her focus was on completing the work, not on learning the content or carefully conveying the message.

Motivation and engagement are contagious, and when students get excited, learning gains momentum. Wendy Yount is a fourth-grade teacher at Rocky Branch Elementary School in Bogart, Georgia, and Alisa was a student in her class. The following is a blog entry Mrs. Yount posted describing the project and students' enthusiasm for it:

> A note to you all regarding the Native American "Projects": This quarter we have studied different types of maps, US regions, and Native Americans. There are very limited resources available here at school so I do the bulk of the instruction. I had the students choose one of the tribes we studied and gave them the choice of doing a poster or a PowerPoint in school. Honestly, they begged me to let them build things and work at home. Students who created a project at home did it because they wanted to, not because I assigned it. When I give a project, the children will receive specific guidelines and expectations, a grading rubric, and YOU will have to sign it! I feel the need to clarify this!
>
> With that said, it was quite exciting for me to see the obvious enthusiasm of the class as they dove into this self-selected project. One parent told me that her daughter spent more time and effort on this than she ever had on a project that had been assigned for a grade! The 4th grade team will be adding some self-selected components to our upcoming units. We want them to stay so motivated! (Yount, 2009, used with permission)

How can we create more classroom moments such as this, when students are so engaged, they just cannot help themselves? Passion for learning, the content, and the topic is the foundation for adventure. When learners are intrigued by the topic and see connection to why people study, work, or learn about the concepts at hand, the fire of engagement is lit. The adventure continues as students "try it on for size" or make their own connections to the topic, because they want to explore and learn more. Ultimately, their own passions surface.

With standards and assessments, accountability, grading, lesson planning, and many other responsibilities, it is easy to forget about the need to experience excitement in learning. A teacher's passion and excitement go a long way in motivating students. While testing and standards are part of our reality, we can still help students connect ideas and learning goals to life beyond the test. But if the teacher does not feel or project excitement, students will have a difficult time making the leap. Learners take cues from teachers. If you are struggling to find the relevance, excitement, or passion in a topic, student attitudes and interest will surely follow suit. Without passion, students may chalk up the lesson to another hoop they have to jump through or another activity solely focused on preparing them for a test.

Make learning irresistible. Clearly illustrate relevance through fascinating people, stories, and facts. Teachers who reach students take them on an adventure every day. Through rigor and passion, the content comes alive. Adventurous classrooms are filled with activities and lessons that fuel the minds of learners. As students enter these spaces, they are excited, intrigued, and anticipating the day's learning adventure.

Quality engagement is not designed to merely entertain learners. Going to a favorite movie is passive enjoyment. *Engagement* is a way to connect with students and motivate them to work and learn from the experience. The adventures suggested in this chapter are designed to promote active interaction, while inspiring students to engage in their learning. Adventurous learning requires much more than entertainment. As H. Jackson Brown Jr. so deftly put it, "You can get by on charm for about fifteen minutes. After that you had better know something" (Simple Truths, 2008, p. 33).

An adventurous classroom engages all students. The strategies in this chapter support your planning to make learning a motivating adventure.

> Strategy 11:   Use Irresistible Hooks and Clever Closures
>
> Strategy 12:   Get Plugged In
>
> Strategy 13:   Play Games to Learn, Review, and Remember
>
> Strategy 14:   Spice It Up
>
> Strategy 15:   Create Optimism and Celebrate!

Strategy 11: Use Irresistible Hooks and Clever Closures

When teachers use hooks and closures to make kids wonder, ask questions, laugh, or make connections to their lives now or in the future, we create a sense of novelty intended to entice students. Novelty activates the brain and prepares learners to explore new information while making connections with what they bring with them. It also creates encouraging emotions that positively influence students' readiness to learn (Wolfe, 2001).

There is a reason why people become addicted to television shows that offer an ongoing saga the entire season long. At the end of every episode, we are left wondering what will happen next, usually through cliffhangers and sneak previews—clever closures—that keep us wanting more.

This strategy is all about tapping the wonder and intrigue in our topic or learning goal by getting students thinking about and predicting what will happen. It's best used as a lesson-planning tool to engage the whole class. However, after you get to know your most disengaged students, you may structure these moments based on their interests, prior knowledge, or experiences.

Irresistible hooks jump-start lessons and create anticipation. Depending on how the teacher frames the lesson, students may feel excitement, fear, or even dread. Begin a lesson, a unit, a class period, or the day with irresistible hooks that actively engage students and get them curious about the topic. Students begin to see the possibility, fun, and excitement in learning by the questions we ask, the examples we use, and the stories we tell.

Consider the following sample irresistible hooks.

- Do an unexpected movement, mime, or role-play to introduce a topic.

- Become a character in the text to start a conversation about characterization.

- Create movements to represent concepts. For example, use quick, tiny steps to teach staccato in music, or walk around the classroom backward to teach negative numbers.

- Draw a sketch or word on the board for students to secretly guess.

- Begin writing a word, rule, or sentence, and let students discuss to find the meaning or the connection. Consider the following examples:

  - The class play was filled with *jollity*. This means _____.

  - *Indignation* is a good word to describe _____.

  - Use *capital letters* in your writing when _____.

- Draw picture clues to introduce and connect a definition, a rule, or important information.

- Post a word, a fact, or a question a few days before teaching the lesson. Instruct students to find the word's meaning, seek additional facts to connect to the posted statement, and suggest possible answers.

- Offer a problem that requires students to use the information being taught. For example, if students are studying the economy, offer a scenario wherein something happens in the world, such as the stock market dipping or a hurricane hitting Florida. Then, have students predict the influence on the U.S. economy.

- Present a puzzle to solve.

- Ask a variety of questions. Make learners think by beginning questions with "why" or "how."

- Describe a situation relevant to your topic, and ask students to respond to questions like "What would you do?" and "If you were in charge, how would you respond?"

- Find examples of cause and effect in the newspaper.

- Give clues and hints instead of answers.

- Wear or display a prop or artifact from the unit or topic, and have students guess its significance.

➤ Have students brainstorm why the upcoming task is important and what it will help them do.

Clever closures create an upbeat ending for a class that celebrates learning and builds anticipation for the next day. Students will leave class happy. When teachers exude enthusiasm and plant a seed of inquiry and interest, we give learners something to look forward to hearing or doing upon their return.

Consider the following sample closures.

➤ Celebrate that day's learning with cheers, songs, or raps. (See strategy 16, page 134, for more ideas.)

➤ Use exit tickets to gather student responses to the learning goal for the day. Have students spend a few minutes at the close of the day or class period responding to a specific question such as "How do adjectives help us write better?" Students may also write or draw something they learned or a question that is still lingering. Exit tickets highlight for them and for you what they are taking away from that day's lesson.

➤ Have students write journal entries reflecting on the learning that occurred, the activities for the day, or their progress.

➤ Ask students to discuss highlights from the lesson with a partner or a small group.

➤ Have students write the day's biggest highlight on sticky notes and put them in a special place—in a personal agenda, on a graphic organizer, or on a bulletin board. Alternatively, ask students to categorize the highlights and talk about the effectiveness of the lesson using evidence from the sticky notes.

➤ Have students form small talk circles to stand together and share an insight or idea from the day.

➤ Have students work in small groups or pairs to create a symbol that represents the big idea from the day.

➤ Ask students to find examples of the concept in the newspaper or in places outside of school. For example, ask elementary students studying patterns to list all the different patterns they encounter during the day.

➤ Give students an interesting problem to solve. What if the characters in a story had done something else instead of what the author wrote? Alternatively, take real problems from news headlines, and ask students to propose a plan.

➤ Pass around a cool, interesting object that the student must hold to speak. This activity allows students to share and ensures everyone hears and listens. Examples include:

  ➤ Pass around a ball to express the "ball" students had while learning.

  ➤ Share a bright idea while holding a lightbulb.

  ➤ Wave a magic wand to contribute to the "magic brain circle."

  ➤ Pass around an artifact that represents the content, and have students each state a fact they learned from the study.

Here are some examples for building anticipation for the next day's learning.

- Frame the closure of the lesson with "You will not believe what we are going to do tomorrow!" or "I can't wait to show you this tomorrow!"
- Ask them to bring something from home to use in class. Say, "Tomorrow, remember to bring _____, because we are going to use it in an exciting way."
- Announce a special event: "Monday is a special day because . . ."
- Make an announcement: "Tomorrow, we will . . ."
- Build anticipation: "During the next unit or story, we will get to . . ."

To create a sense of adventure in the classroom using irresistible hooks and clever closures, follow these four steps.

1 Identify the topic and learning goal for the lesson. Then, consider the following questions.

- How is this learning going to help students in their future coursework or in life?
- Why is this content or skill important to learn?
- What role does it play in the community, online, at school, in families, or in businesses?
- Who uses this information or these skills in their work? How?
- What would happen if someone didn't have the skill or knowledge? Would something funny or weird happen?

2 Using table 4.1 (see page 129 for a reproducible), choose a purpose for the activity, and write down possible ideas for corresponding hooks and closures.

Table 4.1: Planning Irresistible Hooks and Clever Closures

Purpose	Description	Hook or Closure Idea
To connect	Connect the topic and the learning to what students already know, prior experiences, a previous lesson or learning goal, or students' backgrounds.	
To excite	Facilitate an activity or discussion to foster student excitement about the topic at hand.	
To celebrate	Celebrate successful learning experiences and engaging activities.	
To remember	Use activities and instruction to trigger students' knowledge and assist them in remembering.	

3 Choose a classroom management structure for implementing the hook or closure.

- Whole class
- Small groups, pairs, or trios
- Standing up or sitting down
- Circles, concentric circles, rows, or groups

4 Remember to structure groups to create a random mix of students and to safely involve learners who are uncomfortable choosing a group or being chosen.

- Number the class members so that there will be about three to a group. For example, if you have thirty students in your class, number off from 1 to 10. All the ones go to one place in the room, twos to another, threes to another, and so on.

- Hand each student one card from a deck. Depending on the size of the group desired, students organize based on the color, number, or suit on the card.

Tips and Traps

Hooks and closures that are overused lose their power to draw students into the work of the classroom. Change it up!

Hooks and closures that are too simple and obvious fall flat quickly, but hooks and closures that are too loosely related are not as meaningful. If the connection is too farfetched, students will disengage quickly. A bad hook may end up backfiring or having the opposite effect, as students' connections may draw the conversation off topic.

Use the questions or responses from the exit slips at the end of a lesson to frame the hook for the following day. Be sure to follow through on it the next day so student anticipation is satisfied.

Putting It Into Practice

Let's examine some specific activities to use as irresistible hooks and clever closures. Quotes, "I wonder" statements, music, short readings, humor, and predictions are ways to implement irresistible hooks and clever closures into the classroom to motivate students to engage.

Quote It!

Give students a quote, and ask them to say, draw, or write their ideas about how the quote is related to the topic, the text, or the investigation. When studying war, for example, use the following quotes to start conversations about the issues involved with war (BrainyMedia, 2010):

- "All war is deception." —Sun Tzu

- "An unjust peace is better than a just war." —Marcus Tullius Cicero

When studying geometry, use the following quotes:

- "I don't divide architecture, landscape and gardening; to me they are one." —Luis Barragán

- "It is essential to an architect to know how to see: I mean to see in such a way that the vision is not overpowered by rational analysis." —Luis Barragán

Create "I Wonder . . ." Statements

Tell students the topic, and have them complete a top-ten list of "I wonder . . ." statements. Be sure to give them a sample list so they can see how to do it. This activity could start or end a lesson. Some sample student "I wonder" statements when studying plants are:

- I wonder how long plants can go without water.

- I wonder what kinds of plants grow in Poland.

- I wonder what would happen if I used apple juice to water my plants.

- I wonder if plants can make people laugh.

- I wonder what plants live through snow.

Some sample student "I wonder" statements when reading a story about stars might be:

- I wonder how many stars are in the sky.
- I wonder if stars still are in the sky when it is daytime.
- I wonder if stars are hot.
- I wonder if stars could ever come to Earth.
- I wonder what it is like to be an astronaut traveling in a spacecraft.
- I wonder what it would be like to live in a home that uses solar energy.

Use Music

Use music to depict a tone, mood, feeling, or setting:

- Select a "golden oldie" most students will not recognize, and play it as one of your favorite songs. Ask the class members to brainstorm how it links to the lesson or predict why you chose this particular song.

- Introduce the topic, and then ask students to bring in a song or musical selection from their world that fits the tone or message. You could play the songs or simply have students name them. The next day, have students discuss the relationship between the topic and their musical selection as a whole class, in small groups, or with partners.

- Play a selection that fits the day's learning; call it the "soundtrack" for the lesson.

Use a Short Reading

Read a portion or all of a newspaper article, a children's story, or another selection to set the stage and connect to the learning through feelings, emotions, or content. For example, before studying the life cycle, read *A Very Hungry Caterpillar* (Carle, 1969). (Visit www.hbook.com/resources/books/concept.asp for more ideas of books to read to accompany class concepts.) Have students search online for newspaper articles related to the content. For example, when studying genetics, the newspaper article "Study Says Genetic Marker Not Predictor of Heart Disease" (Inman, 2010) could spark great discussion. Read a newsflash from a local newspaper about a soldier receiving an honor in the war in Afghanistan before reading about a battle in a previous war.

Use Humor

Humor can produce an emotional experience that engages students and helps students remember. The best humor brings the class together in laughter, not tears. Avoid sarcasm, and hold that expectation for learners, too. When humor crosses the line to sarcasm, even with no malicious intent, it can change the adventurous tone of the classroom and negatively impact trust and, in turn, learning.

There are many ways to use humor effectively. You can:

- Tell a personal funny story as an example.
- Share a cartoon, joke, or riddle that relates to the topic.
- Make up a silly poem using the content.

Do something "crazy" or unexpected! We know of one instance when, for the first few minutes of class, a math teacher walked around backward. The students did not know why, but they all giggled quietly in wonderment. After the initial routines of the class were complete, the teacher revealed the day's math topic was negative numbers. The learners laughed as they made the mental connection between their teacher walking backward with the concept of negative numbers on a number line. To close the class, the learners reflected on the day's learning while walking backward. They will remember that when working problems with negative numbers.

Make Predictions

Using a fictional text as a reference, have students write or discuss predictions. When using a nonfiction text, learners can consider questions such as, "Given this news story or world event, what do you think might happen to our economy? To middle-class families? To those without homes?"

Strategy 12: Get Plugged In

At any moment, in any given location, countless numbers of people are engaged in some type of media use. With the advent of cell phones that provide connections to television, Internet, and other interactive technologies, our "plugged in" time has increased dramatically. Our tweens and teenagers are no different. In fact, according to a recent Kaiser Family Foundation report by Victoria Rideout, Ulla Foehr, and Donald Roberts (2010), they are more connected than ever!

As anyone who knows a teen or a tween can attest, media is among the most powerful forces in young people's lives today. Eight- to eighteen-year-olds spend more time using media than any other activity besides—maybe—sleeping. (They sleep an average of seven and a half hours a day, seven days a week, which is less than the amount of time some of them spend on the grid.) The television shows they watch, video games they play, songs they listen to, books they read, and websites they visit are an enormous part of their lives. These activities offer a constant stream of messages about families, peers, relationships, gender roles, sex, violence, food, values, clothes, and an abundance of other topics too long to list (Rideout et al., 2010).

Children between the ages of eight and eighteen increased their daily media exposure from eight hours and thirty-four minutes (8:34) to ten hours and forty-five minutes (10:45) between 2004 and 2009 (Rideout et al., 2010). This means that on average, the students in our classrooms are spending over seventy hours a week engaged in some sort of media use. They are connecting and communicating with friends and others on social networking sites and through text messages, playing video games at home and globally on the Internet, and being entertained by listening to music or watching movies, television, and videos posted online (Rideout et al., 2010).

This reveals a clear pattern that new media is capturing more and more of our students' time. Table 4.2 describes the Kaiser report's findings (Rideout et al., 2010) of surveying two thousand eight- to eighteen-year-old students on various aspects of their media use per day.

When multitasking was taken into account, such as listening to music while playing on the computer or watching television while reading a magazine, students spent an average of seven hours and thirty-eight minutes (7:38) per day in 2009—an increase from six hours and twenty-one minutes (6:21) in 2004.

Table 4.2: Eight- to Eighteen-Year-Olds' Media Use Over Time

Type of Media	Average Amount of Time Per Day in 2004	Average Amount of Time Per Day in 2009	Time Difference
Television	3 hours 51 minutes	4 hours 29 minutes	Increase of 38 minutes
Music/Audio	1 hour 44 minutes	2 hours 31 minutes	Increase of 47 minutes
Computers	1 hour 2 minutes	1 hour 29 minutes	Increase of 27 minutes
Video Games	49 minutes	1 hour 13 minutes	Increase of 24 minutes
Print	43 minutes	38 minutes	Decrease of 5 minutes
Movies	25 minutes	25 minutes	0
Grand Total	8 hours 34 minutes	10 hours 45 minutes	Increase of 2 hours and 11 minutes

Source: Adapted from Rideout et al., 2010.

The brain is constantly active in today's world of gidgets, gadgets, and technology. Students have to "power down" to come to school, where there are no game machines, touch screens, cell phones, or action films. In most classrooms, there is limited access to the Internet to socially connect through MySpace, Facebook, or blogs. How much sitting, listening, and other passive activity do students endure in a day? Calculate the number of minutes students spend listening or sitting in class versus the number of minutes they spend talking and working. How does it compare? Better yet, shadow a student for a day, and tally the various kinds of activity in which the student engages.

Using technology in the classroom challenges us to understand students' media use outside of school and what it reveals to educators about their communication styles, needs, and interests. Given the reality of learners' relationship with technology and media, how can we, as educators, get plugged in and take advantage of the tremendous influence media has on our students?

Use technology to re-engage unmotivated students and proactively engage *all* students of the iGeneration. However, building tech resources and an online classroom community may take time. Many schools are still grappling with how to give access to and effectively use technology to support learning. There are many policies to reduce the distractions of cell phones, computers, iPods, iPads, MP3 players, and more. Given the nature of how the iGeneration communicates and interacts through media, integrating the power of media may be a better way to spend our energy. Work on the computer inspires many learners to excel. Students often have more expertise in the use of computers and other electronic gadgets than educators. Technology tools capture their attention, teach difficult skills, provide opportunities to research and make discoveries, provide access to resources and people, and open the potential for communication in unique and interactive ways.

Creating an Online Community

Creating an online space for your class gives students access to content at anytime—day or night. This dynamic community resource provides learners a place to find information, links, and media that teachers selected or students have shared; to check assigned work or project criteria; or to view a podcast of the day's lecture or discussion. Creating an online classroom provides learners a place to visit, learn, share, discuss, and evaluate learning before and after being in class. Web 2.0 tools harness the power of the Internet and bring learning readily to the student.

Some schools have access to some online course or collaboration software or tool. Moodle is a free, open-source course-management software that has significant market share. Some schools may have access to Moodle, Blackboard, WebCT, or other software. In general, the tools are similar. Using online-course software in conjunction with a traditional class allows students to learn to use Web 2.0 tools as well as to learn specific content. Each student has his or her own log-in and password. Therefore, access is restricted to those in the class. The course is a clearly defined learning space.

The first step is to explore various technology resources available to you. Table 4.3 describes some of the tools available. For more examples and practical implementation tips to get plugged in, see *Teaching the iGeneration* (Ferriter & Garry, 2010) and *Creating a Digital-Rich Classroom* (Ormiston, 2011).

Tips and Traps

Check the capacity of the hardware and software available and the speed of the connections before using technology in the classroom.

Sometimes students do not have access at home or outside of class to the type of technology being used or considered. Requiring the use of a technology to which not all students have access can cause students to disengage quickly. Check to be sure all students have access to what's needed. Provide options through the local library, community center, or before- and after-school programs.

Remember, meeting students in an online community is not a social setting, but a designated academic space. Present yourself professionally online as if it is your classroom.

Putting It Into Practice

Technology is a useful and attainable way to engage learners in the content. The dynamic, interactive nature of technology mirrors the excitement and mystery often experienced in an adventure. To engage learners, create an online course page, use electronic responders during class, attack boredom for individual learners, and use video-game mania. These tools can be engaging for all students but especially those wearing the been there, done that wrapper.

Create an Online Course Page

Teaching with an online course page allows students to go home and connect with all the websites, video links, online textbooks, and videos created for and by them in the course. They contribute to discussions that started in class, give opinions on a poll, help define the concepts of the day in the glossary, check for the next assignment, and learn a little more about today's topic. Teaching in the 21st century without online support leaves the material one-dimensional and lifeless. Online tools enhance instruction with differentiation, acceleration, intervention, and remediation. If your school does not provide you a webpage, consider the following resources to create one:

- ➤ http://docs.moodle.org/en/Teaching_with_Moodle
- ➤ http://teacher.pageflakes.com

Table 4.3: Web 2.0 Tools

Tool	Description	Examples
Social Bookmarking	Share resources with students using a social-bookmarking site. Tag resources for learners to lessen their time searching through irrelevant material and increase their time reading pertinent material. Choose content-specific text at appropriate reading levels. Add sites the students find, filtering first to ensure quality.	http://delicious.com http://digg.com www.diigo.com/education
Discussion Boards	Use an electronic discussion board to level the playing field for students who take longer to process material, struggle with language, or fear public speaking. An online space bolsters self-confidence and reveals the skills of quieter students. Provide time in class to be online to jump-start discussions.	http://moodle.org/forums www.ning.com http://wave.google.com
Polls and Surveys	Polls give teachers a sense of where the class stands on an issue prior to the discussion, how students feel about the homework, what students are looking forward to, or how they are feeling about a particular unit. This is an excellent tool for preassessment.	www.micropoll.com http://quizilla.teennick.com/polls www.stellarsurvey.com http://zohopolls.com
Blogs	Have students blog from the perspective of characters in a book or historical figures from a certain time period. Use contemporary Web 2.0 tools to explore historical events and people so students make connections and gain deeper understanding.	http://21classes.com http://edublogs.org www.plurk.com
Wikis	Use a wiki to create collaborative notes for a course. Have students use the learning goals, class collaborative notes, and activities to create an online textbook. This interactive communication reveals students' understanding as the course progresses. Modify and adjust your lesson based on what is being published or not published. Students can conduct their own research and link additional resources.	http://pbworks.com www.wikispaces.com www.wetpaint.com
Online Assessments	Have learners get online and complete an assessment to inform you and themselves how their learning matched up with the lesson objectives. Use this information to start a class talking about learning objectives for the day. Use online quizzes to maximize class time for more meaningful teacher-student interaction. Shift homework to include online components to help students enjoy homework while learning. The dynamic nature of these online tools engages and motivates students. Teach learners how to use online assessments for self-improvement.	www.arcademicskillbuilders.com http://persuadestar.4teachers.org http://quizstar.4teachers.org
Lessons	Use a lesson module on an online learning site to bring self-paced learning into class. These activities are decision-based simulations students do once or as often as they want or need. Online learning is a productive remediation tool for skills-based content. Post podcasts online for students to review a lecturette, work a problem, or explain a concept.	http://kidsvid.4teachers.org http://moodle.org www.thinkquest.org/en http://trackstar.4teachers.org/trackstar
Assignments	Move into the electronic age and away from the traditional wire basket. Have students electronically submit assignments. The electronic path creates a record for the teacher and student, making it easier to follow the progress of a project. Some learners are more apt to turn in assignments electronically than in person. Removing requirements for printed assignments surprises and inspires learners to complete work and meet deadlines.	www.blackboard.com http://poster.4teachers.org http://schooltown.net http://turnitin.com

continued →

Tool	Description	Examples
RSS Feeds	An RSS feed is a syndicated list of headlines with links to stories from a news site, blog, or journal. Link to professional journals or news sites, perhaps even in a foreign language the students are learning, to bring life to the classroom. Link magazine articles for 24/7 access. Automatically sort with settings on the feed. For example, government class can be exciting when students connect with current events and legislation rather than just history as written in the textbook.	http://friendfeed.com www.google.com/reader www.newsgator.com
Glossaries	Have students create a course glossary to assess topics and terms they understand and areas to revisit. Learners create a visual reminder of the vocabulary each time they visit the course page.	http://docs.moodle.org/en/Glossaries http://glossword.biz www.studystack.com

Source: Adapted from Jennifer Nelson, Eden Prairie Schools, February 15, 2010.

Use Electronic Responders

Electronic responders provide an opportunity for students to respond simultaneously to a teacher-posed question. Responses are most often sent directly to the computer and displayed for the teacher and/or the class to view and discuss. Suppose that in a middle school English classroom, students are studying how to read and interpret graphs in nonfiction text. The teacher prepares questions to assess students' understanding of graphs, and each student answers using electronic responders that send their responses directly to the teacher's computer. With the click of a button, a graph appears displaying the range of students' responses. After practicing with a series of questions, students have a better handle on how to read a graph. Then the teacher asks, "If you were an executive and asked for a report on the buyer trends for a product you were trying to sell, would you want to see a graph like the ones we have been reviewing or read a three-page written report?" A discussion follows focusing not only on how to read a graph, but also the best way to display information. Students are now poised to take their learning to a deeper level and create their own graphs for a report or to communicate ideas to another audience.

Attack Boredom!

If students lack motivation because they are bored (such as with been there, done that wrappers), they may engage using a technology tool. For the tech-savvy student who does not understand the material, such as the learner wearing the "I don't know" wrapper, Web 2.0 tools help collect thoughts or ideas to make sense of the content. As a bonus, anything an individual learner creates has potential to help classmates understand. Interactive presentations, papers, and so on may be used as discussion points or activities for other students as well.

To differentiate assignments for frustrated students, consider having them build a website, start a blog, text, or use a Twitter page. Connect with these students to learn more about their favorite media tools and about how to motivate them.

- For the disruptive, bored student who could be wearing the class clown wrapper or the "I don't care" wrapper, assign him or her to create a blog based on the content. Make the learner responsible for posting the highlights from a class discussion, or collecting questions that the class has about solving a problem or completing an assignment.

- For the bored learner who knows the content, design a task for the student to use a technology tool such as PowerPoint or a video to teach other students the concept being taught.

- For students who are bored in general, ask them to use technology to track their personal progress. For example, have students record and track their reading fluency on the computer, or ask them to produce a video related to the topic, such as a video documenting a scientific investigation.

Use Video-Game Mania

Students are enthralled with high-interest interactive video games. Games lure them in and challenge them to achieve more—they just cannot help but try to get to the next level. What is it about video games that make them so popular, engaging, and sometimes addictive? What if our students showed the same persistence in learning in the classroom? Use key aspects of video games to capture the interest of our unmotivated students.

- **Clear purpose and direction:** Video games set clear goals for students to get to the next level or beat a previous score.

- **Immediate feedback:** When students fail or make a mistake, the game provides information about what happened. Usually, students can try as many times as they need to reach a higher level.

- **Choice and competition:** Players choose the level of competition so they can compete against themselves, friends, or other players on the web.

- **Multimedia:** There are multiple methods of communication. Pictures, videos, music, and words are all used to support the success of the players and give feedback on mistakes.

Students may be your best resource here. Ask them to name some of the most popular video games they play. Discuss how these games could be used in the classroom. In a blog entry, Jarrod Robinson (2008, used with permission) describes how using math-, brain-, and sight-training Nintendo DS games enhanced learning and engaged students in his classroom:

> Each week we set time for a variety of activities including homework catch-up and skill builders over a variety of subjects along with a double period working on a community or school based project. Across the course of the year the students self esteem and confidence has also improved substantially which has been fantastic.
>
> The Nintendo DS systems have been integrated to work on their skills in a engaging and fun way. . . . In a class that was almost impossible to get them to sit still to complete anything, they are now sitting through entire lessons without saying a word, completely focused on their work and their progress. Are they engaged? They sure are.

Strategy 13: Play Games to Learn, Review, and Remember

Do you need a way to make difficult or boring information become an interesting and motivating lesson? Using game formats and manipulatives involves and energizes students to learn. These engaging activities can be used to teach new information or review materials. Games are not only fun, they can also result in increased achievement: "Teacher-conducted research indicates that games can have a significant effect on student achievement when teachers use them purposefully and thoughtfully" (Marzano, 2010, p. 71).

When playing games, students are actively involved and working with the material or content; at the close of the game, they can reflect on new insights, the purpose, and next steps. This type of reflection is a productive use of time. Marzano (2010) summarizes the power of properly playing games and describes four components of classroom games that research shows have the biggest impact on student achievement:

1　Use competition that is low risk.

2　Target essential academic content.

3　Reflect on the learning that has occurred or the new questions that have emerged.

4　Have students revise their notes accordingly afterward.

Note that the critical factors center around debriefing, reflecting, and using the reflection to expand student learning tools and understanding of the material. Try this planning process for using games in your classroom:

1　Identify the purpose for the game, such as to learn new concepts or to review and practice previous lessons.

2　Select the learning goals or concepts to include in the game. Assess students to find out what they understand and what they need to practice.

3　Determine the most workable activity. Consider the learning styles of your students, the purpose, and the targeted learning goal.

4　Decide if players will work alone, with a partner or small group, or as two class teams.

5　Prepare probing questions and facts. A quick written response, problems from a previous quiz, or samples of student work from past years contribute to making the game more meaningful and effective.

6　Plan set-up needs.

7　Determine the best time to play.

- Where does the game fit best in the learning plan?

- How much class time will be used?

8　Explain the game purpose, procedure, and rules to players.

9　Play the game.

10　Elicit reflections. Have learners discuss the discovered facts or information they need to remember.

Tips and Traps

Identify the academic goal and then select a game format to reinforce or review the standards, skills, or concepts. Make sure the game has an academic purpose. Sponge activities are designed as a break from the academic routine. They are fun but often have no academic focus to support the standards being taught. In those cases, Marzano (2010) found the games were not as effective in increasing learning. However, if the lesson has been intense, a sponge activity can energize learners! Some examples of sponge activities include providing a stretch break, conducting a short exercise routine, dancing to a song, telling a funny story, providing show-and-tell time, or taking a walk outside for some fresh air.

Use or modify a familiar game format so your valuable time is devoted to the content, not the rules. Use games such as hangman, *Boggle*, *Scrabble*, crossword puzzles, competitive races, *Jeopardy!*, *Wheel of Fortune*, and *Pictionary*. The class can spend more time playing the game and learning or reviewing important content. In the future, use the same game for facts from another unit.

After playing the game with the whole class, consider placing its tools and artifacts in a station as a small-group or partner activity when one or a few learners need to master targeted concepts. Then learners can continue to review the academic material using the game format. For targeted concepts that only a few students need work to master, find a computer game or pre-designed game to help them learn.

Divide the class into competitive teams. Each time the team answers a question correctly, the players get to take another turn. Call on an unmotivated student or someone who is least likely to be chosen by their classmates to be the scorekeeper.

Consider having an unmotivated student design a game as a study activity. Engage this learner in crafting questions or choosing a format to plan the game for the class.

Engage students in the planning of the game. Small groups of learners may create tasks or questions to use in playing the game. The preparation and creation of the game may be just as beneficial to student engagement and learning as actually playing it.

After the game, praise students and cheer for everyone. Remember to save time for reflection. Debriefing the game is essential for learning. Time can easily slip away, so provide ample time for students to reflect.

Putting It Into Practice

Here we discuss games to engage students in the content: classroom Jeopardy, student-designed games, quiz-bowl competitions, and mystery quests are examples of using quality academic games for effective learning opportunities.

Classroom Jeopardy

Classroom Jeopardy is a familiar tool used to review content. Similar to the popular television game show, six to eight categories cover the content to be reviewed or studied in this game. Each category contains a list of answers hidden beneath a dollar level. The higher the dollar amount noted on the card, the more difficult the response required. Individually or in teams, students take turns naming a category and level. An answer is revealed, and the individual or team must phrase a corresponding question. Each time an answer is revealed, teams or individuals compete to respond with the accurate question. The teacher or moderator confirms it correct or incorrect. If correct, the team continues to choose another category.

Rami Hoaglin, a high school mathematics teacher, described the impact of playing *Jeopardy!* in her geometry classroom after doing action research and collecting student responses:

After playing "Geopardy"—a mathematical version of the game show Jeopardy—in my Geometry classes, many students who normally did not participate in class discussions began to perk up and eagerly participate in this game. Comments that students made included the following: "This is fun!" "I am going to get the answer first this time." "Come on Joe, you can get it!" "Oh, I get it now." "This is a fun way to review for a test." (1999, p. 106)

Student-Designed Games

Engage students in the content by having them create their own academic games based on an identified learning goal. Individually or in small groups, have learners design games for the class to play. Each group focuses on a different learning goal. Provide students with the following four-step process to focus their planning.

1 Identify the learning goal.

2 Determine what kinds of questions you will ask, making sure they are focused on the learning goals. Design questions that ask classmates to:

- Recall facts, events, or important people
- Describe the key players or people
- Solve problems
- Make choices

3 Determine the structure your game will use. If it is a board game, you will need to:

- Design a board with starting and ending points
- Create or find game pieces
- Create or find dice, a spinner, or other contraption to move players along the board
- Create cards with questions and possible answers
- Develop tasks
- List actions to perform
- Make objects, symbols, or people with Play-Doh® or drawings

4 Define the logistics of the game. Do the following:

- Identify the number of players.
- Decide whether the game is played in teams or individually.
- Establish an object to the game.
- Clarify what the players need to do.
- Write the rules.

Quiz-Bowl Competitions

Quiz-bowl competitions are designed for students to engage in the content in a fun, motivating way. Questions drive students to talk to each other and think through the current topics. A quiz bowl is an innovative formative assessment for teachers to see what learners understand and what they need for next-step planning. In teams, students formulate responses to questions or solutions to problems. For example, a middle school mathematics team analyzed quiz data from their seventh-grade classes. They arranged students by the type of problem they needed to review, based on incorrect responses from the quiz. One group of students needed to work on solving one-step equations, while another focused on solving two-step equations. The third group needed to work on setting up equations. As a classroom instructional activity, the student groups worked on fixing the items they missed on the quiz to clarify their misunderstandings. Then, they were charged with creating a few problems to share with the class. Each group presented their examples to the other class members for a quiz-bowl competition.

Mystery Quests

Framing learning as a mystery creates a sense of adventure and capitalizes on the curious nature of students. Use these ideas or frame one of your own to create a game that sparks excitement and ignites learning.

- Give students a set of clues such as facts, characteristics, or statistics, and have them try to figure out the mystery object, animal, or topic.

- Go on a scavenger hunt to find the answers or possible solutions to problems:

  - Pick a focus, and define what you want students to learn.

  - Set the boundaries for the scavenger hunt—texts, websites, books, school grounds, the classroom, or even an after-school nature hike.

  - Describe what students should look for, and send them off in pairs or small groups.

  - When students reconvene, have them draw supportive conclusions using evidence from their hunt.

- Be a private detective and discover the most important aspects of a topic, a historical event, or a scientific discovery.

- Use characters in a movie or television show. For example, stage a scene from the movie *National Treasure*. For younger students, put blue paws around the room, and have students play *Blue's Clues* and use the items with the paw prints to unlock the mystery.

Strategy 14: Spice It Up

Add spice at the beginning of a lesson, during an activity, or at the close of a lesson to give students memorable connections to the ideas, to generate interest or curiosity, and to provide feedback that stretches their thinking and moves them beyond their current potential.

We add spice and expand skills by integrating innovation, collaboration, information gathering, and problem solving into the fabric of our instruction and lessons. Students need to be creative and have opportunities to be innovative to learn and be successful in the future.

We add spice when learning becomes an opportunity by turning the mundane and boring into challenge, excitement, and anticipation. Twist lessons and topics to turn student passions and interests into more of those learning opportunities. Increase the interaction between students and teachers to positively influence students' attitudes. Make them yearn to cooperate, participate, and learn.

Tips and Traps

During planning, practice selective abandonment and throw out the boring parts. Teach in a way that captures the learners and is at the appropriate level for growth. The following techniques are samples of spicing up assignments.

- Use video clips, quotes, song lyrics, or television shows to introduce topics.

- Have students brainstorm content or skill connections to video, music, television, or other experiences.

- Use topics of interest to students to plan the spice. See chapter 3 (page 69) for additional ideas to identify the learners' areas of interest and passion. Do not assume you know!

- Plan activities using flexible-grouping designs. Use a blending of small groups, large groups, individual activities, and pairs to perform assignments and tasks. See chapter 3 (page 69) for more ideas on integrating student learning styles.

- Incorporate technology such as ebooks, networking, Internet searches, interactive boards, online portfolios, and blogging. See strategy 12, Get Plugged In (page 110), for more ideas.

- Ask students to brainstorm and plan different ways to present a lesson with "spice." They will be learning and motivated at the same time!

Remember, adding spice does not mean adding fluff. Cutesy lessons do not stimulate minds. They may be interesting at first, but they are too shallow, and the energy wears off. Learners do not have time for fluff. The spice and fun added must relate to the content.

Stimulating activities should be used with *all* students to teach, practice, and learn. When we use highly engaging activities as rewards alone, we communicate that fun only happens *after* learning rather than promote learning itself as fun. When engaging in these activities, students are exploring, discovering, inventing, problem solving, and learning while being motivated.

Mundane, filler activities and worksheets with no clear purpose bore students and send them the wrong messages about the use of school, the value of their time, and the importance of learning. Teachers sometimes see worksheets as meaningful practice, while students see them as unrelated to anything they are learning and shut down. Eliminate busywork, boring worksheets, and lectures. A worksheet must have a clear purpose and a defined learning goal. Chunk it so that it feels doable and possible.

Putting It Into Practice

Use effective lecturettes and revitalized worksheets to spice up lessons and engage learners.

Give Effective Lecturettes, Not Ineffective Lectures!

For true engagement that produces learning, students must see the lesson's personal value and relevance to their future success and be interested in the content as it is presented. Lectures can be ineffective and boring when they are teacher-directed and have no real hook to pique student interest. In this type of lecture, students act as passive listeners as the teacher follows the textbook instead of personalizing the lesson so learners can relate. While students may read the text or work the problems aloud, they usually do so without processing the learning or highlighting important aspects of the work. When the bell rings or the text ends, the lesson is over, regardless of student misunderstanding. Sound familiar? Alternatively, *lecturettes* are short, engaging presentations teachers offer to introduce concepts and assist students in thinking about the learning "on tap." Lecturettes provide the right balance of teacher-explained content and student reflection. Figure 4.1 (page 122) is a checklist for planning, introducing, and evaluating effective lecturettes in your classroom.

Revitalize Worksheets

Sachi came off the bus one day and sat down next to her mother, ready to do her homework. She immediately burst into tears when she opened her homework. She had no idea what to do. The first words out of her mouth were, "They don't teach us. They just give us worksheets and tell us to do it. We just have to teach ourselves."

If we were to revitalize the worksheet tasks, what could they look like? Consider the following as you plan the next worksheet assignments.

- What are the learning goals for the worksheet?
- What is the purpose of the worksheet?
  - Practice?
  - Create interest?
  - Check for understanding?
  - Offer as an option after students complete a task?
- How can you structure the worksheet to work for the whole class? Do you need to provide different options based on student understanding? For example, if some students already understand nouns, assigning more work to identify nouns is not as appropriate as having students write their own paragraphs using what they know about nouns.
  - What process, response, reflection, or comment boxes can you add to collect student input?

Assign worksheets that are absolutely essential and serve a very specific purpose. If you are using a textbook lesson, allow students to skip the questions that don't address the standards and concepts being taught—no student will mind! This option is also needed if certain questions reflect learning that students have already mastered.

Consider the following strategies to spice up worksheets, focus on essential information, and encourage deep thinking.

- Cut the worksheet in smaller strips, chunks, or pieces. Breaking it down into more manageable segments can be especially motivating for struggling students because they see progress in a shorter amount of time with each completed piece. This makes the learners feel capable of doing the work and raises self-confidence.

- Distribute one or two questions to each student rather than having all learners answer a long list of questions. After they complete their questions, students share their thinking process and the answers.

- Seat learners in a circle for a round-robin activity. One student answers the first question, and then passes the worksheet to another student, who answers the second

Directions: Use the following checklist to plan, introduce, and evaluate effective lecturettes in your classroom. Read each item and check the statements as you complete them.

Before the Lecturette: Planning

- ☐ Identify appropriate standards, skills, and/or concepts to include in the presentation.
- ☐ Preassess the students to find out their knowledge base, feelings, and interests.
- ☐ Use the data from the preassessment in planning.
- ☐ Divide the information into manageable chunks.

During the Lecturette: Introducing and Teaching

- ☐ Post the standards, objectives, or benchmarks to be introduced.
- ☐ Use a creative, unexpected hook.
- ☐ Explain the purpose of the lesson; introduce and refer to the posted standards.
- ☐ Introduce appropriate chunks of the material.
- ☐ Allow students to be active participants and interact with the information.
- ☐ Use personal stories or experiences that are age, context, and content appropriate.
- ☐ Allow time for students to share their personal experiences and make connections.
- ☐ Teach the important, beneficial chunks in a meaningful sequence.
- ☐ Use a variety of strategies to promote student interaction and movement.
- ☐ Strategically build in stopping points for effective student input, sharing, and processing.
- ☐ Move around the room.
- ☐ Have learners work through concepts with guided practice.
- ☐ End the teaching segment with a valuable, reflective piece about the learning, determining what was taken from the lecturette.

After the Lecturette: Processing and Learning

- ☐ Plan activities for learners to work with the information that has been introduced.
- ☐ Assign student-focused adjustable assignments according to the assessment data.
- ☐ Decide whether the learners will work alone, with partners, or in small groups.
- ☐ Work with the individuals or small groups who need intervention.
- ☐ Assess learners with a formative postassessment to determine the next step.
- ☐ Celebrate!

Additional Comments:

*Visit **go.solution-tree.com/instruction** for a reproducible of this figure.*

Figure 4.1: Checklist for engaging, motivating lecturettes.

question. Prompt learners to review the previous responses on the sheet and do any of the following depending on the nature of the question:

- Add another sentence offering more detail or another perspective.
- Check the work, and write one idea that seems interesting or accurate.
- Review the work, and write one question about it.
- Create a symbol to represent the idea or response.
- Describe the thinking process another student used to arrive at the answer or response.
- Summarize the responses in their own words.

- Students continue passing the worksheet or question to another person as long as the teacher directs. Each time the worksheet is passed, provide new ways to respond.

Strategy 15: Create Optimism and Celebrate!

To be motivated, a learner has to feel success. Plan each learning opportunity for students to achieve success. Recognize large and small accomplishments, and be specific about the focus of the celebration. Celebrate in a meaningful way so students begin to connect what they are doing with what they are learning and begin to feel their effort is producing results. With this sense of optimism, students are excited to take even more steps toward achievement. Celebration affirms achievement and influences a person's emotional reactions to his or her own accomplishments, all of which build self-esteem (Linnenbrink & Pintrich, 2003).

Some educators believe we do not have time to stop and celebrate. Frankly, we do not have time *not* to celebrate and observe the progress made. It is essential for learners to recognize and internalize success. Celebrating success goes a long way to building hope and confidence. When students have hope, they see possibility. When they see possibility, they try. As their small successes become transparent, they build confidence, and with that confidence, they take more risks, make mistakes, and learn more! Celebration also builds rapport between the teacher and the student. Celebrate the successes of students to show students that you care about them. Acknowledge their successes and progress.

It is easy to focus on everything that isn't "right" about a student's achievement, behavior, effort, or work. The problem with this approach is two-fold. First, students are overwhelmed with the sheer amount of negative feedback and become paralyzed; they simply do not know where to start. Second, negative comments often omit information telling students what to do to fix the mistake, misunderstanding, or behavior. When students do not know what to do next, the result is often disengagement, which can manifest in disruptive behavior, clowning around, or inaction. Probably even more problematic are the unseen consequences. Students may begin to think that something is wrong with them personally and that there is really nothing they can do to fix it or move forward (Hattie & Timperley, 2007). At this point, some students may throw their hands in the air and exclaim, "I don't care!," "This is stupid," or "I quit!" These feelings lead to shame and despair. What if a learner goes for an hour, a day, a week, months, a whole year, or a whole school career and has few "aha" moments? These students become convinced that school is not the place to be. They may sit in the classroom physically, but mentally and emotionally, these are our lost students.

Start from a place of strength, and then move to addressing areas to work on. Get to know what the student knows. Ask yourself, do I build on strengths or focus on weaknesses and challenges? Success is contagious. It breeds confidence and hope so that students will take risks. When a student understands the information or experiences an aha moment, it is a motivating adventure not only for the learner, but also for the teacher. In fact, this feeling is a huge part of the joy of teaching.

Tips and Traps

Celebrate good classroom discussions and successful activities as well as individual achievement. Let students help plan and prepare celebrations. For example, students can brainstorm and help prepare certificates that describe in specific terms the achievement of each student.

Beware of empty celebrations, parties, comments, hooks, or exclamations that do not have a clear reason.

Plan celebrations to work with your style and that feel comfortable for you. If you would struggle to lead a group cheer, have someone else do it, or choose another method of celebration.

Putting It Into Practice

Bring adventure into the class, celebrate success, and create optimism by using chants and cheers, putting up motivational visuals, and even dancing!

Use Chants and Cheers

Use chants and cheers to celebrate success, encourage students, and get them fired up to learn. Celebrate great ideas and "I get it!" moments that students experience. Try the following as appropriate for your style, your students, and their age level:

- "We got it! We got it! Yes!"
- "You got it! You got it! Yes!"
- "We rock! We rock! Yes we do!"
- "Team work! Team work! Go team!"
- "You are great and getting greater!"
- "It's going to be a great day!"
- "We are the *best*!"
- "Great job!"
- "Hurrah!"
- "You go, girl!"
- "Good job, good buddy!"
- "Keep on keepin' on!"
- "Yippee!"
- "Uh-huh, uh-huh, uh-huh!"
- "You did it! Whoo hoo!"
- "Yes, yes, yes! Wow!"

Ask students to make up their own cheers.

You can accompany cheers with physical movements such as high fives and standing ovations. Create movements or actions that kids perform or that signal "It's time for a celebration."

The following are sample celebration claps, cheers, and movements (Chapman & King, 2009a).

- **Fish clap:** Open your left hand. Flap your right hand front to back several times like a fish flapping in the palm of your hand.
- **Ketchup-bottle clap:** Ball your right hand into a fist to represent the bottle. Tap on the top of the fist with your left hand like getting ketchup out of a bottle.
- **Table-rap clap:** Rap on the table twice while saying "table rap," and then clap your hands once while saying, "Clap."
- **Excellent guitar:** Pretend to strum a guitar and have everyone yell, "Excellent!" Repeat the sequence. Then pose like Elvis and say, "Thank you very much!"
- **Trucker cheer:** Hold your hand to your mouth as if you are talking on a CB radio and say, "Good job, good buddy!"
- **Happy clam:** With a finger at each corner of your mouth, make a big smile.
- **Micro-wave:** Wave with the pinkie finger.
- **Roller coaster:** Travel both hands up, up, up, and then go down quickly into a dip and back up again like a roller-coaster ride.

Put Up Signs and Motivational Posters

Motivational signs and posters can also engage and inspire students. Accompany the messages with pictures and visuals reflecting the culture and landscape of your classroom and school. Learners may help you create the signs, photographing inspiring moments in the classroom or in the school. Encourage students to make signs for room displays with their own motivating statements. Following are suggestions for signs that promote goal setting, work, and perseverance.

Examples of signs that promote goal setting:

- Believe in yourself!
- Tomorrow holds the key to your dreams.
- Never quit dreaming!
- Today's goals are tomorrow's successes!
- Anything is possible!
- Dare to dream!

Examples of signs that promote work and perseverance:

- Meet the challenge!
- You can do it!
- Go for it!
- Within you is the strength to meet life's challenges.
- You are great and getting greater every day!

➤ Do your best!

Stand Up and Dance

Picture Ellen DeGeneres, daytime talk-show host, dancing on the set. She motivates everyone in the audience and at home to dance, move to the beat, and smile while enjoying the activity. Instead of the renowned "Ellen time," call it "Dance time." Select a song with a good beat for you and your students, for example, Aly and AJ's "Walking on Sunshine," Reel 2 Real's "I Like to Move It," or ABBA's "Dancing Queen." Students will laugh, giggle, and look around uncomfortably, and everyone will enjoy the experience. When they sit down to tackle the next topic, their minds will be open and refreshed.

Chapter 4 Campfire Talk

This chapter described strategies to find adventure in learning. Consider your own understanding, perceptions, and experiences about what works to make students feel that learning is exciting and fun. Discuss the following questions, statements, and activities in your professional learning community, department, grade-level team, or a staff meeting.

1   What is the most memorable classroom experience you had as a student? Describe it. What were you doing? What was the teacher doing? How did you feel? How could you adapt this in your classroom?

2   How would you want students to describe your class? What are some strategies you could employ to create this reality in your classroom?

3   Try one of the strategies in this chapter either with an individual student or with the entire class. Get together with colleagues, and reflect on your experience with this strategy:

   - Did it work? Did it result in the behavior or task you were trying to impact?

   - How did students' attitudes change?

   - Did students accomplish the assigned task? Why or why not?

   - What worked? How do you know?

   - What did not work so well? Why?

   - How could you change the strategy to make it more effective next time?

4   In what ways do you currently celebrate the success of your students?

5   List learning experiences you could use as opportunities to celebrate.

6   Use the Policies and Practices reproducible (page 130) to list the policies and practices in your classroom. How do these policies send messages of hope and possibility to students? Are there ways to revise your practices to intentionally send messages of efficacy?

7   Use the Plan for Student Motivation reproducible (page 128) to discover, diagnose, and plan to address the needs of individual unmotivated students through finding adventures in learning.

Plan for Student Motivation

Strategy	Name the Unmotivated Student(s) in Need of the Strategy	Identify the Wrapper the Student Is Wearing	List Observable Evidence, Behavior, Habits, or Traits	Develop an Action to Address the Need	Assess and Reflect on Implemen-tation	Additional Comments
11. Use Irresistible Hooks and Clever Closures (page 104)						
12. Get Plugged In (page 110)						
13. Play Games to Learn, Review, and Remember (page 115)						
14. Spice It Up (page 119)						
15. Create Optimism and Celebrate! (page 123)						

Planning Irresistible Hooks and Clever Closures

Using the table, choose a purpose for the activity, and write down possible ideas for corresponding hooks and closures.

Purpose	Description	Hook or Closure Idea
To connect	Connect the topic and the learning to what students already know, prior experiences, a previous lesson or learning goal, or students' backgrounds.	
To excite	Facilitate an activity or discussion to foster student excitement about the topic at hand.	
To celebrate	Celebrate successful learning experiences and engaging activities.	
To remember	Use activities and instruction to trigger students' knowledge and assist them in remembering.	

Policies and Practices

Use the table to list the policies and practices in your classroom. How do these policies send messages to students of hope and possibility? Are there ways to revise your practices to intentionally send messages of hope and efficacy?

Policy or Practice	Explicit or Implicit Message to Students	Changes to Instill Hope and Self-Efficacy
Late-work policy		
Tardy policy		
Celebrations		
Homework policy		
Grading practices or policies		
In-class discussion practices		
Handling disruptive comments or behavior		

Promoting Choice and Control

Andre was a quiet and reserved tenth grader. Whether in small groups or whole-class discussion, Andre remained mostly silent. His mother heard the same thing over and over at student-teacher conferences: "He needs to participate in class more often." No amount of persuading or consequence changed Andre's participation in class.

One day Andre's teacher noticed his notebooks were covered with intricate and beautiful drawings of events described in class, interactions among classmates, and words and phrases taken directly from discussions or related to the content of the course. The teacher began to offer students choice about how they reflected on the content and participated in discussions. She asked Andre to share his drawing and how it related to the content. Thirty-two students sat captivated as this quiet student shared deep insight about the impact of WWII on a family living in rural California. The image revealed not only the hardships of the time, but also the emotional wear and tear on families during that time period. The class erupted in applause. From that day on, Andre sat straighter in his chair and offered his thoughts in discussions more often.

What choices do students have in school? Do they have any control over their learning? Can they, with effort and persistence, impact their success? What opportunities are provided for students to choose and be in control of their learning? When teachers consider these questions, they reflect on the passive world of school that students often experience.

Life is filled with choices. The everyday decisions we make mold us into the people we become. We make decisions throughout life: the people we select as friends; the hobbies we spend time on; the careers we choose to pursue. But many classrooms do not offer choices and opportunities for learners to make decisions. As a result, students often rebel because the teacher is always in control. The decision not to do an assignment or engage may be the only control a student can exercise. When teachers provide choice, the learner is in control. The student becomes more eager to work on assignments and activities. Sometimes this happens because he or she has the control to select his or her favorite way to complete the task.

When teams of teachers or groups of students spend too much time focused on things outside of their control, morale sinks, confidence wavers, and motivation evaporates. Time spent in school seems like a string of cloudy days. But when we spend a small amount of time on things outside of our control and the majority of time on things in our control, by contrast, our morale increases; possibility and excitement develop. Though we cannot change things like weather, it is fine to talk about these "out of our control" issues because they often impact our lives in significant ways. We can learn from them. When the rain passes and the sun comes out again, the day looks bright, hopeful, and full of possibilities.

What a learner experiences outside the school day—activities, home life, personal beliefs, friends, habits, food, and actions—is out of an educator's control. Learners' personal experiences, choices, and influences impact their motivation, attitudes, and actions. School staff can do nothing about what happens before and after school, but must accept responsibility and proactively plan for what happens during school time. For example, educators must be positive role models. Demonstrate and teach the difference between right and wrong as well as positive and negative attitudes. Students either become motivated to do what the adults at school want or to rebel against the direction, opportunity, task, or assignment. It is their choice.

Tracy Kidder (2010) comments on the work of teachers, naming issues that remain mostly outside of their control and emphasizing the classroom as a place where teachers have some freedom:

> Most teachers have little control over school policy or curriculum or choice of texts or special placement of students, but most have a great deal of autonomy inside the classroom. To a degree shared by only a few other occupations, such as police work, public education rests precariously on the skill and virtue of the people at the bottom of the institutional pyramid.

The classroom is a place where teachers have great power to impact the motivation and engagement of students.

When we perceive many of our daily worries as out of our control, what happens? Take a quick survey from your own experience, using figure 5.1 (see page 152 for a reproducible version). You may find it beneficial to discuss the results of your findings during this exercise with colleagues.

When educators reflect on their work through the lens of what is inside and outside their control, it has potential to lead to specific actions to support students. Our work to motivate learners must begin with things inside our control. There is hope and possibility when we discuss and plan how to move forward or do things differently to affect learning and motivation.

In the same spirit, students benefit from identifying what is in and out of their control. When students feel out of control, they may shut down, complain, become angry, or give up. Whether we give choices or not, students inevitably make the most important decision: whether or not to try. When we offer students opportunities to make decisions and choices, they not only become excited about the content or task, but also accept responsibility, try harder, and become more willing to complete the task. Like adults, students can learn from cloudy, rainy days. When they feel out of control, it is a signal that they are struggling with something and need the teacher to find a ray of sun that will help them see the next steps toward success.

Students can also complete figure 5.1 to examine and list things inside and outside of their control. This activity can be a valuable step toward having more control and choice in their school

1. In the cloud, make a list of all the things outside your control.

2. Now make a list of all the things within your control, and write them in the sun.

3. Consider what percentage of time you spend talking, thinking, and working on things within your control versus outside your control. Write the percentages in the spaces provided.

I spend about _____ % of my time thinking, working on, and talking about aspects outside my control.

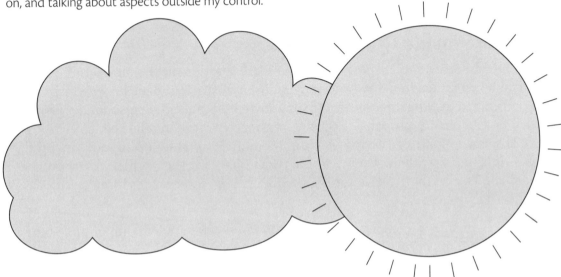

I spend about _____ % of my time thinking, working on, and talking about aspects within my control.

4. Reflect privately, or discuss with peers. What is the balance between time you spend on things within your control compared to those outside your control?

Do you spend too much time talking about things outside your control? If so, what is the possible impact on your work?

How productive are you when spending time on things within your control?

Figure 5.1: Survey on control.

lives. It also acts as a metacognitive tool that helps them get through tough situations by shifting energy away from reacting to situations out of their control and toward recognizing actions that lead to their desired outcome.

When students are more self-directed, they are better able to recognize what is not working and make a new plan. This plan may include involving peers, parents, or teachers to assist in their learning pursuits. Self-directed learners persevere and work through their challenges to learn more. Students who exhibit these behaviors have increased motivation and higher academic achievement (Zimmerman, 2008).

Accordingly, the strategies in this chapter suggest ways to lend students some control and some choice so that they take more ownership in their learning and their work.

Strategy 16:   Provide Quality Choices

Strategy 17:   Set a Goal, Make a Deal

Strategy 18:   Use the Arts

Strategy 16: Provide Quality Choices

When we get to choose, we feel some control over our lives, our success, and our day. Choice in a classroom can be presented in many ways ranging from where a student sits to which assignment he or she will complete. Sometimes learners shut down and make the personal decision not to do the assigned task. This can cause major conflict between the student and the teacher. It stands in the way of academic progress. The reason learners refuse or choose not to do something varies. As educators it is important not to jump to the conclusion that their refusal is intended as disrespect toward adults or authority. Examining the root cause of a student's disengagement can lead to a more effective response.

Offering choice can shift the energy in this conflict and offer students input and some control in their learning. Choices provide learners a way to show what they know and opportunities to work in challenging ways. When we offer choices, we communicate trust and respect: "I trust you to make a decision that is best for you. I understand that individuals learn differently and that we all like to interact in different ways." Taking ownership of these activities is engaging and motivational.

When developing a list of choices for a task, examine the options to be sure each one is a quality choice. Consider the following list when planning effective choices in your classroom.

- Provide information on what students must do to meet the standard, assignment's objective, and achieve the expected outcome. After assignment instructions are explained, students should be able to make a choice and complete the task with little or no assistance.

- Plan each choice to take approximately the same amount of time.

- Require the same type of reasoning or thinking in each choice. For example, if you offer students four essay questions and they can choose two to complete, be sure all questions require similar thinking. If two items are knowledge focused and two require higher-level reasoning, students may choose to answer only the knowledge questions. Their essays will reflect their understanding of the knowledge objectives, but little will be known about their proficiency in the higher-level thinking that the essays were also intending to measure. Any score assigned will be misleading if represented as achievement on all content objectives.

Tips and Traps

Use visuals to make choices and the act of choosing fun and exciting. For example, list them on a shape that fits the topic, season, or task:

- List project choices on a board in the shape of the theme.

- List article choices on an open-book shape.

- Write homework or class assignment questions on a huge question mark.

- Create assignment choices on a tic-tac-toe grid, and have students select three assignments in a row, vertically, horizontally, or diagonally.

- Provide a choice of open-ended questions to answer at the end of a quiz or test.

Putting It Into Practice

Choices can be presented in different formats. Consider table 5.1 in your planning. Table 5.1 lists common classroom assignments or tasks and presents different ways to encourage choice in how students fulfill requirements.

Table 5.1: Choice in the Classroom

Assignment or Task	Student Choices
Make a presentation.	Give a demonstration, conduct an interview, or create a musical beat, poster, reenactment, PowerPoint, or game show.
Demonstrate knowledge.	Use manipulatives, explain your step-by-step thinking, draw it, act it out, or give a demonstration.
Select how you will work.	Work alone, with a partner, or small group.
Choose a work place.	Work on the floor, at your seat, or at the table.
Write an assignment or test.	Select from a list of questions. Answer the question by drawing an illustration, writing a paragraph, creating a list, or plotting ideas on a graphic organizer.
Choose how to respond.	Write the answers in a list, a poem, a song, a story, or a letter.
Complete a reading assignment.	Choose a book, article, or section from a list to study.
Complete a project, such as a research or science investigation project.	Choose a topic from the list for your project's focus.
Complete a student-focused assignment.	Choose two items from the list of activities to finish your assignment.

In the following sections, we discuss a few ways to provide quality choices in your classroom: use a variety of creative materials, graphic organizers, Foldables™, and learning stations, and give students responsibility.

Use a Variety of Creative Materials

Allowing students to choose materials to complete an assignment can offer variety and motivate learners to act. For example, a quiz can be an unpleasant experience for a learner, causing him or her to shut down or rebel. Help take some of the anxiety out of the situation by using a smaller piece of paper, such as a fourth of a piece of notebook paper. The student thinks, "Maybe I can do this if I just have to write this much."

Consider using a pleasing color or texture of paper to make any assignment a more enticing experience. In addition, offer different types of pens and pencils, markers, colored pencils, and crayons that vary according to size, color, and texture. Students find learning fun and engaging when they get to use their favorite materials. Put a variety of different writing utensils in strategic places around the room for students to select a favorite. Choices in these areas are easy to offer and can be the invitation students need to complete an assignment.

Use Graphic Organizers

Graphic organizers are pictures, tables, charts, or grids that learners use to organize their thoughts and plot information. Graphic organizers can show the relationship between and among ideas and concepts, sequence historical events, organize the plot of a story, or illustrate the influence of major figures. Learners may design their own graphic organizers or choose from a list depending on how much experience they have with them. In any case, demonstrate and teach students how to use each graphic organizer before offering it as a choice.

The following list provides some choices of organizers to use across content areas and grade levels.

- Select or cut out a shape representing the unit theme. Post important facts being learned during a discussion on the shape.

- Use the steps of a ladder, a numbered list, or rectangle frames to communicate each step of a process or sequence.

- Use a T-chart or Venn diagram to compare and contrast two categories.

- Use a timeline or bar graph to plot data, events, or findings, and then explain the organization.

- Use different shapes to create your own graphic organizers using two or more figures.

For example, let's say students have been studying energy. They are focusing on defining, explaining, and identifying different types of energy. In addition, they are exploring how different types of energy may influence the environment. Students will use their notes on energy to create a graphic organizer depicting various energy sources and the impact of each on the environment. They can choose from a variety of shapes to create their own graphic organizer.

For more information on graphic organizers, see Carolyn Chapman and Rita King's (2009b) book *Differentiated Instructional Strategies for Reading in the Content Areas.*

Use Foldables

Foldables provide students with another unique way to organize, remember, and review information. Have students fold paper according to your instructions. Use different sizes, colors, and textures to create variety and offer choice or to carry out a theme. Students may create their own patterns or themes based on the concepts being taught. Assign a task or question for each section of the Foldable, and let them choose either pictures or words to explain it. Consider the following examples:

- When teaching a process or a procedure, have students fold a sheet of paper so the creases divide the paper into the appropriate number of sections. Write one part of the process in each section. For example, when teaching the writing process, the paper would contain six sections: prewriting, organizing, drafting, revising, editing, and polishing. Use your own terminology to frame the steps. Then students either write explanations of the steps or draw symbols to represent each step. This becomes a tool they refer to as they are employing the process.

➤ When teaching concepts, consider folding and cutting the paper to include flaps. Students may use this Foldable to study vocabulary terms, writing the word on top of the flap and the definition underneath. Students may also use this type of creative material to represent cause and effect in nonfiction or fiction texts.

➤ When teaching the sequence of events or connections of people, fold the paper to form multiple flaps to depict connections to concepts, events, or people. For example, when constructing the timeline of events from a literary text, students may fold the paper as an accordion, writing the sequence of events in each fold.

➤ When teaching the relationships among and between concepts, have students fold various shapes and make parts of the shape represent the parts of the concept. For example, have students fold paper airplanes. Use each part to represent a different part of speech, role of characters in a literary text, or the role significant historical figures played in a major world occurrence.

After teaching several different types of Foldables, allow students to select their favorite to write or draw assigned information.

For more examples of this fun and creative activity, consult the following websites:

➤ http://foldables.wikispaces.com

➤ www.catawba.k12.nc.us/c_i_resources/foldables.htm

➤ www.dinah.com

Develop Learning Stations

Learning stations work at all grade levels, in any subject, to provide students choices in how they move their learning forward and how they demonstrate what they know. Learning stations can be set up to introduce ideas or to help students dig in more deeply to the learning goals; in those cases, all students visit every station. If these work areas are designed to help students learn more based on their progress or lack of understanding according to a formative assessment, then students only work at the stations they need. This provides a productive intervention for those needing time to build prior knowledge and for others needing a deeper challenge because they know the information being taught.

Aside from providing students with choice, learning stations are a valuable way to:

➤ Differentiate to meet individual needs

➤ Address the unit standards, skills, and concepts with student-focused tasks

➤ Provide learning experiences that explore, reteach, reinforce, and review content, thus helping students discover, learn, create, and process information

➤ Address different learning modalities, styles, and intelligences

➤ Provide leveled assignments (Use the simple and complex learning goals identified when you unpacked the standards to plan leveled assignments. See strategy 6, page 71.)

➤ Make learning an adventure

➤ Use a variety of materials

➤ Use critical and creative learning opportunities

- Provide hands-on learning
- Offer varied and simultaneous learning opportunities
- Honor differences in completion time, attention span, and need for personal space

Although it takes time to plan and set up quality stations and learning centers, the effort is well worth it when students are engaged and learning more! Table 5.2 offers some sample learning stations with engaging names.

Give Students Responsibility

Students who are unmotivated or disengaged may not expect to be given responsibility. Often they feel removed from the classroom community and do not see themselves as contributing members. When you give students responsibility, you build relationships by sending a message that you believe in them and see them as an important part of the classroom community. The student thinks, "If the teacher trusts me to do this, maybe I can be successful in this class."

Assign roles to help the procedures of the classroom run smoothly. Consider the following ways to give students responsibility and allow them to feel in control of their own learning.

- Provide specific tasks that need to be completed, such as reminding students to get their group presentation ready for the next class period.
- Let them check their own papers for instant feedback against an answer key to see how many they got right and correct their mistakes.
- Have them demonstrate one problem or example on the board and explain their thinking process to the class.
- Delegate chores, such as distributing papers or checking to see who did the homework.

Strategy 17: Set a Goal, Make a Deal

To set a goal, we first break the big picture down into parts and then allow students to have some control over how and when they meet the goal. Students can thus set achievable goals and celebrate their progress. This process builds confidence and gets results.

Goals are often written in terms that make a deal: "When you do X, then the reward will be Y." For example, when you do your homework, you will have free time. There are some tasks that we must do even if we are not all that thrilled to do them. However, by giving students something to look forward to after an unexciting task, we entice them to push through the tough stuff. The reward they receive can be intrinsic or extrinsic, depending on the individual and the situation.

Effective goal setting requires some planning. Figure 5.2 (page 140, see page 153 for a reproducible) is a guide for teachers to use when implementing goal setting. Have students fill out the top section to plan their goal. Then, after the time frame, have them complete the bottom section.

Teachers can use this template for individuals, small groups, or the whole class. Let's examine some of the key planning components.

- **Goal:** Identify the expected task or behavior. Some examples include trying to answer a question independently before asking the teacher, staying on task during class, avoiding side conversations, avoiding sharpening a pencil at the wrong time, keeping

Table 5.2: Examples of Engaging Learning Stations

Station or Center	Use and Purpose	Suggested Materials	Jazzy Names
Reading Resource Center	Read material of choice.	Reference materials Printed materials in different genres Reading selections for pleasure or learning reference	Book Nook Study Corner Discover Spot!
Writing Station	Write fact or fiction assignments. Critically express thoughts and write creatively.	Different sizes, shapes, and colors of writing tools and paper Topic and format choices Computers and gadgets	Author's Desk The Writing Place Wonder Writers' Nook
Reflection Center	Write in journals. Process thoughts. Express feeling and emotions. Assess learning and needs.	Journals Different sizes, shapes, and colors of writing implements and paper Graphic-organizer choices	Wise Words Reflection Celebration Express It!
Technology Station	Use technology to explore, learn, and create.	Computers to do web searches for references and exploration Different programs and games to reinforce learning Calculators, e-books, cameras, scanners, and so on	Gadget Station Computer Lab Techie Place
Manipulative Lab	Use manipulatives for hands-on learning.	Manipulative materials such as play money, wooden blocks, or geometric shapes for math skills and task choices	Skill Center Play It Station
News Center	Learn local, national, and world news. Use reference materials and tools.	Thermometers, rain gauges, and forecasting instruments Dictionaries and thesauruses Word walls Globes, maps, and brochures	Reference Center Resource Shelf What's Up Station
Creative Station	Use different art media to learn, create, discover, and invent.	Junk box that includes old magazines, Popsicle sticks, pens, pencils, office supplies, donated cereal boxes, or empty paper-towel rolls Drawing board Table for experiments Writing and art supplies	Discovery Station Invention Convention Art Spot Project Center
Problem-Solving Station	Unlock mysteries, and process and interpret data.	Brain puzzles Problems to solve Sequencing and processing graphic organizers Data, charts, and graphs Places to record and log discoveries or scores	Brain Table Think Tank

---

Name: _____   Date: _____

Goal (expected task or behavior): _____

Time frame: _____   Reward: _____   Check-in date: _____

Strategies needed to accomplish this goal:

Did the strategies work? Why or why not?

What did you learn? How did it feel to set a goal?

Next steps (if any):

Student thoughts:

Teacher thoughts:

Figure 5.2: Goal-setting template.

hands to oneself, handing in homework, making revisions to a piece of writing, talking respectfully to adults even when angry, and so on.

- **Time frame:** Define the time parameters. Is this a one-time task? Does the behavior need to be seen consistently over a period of time? Decide how long the student has to complete the task or change his or her behavior. Time is important because part of making this goal work includes breaking it down into specifics so that students believe it is possible.

- **Reward:** Identify the reward that will follow completion or consistent evidence of the expected task or behavior. Sometimes there is no need to give an extrinsic reward. The self-fulfillment and celebration of completing the goal are sufficient. Table 5.3 displays some examples of rewards and recognition teachers can give individual students or the whole class if an extrinsic reward is needed. Notice the rewards listed do not cost money. At times students can choose their own reward or type of celebration of accomplishment. (See strategy 15, page 123, for examples of class cheers to use.) Use extrinsic rewards carefully as they can sometimes motivate in the short term, but backfire in the long term. Students need to have a clear sense of why they are setting the goal, and they need to be part of the process to feel control over their learning and success. Connecting this sense of control to success will allow students to experience long-term motivation.

- **Check-in date:** Set a time and day that you will check in with the student about the effectiveness of the deal or the goal. These are checkpoints, or the written reflections or verbal conversations, for gathering formative feedback. These data include reviewing the

Table 5.3: Examples of Rewards and Recognition

Individual Students	Whole Class
Pass to get out of one night of homework	Class or small-group cheers of celebration
Coupon for extra time to work with a partner	Acknowledgement on a bulletin board, door, or assigned place in the classroom or hall
Pat on back	
Verbal praise	Extra station time
Verbal specific praise and compliments	Time to develop a bulletin board or decorate a door
Nonverbal signals, facial expressions, and gestures	Choice of assignment from list provided by the teacher
Personalized note from the teacher	Choice of story or text to read independently or for the teacher to read to the class
Work posted in a special place	
Stickers, stamps, or toys	Redeemable points
Redeemable coupons from local merchants	Pizza or ice cream party (sometimes local restaurants are willing to donate these items)
Chance to wear music headphones	
Awards or certificates	Choice of activity for a segment of a class period—a game, free time to talk with friends, and so on
Ticket to have lunch with an adult (principal, counselor, teacher, and so on)	Free time for a short period of time
	Class walk time around the school or outside
Parent call to report the accomplishments	Group dance to a favorite song
Release time to go to media center, work on a project, or work on computer	Personal time to share an out-of-class experience
Free talk time	Activity to share future goals, dreams, and visions
Opportunity to be teacher helper, office runner, or materials distributor	Stretch or exercise time
	Oral list of accomplishments and celebrations
Line leader	
Preferred seating	
Seating by the teacher	
Captain of the group	

goal and the effectiveness of the strategies. A target date and time motivate the learner to meet time frames for accomplishing goals and assignments.

- **Strategies needed to accomplish the goal:** Clarify the steps the student may take to reach the goal. Sometimes students struggle to do something because they do not know how, or they have a hard time controlling an emotion and they lack options. This component allows for some concrete planning that will help the student know exactly how to accomplish the task or behavior.

- **Did the strategies work? Why or why not?** Have students identify the strategies that led to success, caused them to stumble, or that were confusing. Brainstorm why this happened, what would have made it easier, and what assistance is needed.

- **What did you learn? How did you feel?** An extrinsic reward such as pizza or a prize may be fun and motivating, but completing the task will give the student an intrinsic sense of accomplishment. This question asks the student to consider how completing the task felt and how it might affect his or her future.

- **Next steps:** If the goal-setting process worked, this may be an opportunity to set a new goal. If it did not, next steps should outline what went wrong, why, and what the new plan will be. The new plan should involve a new goal and/or a new strategy, depending on the reasons why the original plan did not work.

- **Student/teacher thoughts:** Articulate ideas regarding the goal. The students can either describe what the teacher says about their plan or share their own ideas.

The goal-setting template can be used in multiple ways:

- **Teacher directed:** The teacher completes the goal components and presents them to the learner, small group, or entire class as an assignment.
- **Teacher-student partnership:** The teacher conferences with the student to set the goal together.
- **Student directed:** The student sets a personal goal, lists strategies, and establishes time frames for accomplishment. This proposal is submitted to the teacher for approval before moving forward with the plan. See figure 5.3 for an example of this option.

Any combination of the teacher and students sharing the planning can be effective. The more responsibility students have in planning, the more invested they will be in completing the goal. By involving students in the planning and execution process, we provide them both choice and control over their success.

Tips and Traps

Say "when" instead of "if" when framing the deal or the goal for students. Although a subtle nuance, the message is different—"if" signals that students have the *option* to act; "when" suggests that the action is *expected* and the timing is within students' control. The task you are asking students to do must be clear and aligned with what you want them to learn or how you expect they will behave. Consider having students brainstorm why the task is important and what it will help them do. This information can be written in the goal section on the planning template. For younger students, use pictures instead of words to help them identify tasks and possible rewards.

Break the task down into strategies students understand. If the task or behavior is too complex or difficult or if students do not understand how to do it, they may fail to change, not because they don't want to, but because they don't know where to start. Be sure the task is something possible that students know how to do. These discoveries are made using quality formative preassessment data.

If you want the task done in a certain amount of time, brainstorm with the students. Have them list what it will take to meet the deadline, and negotiate a time frame. We sometimes expect change overnight. Be sure the timeline is reasonable and doable. Too little time makes the change difficult. Too much time allows for complacency. Take the learner's suggestions, but make the final decision using their input.

Follow through consistently and immediately with the celebration or reward. Any delay or change will make the strategy useless in the future because students will not trust that if they complete goals, they will actually get the reward. Never make a plan you are not prepared to employ.

The goal-setting strategy could involve students co-planning goals and co-designing rewards. This promotes ownership and excitement, and also allows room for a little fun. If students do not participate in planning and just review the process, it is critical that they comment in their own words on the "student thoughts" section of the template. At the close of the task, have students self-reflect

---

Name: *Sam*   **Date:** *September 28*

Goal (expected task or behavior): *I will turn my homework in on time.*

Time frame: *Two weeks*   **Reward:** *Parent call to report accomplishments*

Check-in date: *October 5*

Strategies needed to accomplish this goal:
Doing homework at home is tough because sometimes I don't understand or get distracted by other things. So, I will start the homework before I leave school to be sure I know what to do. I will also come to class right away in the morning and finish the homework.

Did the strategies work? Why or why not?
It worked to start homework before I left school. I ended up completing it most often before I went home. Even if I didn't finish at school, it was easier to do it at home when I had started it already.

Coming in early did not work because I wanted to talk with friends, but because I had mostly finished it before I left school, I didn't really need to do this.

What did you learn? How did it feel to set a goal?
I learned that when I know what to do it is easier to do the homework on time.

I learned that I don't feel as stressed when I start the homework at school.

Next steps (if any):
I will continue to start my homework right after school.

Student thoughts:
I think the teacher thought this worked and that it not only helped me do my homework but also helped me feel more comfortable in class.

Teacher thoughts:
I am proud of you, Sam! Clearly, you have found a strategy that helps you get your work done, but more importantly learn more. I observed that when you started your homework during school you asked more questions in class. In fact, as time went on, you were more confident about your homework when starting it in school.

Figure 5.3: Sample student goal-setting worksheet.

on how the experience went and their next steps. The planning template specifically outlines these components as part of the planning and implementation process of effective goal setting.

If the goal was not met, there is powerful learning in reflecting on why it did not work. Do not skip the step of asking for student thoughts on the template, and remember to assess your own satisfaction with the process and the strategies. If the plan did not work, you may need to tweak the process or try a new strategy. Consider the following questions to guide your assessment:

- Did the goal work? Why or why not? Did it result in the behavior or task you were trying to impact?

- What worked about the goal-setting process? How do you know?

- What didn't work? How do you know?
- How did the student's attitude change?
- How could you change the process to make it more effective next time? Is there anything in the set up or execution of the goal that could be done differently to ensure a different result, such as a different timeline, more student planning, or more teacher-directed interventions?

Too much deal making can create situations where students are always asking what they will get in return for anything they do. Linda Lambert warns that students may become dependent for motivation upon external praise and rewards when they are used too often. Motivation needs to be intrinsic with an inward drive (Lambert, 2003).

Putting It Into Practice

The goal-setting template and process can be used for long-term fixes, but when a quick fix or fast turnaround in terms of behavior or task completion is needed, use a short-form template similar to the example in figure 5.4 (see page 154 for a blank reproducible version). For example, if the objective is staying on task during class, the task or goal might read, "When I feel restless, I'll doodle on a scratch sheet of paper instead of talking to the person next to me."

Creating a treasure chest and setting academic goals are two more helpful tools to further the goal-setting process through choice and control.

Create a Treasure Chest

A treasure chest of donated or recycled items can be used to motivate an individual or a whole class. For example, an elementary classroom can co-create the classroom rules (see strategy 10, page 94) and use the treasure chest as rewards. When students follow rules, they can go to the treasure chest each Friday and choose a simple toy, sticker, pencil, or other treasure that parents, the community, or others donated. If a student consistently does not earn a trip to the treasure chest, the teacher can sit down with that student and make a plan, identifying strategies and expected behavior.

Set Academic Goals

Setting goals as a whole class can build a strong sense of community and control. When students believe that not only the teacher but the class as a whole believes in them, confidence increases. When a classroom community builds trust, an individual student knows that he or she has choices in terms of who to go to for support. It isn't just teacher directed anymore. The classroom as a whole provides support for learning and success. This sense of confidence can instill an intrinsic feeling of control over one's own achievement, success, and circumstances.

For example, a seventh-grade language arts teacher had his students describe the learning they were to achieve using the language of the standard. Together, the class set a goal (achieve 85 percent or higher on the final test) and identified strategies that the students would use to meet their goal (practicing, trying their best, strengthening their weaknesses, and developing their strong points). The goal involved setting a time frame (two weeks) and establishing a reward (pizza party).

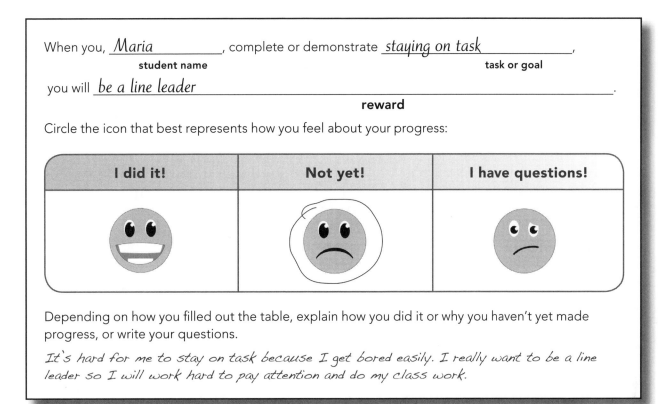

When you, _Maria_ , complete or demonstrate _staying on task_ ,
student name   task or goal
you will _be a line leader_ .
reward

Circle the icon that best represents how you feel about your progress:

I did it!	Not yet!	I have questions!

Depending on how you filled out the table, explain how you did it or why you haven't yet made progress, or write your questions.

It's hard for me to stay on task because I get bored easily. I really want to be a line leader so I will work hard to pay attention and do my class work.

Figure 5.4: A sample template for quick task or behavior goal completion.

Strategy 18: Use the Arts

The arts provide students unique ways to express their thinking and learning, and provide teachers options to help students understand concepts and link them to what they already know and understand. Music, visuals, drama, role-play, poetry, graphic arts, woodworking, and more provide opportunities for students' choice and control over their work and their learning.

Jensen (2001) reports that students who are engaged in visual-arts activities become more self-directed and engaged learners. Fine arts programs are interesting to students; learners want to be included and involved in these hands-on activities, especially students who are talented in the arts. Creative drama activities and movement have been shown to increase achievement, especially in younger children (Conrad, 1992; Kardash & Wright, 1987; Hattie, 2009).

Music is a learning tool and medium that can be used to offer students choice and control when planning assessments; learners may choose to create songs, poems, jingles, raps, or cheers about relevant topic information. This choice may engage students based on their interests or passions. For example, one student may write a song about the concepts of mitosis and meiosis, while another may prefer to create a game or a PowerPoint. Including a musical option in instruction and assessment reaches out to students who have more creative tendencies. Because they are more interested in something such as music or drama, they may persevere longer in attending to the task as well as feel more control over how they demonstrate and show their learning.

Music can also establish noise-level control. Some classrooms have music playing during certain work time. If the classmates can no longer hear the music, they are taught that they need to work more quietly.

One of the first steps to using the arts effectively is to ensure you are clear about what students should learn. The verb in the standard or learning objective is extremely important because it indicates the thinking in which you want students to engage. This verb is what drives the activities or demonstrations of students understanding in multiple mediums. "Students will identify and explain the five themes of geography" is an example of a learning objective. The verbs *identify* and *explain* mean that students have to describe those five themes of geography. An instructional activity that is arts focused might have learners create a symbol to represent each of the five themes. "Students will apply and solve problems using the five themes of geography" is another learning objective. However, the verbs *apply* and *solve* suggest the instructional activity and assessment are not just about explaining the information, but also relating it to real-life situations. For example, an arts-focused activity using those learning objectives might include students in small groups writing a simulated meeting among a cell-phone company and a city council to determine the best location for an additional cell tower. The simulated meeting must include information about how the five themes of geography influence this decision: for example, if the region is mountainous, signals may be interrupted and that would change the location of a cell tower.

The next step is to define how students will use the arts to learn. Depending on your time frame, purpose, and learning goal, use different forms of the arts to offer students choices in instruction and assessment. Consider using the arts to:

- Assist students in understanding a concept. For example, when studying a particular time period in a history class, it may be worthwhile to explore the paintings or drawings of the time, as they often tell a visual story of the main events. In the same way, music is often a way to express feelings and remember events. Finding the music of the period may add deeper meaning and help students recall some of the era's significant themes. Offer students either of these choices when exploring a historical time period, a scientific concept, or even a literary text. Provide some time in class to work on making these connections. Students culminate the activity or project by sharing their insights gained and connections made.

- Create real-world connections. Send students on an adventure to search for evidence of concepts, themes, or examples of the unit or lesson topic. Art is all around us! The radio, the Internet, iPods, cell phones, newspapers, billboards, shopping malls, museums, restaurants, and homes all use art to create a mood, send a message, or inform. When studying narrative text as stories, ask students to find examples of stories in music, art, magazines, and television advertisements. Students may choose to explore areas of interest. For example, musicians may tell stories through their song lyrics. Graffiti might represent stories in images and phrases. Providing options and connections gives students pathways to connect to the material and content.

- Provide students opportunities to use different mediums to create their own products to demonstrate understanding. Some learners may make brochures, PowerPoint presentations, sculptures, advertisements, music, or other things to represent their understanding. Consider the possible mediums that students can choose to understand, represent, or learn the intended learning.

  - **Visual arts:** Draw, paint, sculpt, or graphic design.

  - **Musical arts:** Sing, play an instrument, rap, chant, cheer, or recite poetry.

  - **Art of movement:** Perform, role-play, demonstrate, or mime.

Tips and Traps

As with all learning, the art or performance tasks students complete should be clear and aligned with what they need to learn or how they should behave. Ask the fine arts department in your school to help design a project or an assignment option. The fine arts teachers may be willing to support the project in their own classes. Ask parents, community organizations, or businesses to provide authentic examples of the arts.

At times the arts engage students' learning in new and interesting ways that open doors to understanding. If students create something interesting or cool that is disconnected from the learning goal, but meaningful, ask them to describe their thinking and the connection to the learning goal to focus on their thought processes.

Putting It Into Practice

Use role-play and music in the classroom as effective ways to infuse the arts into learning, give students choice and control, and motivate student engagement.

Role-Play

Role-play can enhance engagement and deepen understanding when used effectively. It can help students understand a text more deeply. Break students into small groups, and have them choose one scene from the text to act out for the class. Students might choose to make the characters puppets and act out a puppet show, decide to write a brief script based on a section of the text and take on the roles of the key players. Role-playing offers learners opportunities to experience the emotion of the situation while making the story or event come alive.

In other cases, role-play can help students apply, analyze, and synthesize content. If studying history, specifically legislation, students could act out a debate such as the pros and cons of a later school start time, or legislative process such as how a bill becomes a law. Students study the content of an issue, and each chooses a role such as a lawyer, reporter, or expert witness. Depending on their roles, students write up their arguments or stories representing the issue. Similarly, in science class, students studying genetics could read a series of case studies and role-play counseling sessions with couples or presentations to their scientist colleagues.

Additionally, role-play helps students practice effective engagement in classroom tasks such as peer editing and revising, group work, and collaborative problem solving. In this way, role-play can be used as a tool to reinforce how to engage in a process. For example, students can act out appropriate and inappropriate behavior for group work, such as showing that one student should not dominate the group, because it should be a collaborative effort. Role-playing and troubleshooting situations like these can help students feel more in control of their learning and classroom participation. When these issues come up, students have choices regarding how to respond, and even more importantly, they feel like they have a say in their learning and the effectiveness of working in groups.

Whether you use role-play to deepen understanding of a text, flesh out a topic, or demonstrate classroom expectations, this process allows for choice and control and helps make learning more comfortable, effective, and engaging for all students.

Students will create more effective role-plays with some guidance in their brainstorming and planning. Teachers may find it extremely beneficial to walk through one example with students, modeling how you might address each of the following six steps. This model will help students focus their discussion.

1   **Determine the audience:** Who is the scene speaking to? When creating a role-play, students must determine for whom they are performing. When acting out a scene in the story, if the audience is the class, who has already read the book, students can assume certain things. However, if the audience is the public and the goal is to entertain, students will need to provide more context in setting up their scene. If engaging in a debate, students need to know who to persuade and what they care about in order to use convincing evidence to support the argument.

2   **Identify the targeted objectives:** What is the targeted objective? This question guides students to determine their outcome. Some role-plays are designed to inform the audience about a specific topic, event, character, or process. Others are meant to describe or recount an event. Still others may be designed to persuade or entertain. Establishing this upfront helps focus the role-play.

3   **Describe the issue, events, topic, perspectives, and characteristics:** This step is designed to brainstorm as many ideas as possible. If the target objective is to inform the audience about an event, a character, or an issue, students brainstorm details that describe or explain. If the role-play is designed to persuade or explore various perspectives of an issue, such as the arguments around building more environmentally friendly buildings or revising waste and energy practices to be more environmentally friendly, students should consider the following questions: What are the various perspectives? What are the implications of this topic on students, the world, the community, or learning?

4   **Plan the scene:** In this step, students identify all of the characters, actors, or roles to be included in the scene. Next, they determine the major action or events to act out; discuss the setting, including both time and place; and, finally, describe what the audience should learn, understand, or think from the role-play.

5   **Develop the scene:** During this stage of the process, the group writes the script. In writing the script, students should include a beginning, middle, and end. In the beginning, students set up the role-play, introduce the characters, and catch the audience's attention. In the middle, the important events, most powerful evidence, crisis, and conflict occur. In the end, the role-play resolves the conflict or makes the audience think.

6   **Plan audience reflection questions:** Have students brainstorm questions to ask the audience or class after wrapping up the role-play. For example, advise them to write questions that do the following:

- Guide the audience to understand the facts of the scene.

- Help the audience understand the feelings of the characters in the scene.

- Dig into the cause and effect of the situation and decisions.

- Establish the implications of choices, not only on the individual, but the community, culture, and the world.

- Guide the audience's reflections on the topic and issues associated with it.

- Lead the audience members to reflect on their experiences and choices.

- Assist the audience members to identify possible steps to take.

Role-Play Planning Sheet on page 155 provides a template, prompting students to create their role-play using the preceding six steps.

Music

Music provides students with an engaging medium to explore concepts and demonstrate their understanding. Offering a musical option can be powerful in supporting learning, especially for learners with an appreciation for or an inclination toward music. After reading a text, have students work in groups to turn the story line into a song. Depending on the comfort levels of students, students may change the words to a familiar tune or create their own song. Use music and rhythm in math to help students remember processes or concepts. For example, make up a rhythm to remember the order of operations. Students could also write a song describing the process they used to solve a problem.

Chapter 5 Campfire Talk

This chapter described strategies to promote choice and control. Consider your own understanding, perceptions, and experiences about what works to give students choice and control in their learning. Discuss the following questions and activities in your professional learning community, department, grade-level team, or a staff meeting.

1   Reflect on cloudy and sunny days. Individually or with a group, use the template and directions for figure 5.1 (page 133) to discuss and plan your work on choice and control.

2   How do students perceive their level of choice and control? Does their assessment agree with yours?

- List the experiences, activities, and roles that you perceive might be in students' control in your classroom. List the things outside of their control.

- Have your students complete the survey, and compare your thoughts or decisions with those of your students.

3   Discuss the amount of choice offered in your classroom.

- Are learners getting too much, too little, or just the right amount of choice or control?

- Are students offered meaningful choices?

- What other opportunities are there to include choice in your lessons, instruction, and assessments?

4   Use the Plan for Student Motivation reproducible to discover, diagnose, and plan to address the needs of individual unmotivated students in promoting choice and control.

Plan for Student Motivation

Strategy	Name the Unmotivated Student(s) in Need of the Strategy	Identify the Wrapper the Student Is Wearing	List Observable Evidence, Behavior, Habits, or Traits	Develop an Action to Address the Need	Assess and Reflect on Implementation	Additional Comments
16. Provide Quality Choices (page 134)						
17. Set a Goal, Make a Deal (page 138)						
18. Use the Arts (page 145)						

Survey on Control

1. In the cloud, make a list of all the things outside your control at work.

2. Now make a list of all the things within your control, and write them in the sun.

3. Consider what percentage of time you spend talking, thinking, and working on things within your control versus outside your control. Write the percentages in the spaces provided.

I spend about _____ % of my time thinking, working on, and talking about aspects outside my control.

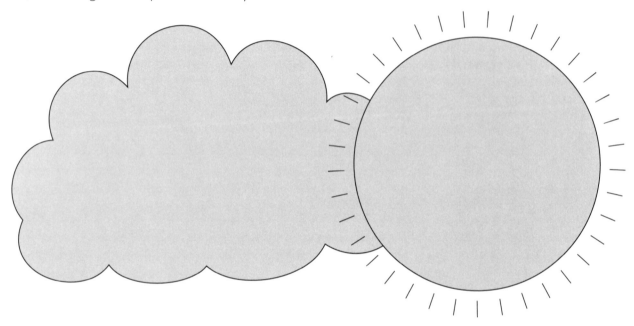

I spend about _____ % of my time thinking, working on, and talking about aspects within my control.

4. Reflect privately, or discuss with peers. What is the balance between time you spend on things within your control compared to those outside your control?

Do you spend too much time talking about things outside your control? If so, what is the possible impact on your work?

How productive are you when spending time on things within your control?

Goal-Setting Template

Name: _____ **Date:** _____

Goal (expected task or behavior): _____

Time frame: _____ **Reward:** _____ **Check-in date:** _____

Strategies needed to accomplish this goal:

Did the strategies work? Why or why not?

What did you learn? How did it feel to set a goal?

Next steps (if any):

Student thoughts:

Teacher thoughts:

Template for Quick Task or Behavior Goal Completion

When you, _____, complete or demonstrate _____,
              student name   **task or goal**

you will _____.
                    reward

Circle the icon that best represents how you feel about your progress:

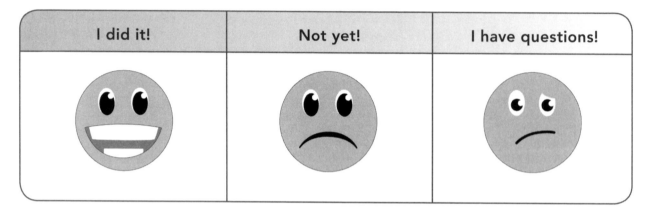

I did it!	Not yet!	I have questions!

Depending on how you filled out the table, explain how you did it or why you haven't yet made progress, or write your questions.

Role-Play Planning Sheet

Directions: Create a role-play using the following six steps.

Role-Play Title: _____ **Role-Play Topic:** _____ **Date:** _____

1. Determine the audience.

2. Identify the targeted objective.
   - To inform the audience of an issue?

   - To describe or recount an event?

   - To persuade an audience?

3. Describe the issue, events, perspectives, and characteristics.
   - What are the various perspectives?

   - What are the implications of this topic on students, the world, the community, or learning?

4. Plan the scene.
   - Major characters, actors, and roles

   - Major action or events of the scene

   - Setting

   - Audience takeaway

5. Develop the scene (write the script).
   - Beginning (introduce characters, draw in the audience)

   - Middle (describe the events, evidence, crisis, and conflict)

   - End (resolve the conflict)

6. Plan audience reflection questions.

Ensuring Learning

As a normal part of Mrs. Busby's assessment practices, she gave all of her math students review problems and spent an entire class period running from student to student to make sure they got them correct. Unfortunately, because of this tiring practice, she never had much time to spend with particular students or really ensure learning. After professional development training on assessment, Mrs. Busby decided to try something new. For the current lesson, she made a short formative assessment on simplifying fractions and mixed numbers. She gave it to her students and afterward was able to identify who understood the concepts and did not need any more instruction. She was also able to pinpoint weaknesses in other students' learning and review with them before the summative assessment. She divided students into groups depending on which objectives they missed. Many were able to work independently to show their learning. This new practice allowed her to work with six students who were completely lost. Mrs. Busby then offered her students a second assessment, and students were much more successful as a result. The summative assessment grade reflected true understanding of simplifying fractions versus a combination of where students were before they were supposed to know the material and how much they gained in the process of instruction. This targeted instruction is an example of how the focus of the classroom shifted from that of teaching to one of learning. The assessments were in direct response to where students were in their learning. In the past, Mrs. Busby planned teaching with little specific attention to how it affected learning. Mrs. Busby's new assessment practices ensured learning and made classroom time more productive for her and her students.

Ensuring learning means helping students believe they can learn. When teachers provide opportunities for students to learn more, they show they care. Students crave real caring and respond to adults who care deeply. This chapter is loaded with strategies that make teaching all about students' learning. Table 6.1 (page 158) describes the fundamental belief shift that happens as teachers move from a focus on teaching to a focus on learning.

Taking on the mission to ensure learning is no small task. It takes perseverance and commitment. Students sense when teachers are serious about their learning through both words and actions. When teachers are serious about the message "Come in this room, and you will learn," they nurture the root source of internal motivation. They get to know their students (chapter 2, page 23) and plan so that each one is successfully moving forward each and every day, learning more and more. Some students require more patience, perseverance, and creativity from the teacher in order to meet their learning needs. The determined teacher does not give up and does not get sidetracked by factors outside his or her control.

Table 6.1: A Focus on Teaching Versus a Focus on Learning

A Teacher Focused on Teaching Thinks . . .	A Teacher Focused on Learning Thinks . . .	Suggestions and Tips to Focus on Learning
"I taught the material; students just didn't get it."	"I find new ways to get my students to understand."	Teach material using a variety of strategies and motivating activities. Provide student engagement opportunities with quality assignments. Constantly adjust based on formative assessment, and persevere until they get it!
"The parents need to be more involved for behavior and actions to change."	"I focus on the time I have students in my classroom because that is what I can control."	Take control of what happens while students are at school, not at home. However, invite parents to school, inform them of their child's progress, and communicate with them so they are involved.
"It takes too much time to do ongoing assessment."	"I figure out what students know and what they need to do next."	Know the individual needs of students by assessing before, during, and after the learning with quality formative assessment tools.
"I work harder than my students in reviewing their assessments."	"I empower students to learn about themselves, get engaged in the learning process, and become more instrumental in their own success."	Provide motivating learning opportunities that target standards and require student engagement. Have students analyze their assessments and set goals to involve them in their learning.
"I don't have enough time to teach the material, let alone ensure students learn it."	"I prioritize what is most important for students to learn and spend time ensuring learning on the essentials."	Weed out the time wasters, and focus on the standards. Make sure students use the best resources available.
"My students have such diverse needs, and it is difficult to reach them all."	"I am clear about the standards I am teaching and use those learning objectives to drive my instruction, assessment, and student involvement."	Assess, interpret the information, and plan adjustable assignments based on the data.

Hold High Expectations and Build Self-Efficacy

Teacher expectations influence motivation and achievement (Weinstein, 2002). In fact, Weinstein (2002) discovered that "students know they are treated differently in the classroom due to expectations held by teachers, and are quite accurate in informing on how teachers differ in the degree to which they favor some children over others with higher expectations" (as cited in Hattie, 2009, p. 124). When teachers do not expect success, students often perform to those low expectations. Our actions and words convey and influence expectations. Hattie (2009) concluded that "teachers must stop over-emphasizing ability and start emphasizing progress (steep learning curves are the right of all students regardless of where they start), stop seeking evidence to confirm prior expectations but seek evidence to surprise themselves, [and] find ways to raise achievement of all" (p. 124).

While the actions of teachers signal the level of expectations they hold for students, Todd Whitaker (2003), in *What Great Teachers Do Differently,* has another take on the issue: "Even the *worst* teachers have high expectations for students. They expect students to pay attention no matter how boring and repetitious their classes are. They expect students to be well behaved no matter how the teacher treats them. Now, those are high expectations" (p. 34). Whitaker (2003) suggests that the biggest difference we can make in terms of expectations is to have high expectations of *ourselves*; we "must always work to engage the students. If the students are not focused, great teachers ask what they themselves can do differently" (p. 34).

Doug Reeves's (2007) research puts an exclamation point at the end of Whitaker's statement. He asked administrators and teachers what they felt was the biggest influence on student learning. The schools with educators who identified factors within their control showed three times greater achievement than schools with educators who identified factors outside their control. The notion of efficacy—the confidence we have in our ability as educators to find creative and possible ways of engaging students—plays a tremendously important role in student motivation and engagement.

Students learn because they think they can! They learn because teachers think they can. This intrinsic motivation, this feeling of hope, can compel students to try new things and actively participate in discussions and activities that they otherwise would not. If learners believe they will succeed, they are more likely to put forward the effort to learn or engage in an activity that teachers promise will help them learn. Self-efficacy is absolutely essential for success. As Hattie (2009) wrote, "The notion that increasing achievement is a function of our efforts and interest is critical to success—there is no point, for example, in investing in study or preparation if we do not believe that our efforts can make a difference" (p. 48).

Educators must gain confidence in their ability to motivate learners.

- Believe in yourself and your capacity to influence student learning. Do you believe that you have the capacity to help these unmotivated learners engage? Confidence is the first step to being able to do this well. When you believe in yourself, you will be able to empower your students.

- Believe in students and their capacity to learn. Do you believe that each student has the capacity to learn? What messages do you consciously or unconsciously send to students about the possibility of their progress? When a learner is continuously chosen to answer low-level questions, that student begins to form negative beliefs about his or her ability. Build that "I believe in me" attitude in students (Pajares, 2005; Chapman & King, 2009b).

- Make the unmotivated students a priority. Make it your mission to compel all learners to work with you. Let them know you care and expect them to cooperate and learn. Requiring them to fix their mistakes and revise their work sends the message that learning is possible and really important. These are two critical messages in promoting motivation (Saphier, 2005).

- Exhibit trust, respect, and belief in each learner. Sometimes it is difficult to like and approve of the behavior of certain students. However, it is important to always take the time to respect them, even when you do not approve (Sizer, 2004). How do you think about students after they leave your room? Although some learners are more likeable than others, these feelings cannot show. Each individual needs to be accepted and respected as a person with gifts, talents, and strengths that must be honored and recognized.

- Plan instruction to meet the students where they are in their learning. Adjust assignments according to preassessment data; determine the most appropriate information to provide each individual learner for that particular time (Chapman & King, 2009b). Students feel a gratifying rush from thinking and working on a challenging assignment or problem, then solving it. Give them the "Yes, I did it!" feeling by assigning the appropriate tasks.

- Strategically plan writing, sharing, and conferencing times for students to voice their attitudes and beliefs about school.

- Gain insight into how much they believe in themselves. If students struggle to *think* they can succeed, they are more likely to remain unmotivated, lazy, or defiant about doing schoolwork. Laziness and defiance are often cover-ups for feelings of incompetence. Use regular check-ins to monitor the learner's understanding and progress. Provide second chances to complete work after interventions. Teaching students how to track their own progress will help them believe that their current work will lead to future learning and success. Self-monitoring must be taught.

Carol Dweck (2006) explored students' beliefs about their intelligence and found students who believe their intelligence is already determined have a fixed belief that they cannot learn or be successful in school. They do not believe that improvement can happen, or that they can be successful learners. On the other hand, some students believe they can continue to grow, learn, and develop—and do! It is crucial to reflect on and analyze our classroom practices in relation to learners' expectations and self-efficacy.

Dweck explored the potential of students with fixed mindsets to change and develop growth mindsets; she questioned whether a new way of thinking about learning would change their achievement and motivation. Her findings indicate that it is possible for fixed-mindset students to shift toward a growth mindset to develop "academic resilience," which Dweck describes as students' attitudes of perseverance—any challenge is met with more effort, leading to success (Dweck, 1999).

As teachers, we have the potential to affect a student's mindset through our:

- *Planning* of instruction, assessment, and student involvement
- *Reactions* to their learning, timing, and questions
- *Communication* of their progress

Both student and teacher beliefs about student learning impact achievement and motivation. A teacher's belief can inspire and foster hope in the learner. A learner needs to believe and feel he or she is successful in school and a vital part of the learning culture. As a result, it is crucial that reflection on classroom practice be an ongoing part of our work as teachers.

Take and Provide Time for Learning

One of the biggest challenges to ensuring learning is time, a precious commodity to both teachers and students. Teachers must first take the time to create challenging and engaging assignments derived from standards, plan lessons, and then provide students with the time to tackle the more challenging higher-order thinking required to complete such assignments. In essence, when educators teach students to extend their thinking, and they pose more challenging problems in the context of curriculum, students learn more and become more independent thinkers and learners in the future. Planning time carefully and intentionally is an essential component to creating a classroom where learning is the focus.

There never seems to be enough time. How do we balance all of the things that absolutely require time—both in class and in our planning? Consider the following ideas to help you manage time:

- Sketch out the time you have to plan and to teach. Analyze instructional time spent teaching the material and student-focused time when students are working to learn to achieve mastery.

- List all of the tasks that need to be completed. To prioritize, circle the three items on your list that most impact or support student learning.

- Spend the majority of your time on the top three items. Plan for those tasks strategically. Complete the other tasks in the rest of the allotted time or let them go. If they were essential, they would be in the top three.

- Start small. Choose one lesson to plan targeting at least one of the top three from the prioritized list. Reflect on how it went before trying to make big plans that may be too overwhelming.

Adjust Grading, Feedback, and Grouping Practices

As we have noted, when students don't believe they can succeed, they may not try—they may not hand in assignments or participate in activities. Some common classroom practices regarding grading, feedback, and grouping can inadvertently sabotage student feelings of self-efficacy. Consider the following ideas and strategies to review, revise, and enhance your instructional techniques.

Grading

Grading all tasks and then averaging them as a final grade can impede students' motivation to try. If students turn in an assignment late and receive partial credit, they will weigh the benefits of the partial grade against the amount of time and effort needed to rework or complete the assignment. In some cases, when students receive a significant number of zeros, it is tremendously difficult for them to recover and earn a passing grade. While teachers may use zeros to try to motivate students to complete all work, when there is little or no hope of achieving a passing grade, a zeros policy has the opposite effect (Guskey, 2004; O'Connor, 2002), especially for struggling students who have no idea how to improve their work.

Some assignments do not need a grade; they need analysis by students and teachers. Review mistakes and assess the work to provide instant feedback for learners. In some cases, the teacher may hand back the work, describe common mistakes and how to fix them, and then set the students to work analyzing their assessments. This shifts the thinking to the students and saves the teacher tremendous amounts of time grading individual student work and writing the same comments on numerous papers.

Both Guskey and Bailey (2001) and O'Connor (2002) advocate for using the *most recent* evidence of learning in grading. Suppose students take a quiz and receive a low score. In response to this low score, the teacher creates a fantastic lesson that addresses the misunderstanding. Students receive a second chance to take a new quiz and show mastery. If the teacher averages the second-chance grade with the first, the final grade will not reflect what students understand at this point in time. Instead, the averaging of the first with the second factors in how fast a student became proficient—not how proficient the student ultimately became. Those students who did well the first time will always get a better final grade than the ones who only showed proficiency on the second quiz. Any effort students put forth between the first and second chances will help mitigate a poor first grade, but even 100 percent success on the second test will not result in a strong grade for a student who failed the first test. If, on the other hand, the teacher *replaces* the initial grade with the second score, students see that it is worth putting effort in to learn more, because it matters and is reflected in the grade. When teachers use the most recent evidence of learning, students become motivated to keep learning, because their grade will show their hard work. Using the most recent grade also reflects the growth that teachers have inspired through their practice.

Some worry that the options of a second chance will cause students to blow off the first attempt. Students may think: "Why try? I can always take it again." However, in effective practice, between the first and second chances, students must do something and work hard to fix mistakes or improve and revise their work. Using data from the first chance, students get help or instruction that addresses their misunderstandings. During this instruction, the teacher monitors and observes to be sure that the instruction actually addressed their misunderstandings. During the process, there is an informal observation. Then, when this informal observation reveals more understanding, a second chance or more formal opportunity is provided for students to demonstrate their understanding. Teachers provide a second chance when students have demonstrated more understanding that deserves recognition.

Feedback and Grouping

Feedback is one of the most powerful tools teachers have to increase learning (Hattie & Timperley, 2007; Marzano, 2007). However, if the feedback is evaluative in nature—such as a grade, a percentage, a smiley face, or a vague comment—students will put their own twist on it. As a result, they may avoid the work, misunderstand what to do next, or make an incorrect assumption about their understanding. *Descriptive* feedback provides specific improvements and next steps to move learning forward.

There is a time and a place for an evaluative grade; a grade is a symbol that represents achievement in a class. But feedback for the purpose of learning and fostering self-efficacy needs to be descriptive and specific (Hattie & Timperley, 2007; O'Connor, 2002). For example, a kindergarten classroom's walls might have multiple examples of what different stages of writing should look like. When first learning to write, students might draw pictures to represent a story the teacher read. Next, they might include some letters that represent beginning sounds. As students progress, they will add beginning and ending letters and write words from left to right. Some students will use spaces between words and start to form sentences. Students see the examples on the walls depicting these stages. After the kindergarteners have listened to the story and have written their responses, the teacher may ask students to look at the stages and identify where they think their writing fits. The teacher may have a few anonymous examples that the whole class tries to place.

Then the teacher groups students by their writing stages and has them look at what it will take for them to move to the next stage. (For example, students might work to use spaces between words.) The goal here is that students work on specific skills to move forward, not something generic that may or may not meet their needs. In this example, the learning stages offer teachers the language and examples to provide student feedback that is specific and related to their writing.

Grouping students can send mixed messages about our expectations when some learners are regularly placed in the lower-level groups. Some students become comfortable being in the group that is always struggling or wearing the "at-risk" label. These students may resign themselves to low achievement. Others may become angry and develop the "I don't care" attitude. The actions we take shape our students' self-concepts and their beliefs about their capacities to learn. When students are grouped based on their knowledge related to specific standards, skills, or concepts, the activity produces more learning and the groups are more effective. This is always changing because it is based on students' knowledge of what is being taught at any given time. Appropriate grouping is flexible and based on the assessment data; students work with peers who are at the same stage. This provides teachers a nice way to move everyone forward. For instance, when teaching a unit, a learner may already know some information being introduced but might not know anything about a standard being introduced. This calls for adjusting the groups according to background and knowledge base. This is only accomplished by a strategic assessment. Other ways to group include by knowledge base, peer preference, interests, age, and random scenarios, such as birthday months. Select the most appropriate way to group according to the purpose of the activity and assignment that will best engage the learner.

Recognize Coping Mechanisms

The issues of grading, feedback, and grouping can profoundly influence students' beliefs about themselves. Imagine being in a room and feeling that you cannot learn like the others—feeling that they all understand, and only you do not. This happens to some students day after day and leads to feelings of inadequacy and a sense of failure (Hattie, 2009).

As adults, we usually manipulate our way out of these situations. Failure is demeaning. Naturally, learners look for a way to protect whatever self-worth they have left (Covington, 2002; Martin 2007; Martin & Marsh, 2003). They develop personal ways of coping with failure, often from a young age. Here are some approaches people use to deal with feelings of failure.

- **Quitting:** They do not show up again or find a valid excuse to no longer be involved.

- **Sitting on the sidelines:** Individuals sit quietly outside of the event or to the side of the activity as an onlooker. They try to fly under the radar, hoping no one will bring them in and expose personal feelings of inadequacy and lack of confidence.

- **Finding distractions:** Some people are very good at finding activities they can do to occupy their time and avoid the main event. They are great at finding other important things to do! While others participate, they "prepare," "organize," or find something that "needs" to be reworked.

You may observe students employing these coping mechanisms to cover their own fear of failure. As a result, it is critical that teachers learn to recognize these behaviors as signs of confidence problems rather than of disrespect or apathy. After all, the strategies we employ when a student truly does not care are different than those we use when a student does not understand the material or does not believe he or she can succeed. Students don't always arrive in the classroom with everything they need to be successful. Some bring the prerequisite skills, and others do not have the proper background. Some bring confidence in the classroom and their own learning, and some do not. Strategies to ensure learning build self-efficacy and focus on helping students see possibilities and experience success. Catch 'em being smart!

This chapter's strategies can be used with the whole class or individual students, depending on the need.

Strategy 19: Use Assessment Before, During, and After Learning

In Latin, *assessment* means *to sit beside* (New Horizons for Learning, 2002). Let's take this notion into the classroom; there, assessment is a process of gathering information with the intention of using that information to:

- *Plan* instructional activities—Remember, quality assessment begins with clearly knowing what you want to assess. Determine the individual objectives students need to achieve the standard (strategy 6, page 71). Use assessments designed from these learning objectives. Use the information before and during instruction to plan centers, lecturettes, stations, and group activities.

- *Involve* students in self-assessing during learning to identify their strengths, weaknesses, knowledge levels, and background experiences (strategy 24, page 183)

- *Describe* student proficiency after learning, such as through reflections, marks, grades, and rubric scores

Assess *before* learning to identify students' proficiency levels and make connections to their prior knowledge or passions. This information provides a bridge to what students already know, preparing them to understand more. Assessments before learning can also aid the teacher in flexibly grouping students in order to avoid the been there, done that wrapper, in which students are bored because they clearly already understand.

Assessing *during* learning means that we check in with students on an ongoing basis regarding their learning, and we align our instruction and response to their understanding and misunderstanding. We not only identify what's working and what's not, but we take new and different action; we find a new intervention or a different modality to explain the information.

When our observations and formative assessment data reveal that students understand, it is time to assess after learning. The after-learning assessment is summative and evaluative, meant to communicate to the learner their proficiency at this moment in time. Most often, assessments administered after learning are used as a grade with the intention of moving to the next standard or learning objective.

As a result of this assessment process, at the close of the unit or time frame for a particular learning goal, students are successful, and their marks or grades reflect their proficiency. Plan time for students to practice, process, and learn to gather enough evidence to report proficiency.

The key to this strategy is to adapt and adjust the way you teach concepts based on what the assessment data tell you (Schmoker, 2006; Stiggins et al., 2005; Wiliam, 2007). Plans based on an awareness of student experience and understanding can make a huge difference on motivation and engagement. If instruction hits students too far ahead of where they are, with no connection to where they have been, they will be lost and confused. Some students are determined to understand with little or no help; others don't mind being confused for a while, as long as they eventually understand; and some simply give up. Put yourself in their shoes: imagine how you would feel if you were taking a trip and got lost. Nothing looks familiar, and you have no idea how to get back on the main road, so you call a friend for directions. Instead of giving you the very next turn or exit to take to get back on track, the friend says, "Well, when you get into town, I'm the last house on the left." Some help, please! Would you keep meandering, turn around and go home, or get out a map and try to figure it out alone? Our students go through similar emotions and face similar decisions in their learning.

Assessing Before Instruction

Use preassessments to identify the learners' knowledge level in relation to the upcoming topic, standard, or skill. Ask questions to reveal their feelings, attitudes, and emotions about learning this content as well as their existing content knowledge. Preassessing and screening data inform the teacher about what each student knows and what each student needs to learn next. To avoid frustrated and bored students, prepare to fill in essential gaps in background knowledge and create more challenging assignments for those who show proficiency.

Ask students to respond to the following questions, verbally or in writing. Use these questions with the whole class, or students who lack motivation:

- "What are you curious about?"
- "What do you predict will happen?"
- "Have you ever heard of this topic or concept before? If so, where?"
- "What do you know about _____?" (This might include a short quiz or writing prompt to assess students' proficiency before starting.)

Assessing During Instruction

Check in with students *during* the unit or lesson to see if they are grasping the content the instruction is targeting. Ask yourself, "Are they getting it?" Observe what individuals say, do, and produce to make decisions about how to identify what they know and do not understand. Ask questions to reveal their feelings, attitudes, and emotions about learning this content.

Use daily formal and informal check-ins. As learners engage in the planned activities, look for evidence that they are thinking about the crucial issues. Ask a brief question at the end of the activity, and collect written or oral responses to see if the activity produced the desired results, or use a quiz to identify the extent of understanding. The following questions may be used with the whole class, or just students who lack motivation:

- ➤ "What are you learning?"
- ➤ "What is working and what is not working?"
- ➤ "What do you need?"
- ➤ "What parts do you understand?"
- ➤ "How did you solve a difficult problem?"
- ➤ "What challenges did you encounter?"
- ➤ "How did you solve those challenges?"

Continually ask yourself, "How do I know that my instruction is meeting students' needs?" The answer lies in the information collected during instruction every day, and ultimately, the information gathered after instruction.

Assessing After Instruction

Assess *after* instruction to gather evidence of students' understanding and their perceptions of what worked and how much they learned. Use the data to inform planning for future lessons. Again, be sure to ask questions such as the following to reveal feelings, attitudes, and emotions about learning the content. Collect verbal or written responses; these questions may be used with the whole class, or just students who lack motivation:

- ➤ "What advice would you share with another student in order to learn this concept?"
- ➤ "What did you discover about _____?"
- ➤ "What surprised you?"
- ➤ "What do you need next?"
- ➤ "How do you keep working when you have a difficult task?"
- ➤ "When will you use the information or skills you have learned again?"

Tips and Traps

Read more on quality formative assessment practice: *Differentiated Assessment Strategies* (Chapman & King, 2005), *Balanced Assessment* (Burke, 2010), *Making Classroom Assessment Work* (Davies, 2007b), *Formative Assessment in Action* (Clarke, 2005), *Assessment* for *Learning* (Black et al., 2003), and *Classroom Assessment* for *Student Learning* (Stiggins et al., 2005).

Monitor students regularly and continually using various formative assessment tools. Do not wait until the end of the lesson or unit, when you expect mastery. On a daily basis, check in with students about their progress. Do small checks using one problem or a short paragraph.

Assessment in this context is used to plan instruction or to help students understand their strengths and next steps. Do not collect anything you are not planning to use. If you do that, you will be overwhelmed with scoring and paperwork, and students will also feel overwhelmed and more fragmented.

Do not worry about grading everything. When asking students to complete a problem or write a quick response to a question, use it the next day or later in the class period to help them make the connection and understand.

Keep a chart with students' names, and record observations about their comments or reactions to particular concepts or general class work. You can use this information later to plan instruction and engage students on an individual basis.

Putting It Into Practice

In this section, we discuss a whole-class formative assessment activity. The example used is for elementary math, but it can be adapted to other subjects or grade levels. With formative assessment determining groups, the activity for the day is more meaningful to individual students as they are working at their levels and on the very next step. Usually, when teachers provide whole-class instruction, they can only teach one thing at a time. Because any given objective may have varying levels of engagement, the teacher confuses some and bores others. Therefore, a whole-class *formative* activity during learning helps the teacher meet individual students where they are in their knowledge and understanding.

We also discuss using summative assessment to allow students to take ownership of their learning.

Focus Formative Assessment on Student Learning

Students can be placed into groups based on their performance on a short quiz. In groups, the activities engage them, because they meet their proficiency levels, and students experience success. This feeling of success builds confidence, and that confidence inspires action. In turn, the activities move their learning forward.

The quiz and formative assessment can take many forms. Here we discuss grouping elementary students based on items they got wrong on a math assessment. Students move to one of three tables set up for their corresponding group.

- **Group 1:** Subtraction without renaming and regrouping
- **Group 2:** Early stages of subtraction with renaming and regrouping
- **Group 3:** Complex two-digit subtraction

In the center of each table, write sixteen problems on sticky notes:

- **Group 1:** Write problems in which students subtract numbers with no regrouping or renaming involved, such as $65 - 32 = $ ____.
- **Group 2:** Use subtraction problems with renaming or regrouping, such as $32 - 9 = $ ____.
- **Group 3:** Include more complicated subtraction problems with two-digit numbers and regrouping, such as $45 - 39 = $ ____.

Students start by choosing one of the sticky notes. Students work the problem in one of the boxes on paper divided into boxes (eight down and two across). They work as fast or as slow as needed to solve the problem. Once they finish one problem, they replace the sticky note in the center of the table and choose another sticky note and begin working the new problem. The process continues with students working as many problems as they can from the sticky notes in the allotted amount of time. This provides the teacher opportunity to observe the understanding of each student and offer support when needed.

While working, students do not focus on the number of problems they are solving—instead, they focus on doing problems at their level and just a bit beyond. Every student is challenged, and the activity is not graded. From the teacher's observations, students may be regrouped, or the whole class might reflect on what they learned. This discussion is a good time to talk about what was most difficult and how students made it through the challenging moments. Learners may also share the strategies they used to find the answer or solve the problem.

Focus Summative Assessment on Student Learning

To make assessment *after* instruction informational, Amanda Smith uses student reflection sheets in her fourth-grade math class in Newfoundland, Canada. The sheets ask students to identify and describe their mistakes on the assessment. These reflections allow Smith to take a more in-depth look into students' learning, and they allow students to take ownership of their learning and take pride in their accomplishments. After a summative assessment on number concepts, she assembled four groups according to the test results—the four concepts that stood out as weak areas. Four students mastered all concepts on the test, so each of them "monitored" a group for any misconceptions, while Smith walked around the room offering assistance. After students demonstrated understanding, she allowed them to visit a station of their choice, at which time one student said, "I want to stay at this center, because I feel I am not great at it yet." Moments like this, when a student is engaged in and owns his learning, are exciting for teachers and students alike (A. Smith, personal communication, July 6, 2010)!

Strategy 20: Ignite Thinking With Probing Questions

Do students ask questions about the topics they are studying? Do teacher-directed questions get one-word responses, or do they generate lively conversation among students? How many questions does the *teacher* ask compared to *students*?

Ask appropriate questions that spark constructive discussion and promote thinking. Effective questions create intrigue and provide a clear focus on the learning goals of the classroom. Student interest in the topic is enhanced when a question results in energized dialogue, and their engagement levels during effective questioning sessions are a source of valuable information about their understanding. Consider the type of questions students ask as well as the number of questions. Ask yourself if students are looking for simple answers, or if they are trying to explore or dig deeper into the content.

When teachers plan intentionally and engage students in asking questions, they can gather information regarding students' levels of thinking. In assessing the types of questions students are asking and how they are responding in written and oral form, teachers can respond accordingly and ensure learning in the moment. Student questions can facilitate more discussion in the classroom and provide a more student-centered atmosphere. When learners feel empowered, the classroom culture shifts, and students take on more responsibility for their learning.

An Effective Questioning Process

Ask and elicit the right types of questions, based on your purpose. Be sure to provide learners with time to think after a question is posed and after a student responds (Black et al., 2003; Davies, 2007b). Wait time gives all students a chance to engage.

Follow these guidelines.

1 Ask and elicit questions for a specific purpose. Use both simple and complex questions. Simple questions that teachers and students ask do the following:

   - Check for basic understanding.

⌣ Elicit easy and quick responses.

⌣ Build confidence and lay the foundation for deeper conversations.

⌣ Make easy opportunities for students to generate and ask questions.

More complex questions or statements do the following:

⌣ Explore deeper, more challenging aspects of a topic.

⌣ Require more thought and take more time.

⌣ Result in more engagement and deeper understanding that is meaningful beyond the class period.

⌣ Make connections to background, other topics, or future concepts.

⌣ Require modeling and practice.

⌣ Make opportunities more challenging for students to generate and ask.

Table 6.2 illustrates simple and complex questions that students or teachers could ask. When asking students to generate questions, help them identify simple questions that start with *what*, *when*, or *who*, and the more complex questions that sometimes begin with *why* or *how*.

Table 6.2: Sample Simple and Complex Questions

Simple Questions	Complex Questions
What was the most interesting part of the story or article?	How does the main point of this article connect with other stories or articles you have read?
What is the difference between the legislative branch and the judicial branch of government?	How does the legislative branch serve the people? In what situations would the legislative branch support the ordinary citizen or get in his or her way?
What were the main events that caused the Civil War?	Can you compare and contrast the causes of the Civil War and the war in Afghanistan?
What is photosynthesis?	How could you test the idea of photosynthesis?
What is a noun? Find three examples in the text.	How do understanding nouns help us write better?
What are the rules in volleyball?	Why are rules important? What might happen if we didn't have rules? What might happen if we change the rules?
What is the order of operations?	How could you solve this math problem? Explain the role the order of operations plays in achieving a solution.

2 Ask probing questions, or give prompts to expand students' thinking and take the conversation deeper. These questions and prompts guide students to:

⌣ Explain the "how" and "why" behind their answers

⌣ Talk through their problem-solving process

⌣ Describe their step-by-step thinking

⌣ Provide evidence to support their answers

Some examples of probing questions and prompts include:

⌣ "Give an example."

⌣ "Explain what you mean."

- "Tell me more."

- "How did you arrive at that response or idea?"

- "How can you support your ideas with evidence from the text?"

3 Teach students how to craft and ask questions.

- See if students *understand* a lecture, text, or activity. Have students ask simple questions to engage the class in a discussion about the literal meaning of the content.

- To discover if students understand the thoughts of classmates, characters, or other individuals, teach students how to probe each other for more understanding.

- Allow them to make connections. When students ask questions to make connections, they dive more deeply into the content.

4 Provide thinking scenarios to engage students during questioning.

- Provide quality opportunities to think and develop a question. Students can either write down a thought or silently think it through.

- Pair students to share their thoughts and ideas.

- Establish conversation circles for brainstorming and discussion opportunities.

- Have learners write their personal responses and reflections before sharing them with the class.

Tips and Traps

Remember to allow think time! It takes time to craft careful questions and a thoughtful response. Provide sufficient silent think time for students to process and create effective questions. Students become frustrated without enough time.

Avoid criticizing a student's question or response. Instead, ask a probing question to guide the student in revising the question or response.

Model the struggle to articulate quality questions and to illustrate quality responses. Teach how to juggle and manipulate ideas. Creating questions is a process of organizing thoughts to obtain answers or explore issues.

Provide students with question starters like "What would . . .," "How?," and "Why?"

Sometimes develop a question with a particular student in mind. When listing questions for discussion, jot down a student name by a question he or she will be motivated to answer.

Post higher-order thinking skill vocabulary words, question starters, and student-friendly definitions. For example, define *analyze* as digging deep for explanation, clarification, or understanding. This way, students interpret the use of the terms in assignments and discussions. When asking students to *analyze* the situation, they refer to the definition to frame their responses.

Putting It Into Practice

Effective questioning keeps all students actively engaged. Using interesting problem-oriented work hooks students on the topic as the lesson begins and provides rich context for quality questions. There are many structures that contribute to a classroom culture where effective questioning is used to ensure learning.

Think-pair-share and slates, white boards, and response cards are great ways to incorporate questioning strategies explicitly. Weave in daily questioning activities like character on a stick, research and word walls, role-play, and the question parking lot to involve each class member.

Use Think-Pair-Share

Think-pair-share is a classic activity that encourages questioning and reflection. The *think* step allows each student a chance to engage in individual reasoning on the problem without interference. Unique and varied questions emerge from this opportunity. The *pair* step, in which students share their questions with one other person, gives learners a chance to safely explore what are undoubtedly fragile concepts or solutions in a less-public way. Once each student gets confirmation or clarifies his or her thinking as a result of pair work, the student is more likely to *share* it publicly with the class, which results in higher-quality classroom discussions. When students are more open with their questions—both to clarify and push the conversation deeper— teachers learn more about how to ensure learning and success.

Use Slates, Whiteboards, or Response Cards

Slates, whiteboards, and response cards ensure that each student answers or asks a question. This engages each learner in answering the same question simultaneously versus one student doing all the thinking and responding while the others sit back passively relying on the more vocal members of the class. Present the question, give think time, and then provide the answer. Say, "1, 2, 3 . . . Show me!" to have all students display their answers simultaneously. This activity also can be used with partners and small groups. Provide time after the "reveal" for discussion and consensus.

Integrate Questioning Into Daily Practice

Use the following sample activities to stimulate and engage conversations about an assigned topic or question.

Character on a stick assists students in generating and discussing questions about characterization and points of view by using a factual or real character from a topic or piece of literature. Students or the teacher create images of selected characters and tape them to sticks. As the teacher asks questions, students respond as the characters on their sticks would respond.

Research and word walls honor and celebrate quality. They are eye-catching ways to present important information. Display the important words from the study to reinforce vocabulary and make connections to discussions. Learners or teachers can write the words using different colors or fonts. Illustrate and decorate each word in a personalized way with the picture depicting meaning, a special decoration, or design. These illustrations make each word unique.

Role-play provides opportunities to practice answering questions using higher-order thinking. Modeling and practicing will feel awkward at first, but they are essential for students to learn to use these questioning and critical-thinking skills with the content. Some examples of role-playing probes are pretend to be, depict the scene, show us how, or act out the part. (See strategy 18, page 145, for more discussion of role-playing.)

A *question parking lot* is a designated place for students to post questions throughout the class time. Many times learners do not feel comfortable asking a question or making a comment about the information being taught. This activity is also a beneficial way to defer some questions that usually come directly to the teacher and can lead the class off track. At the close of the class period, the teacher can distribute the questions to pairs of students and have them answer the questions or go home and try to find the answers. The question-and-answer periods and discussions are also effective ways to start the next class.

Strategy 21: Fire Up Understanding

"Learn from your mistakes" is a common saying that holds powerful truth. Teach students that mistakes are learning opportunities rather than embarrassing moments to avoid.

When students make mistakes, analyze them. Work with students to fill in the gaps, find a correct method, and address misconceptions before they have time to settle and become permanent. Confusion can cause learners to tune out, daydream, or quit. A frustrated learner often thinks, "I don't know what this means, so I don't care what it means."

Discover gaps, mistakes, or misunderstandings by assessing learners before, during, and after instruction. (See strategy 19, page 164, for more on this idea.) We see misunderstanding by watching students' faces and expressions; when students appear confused, sad, or nonresponsive, it is time to gather more information to analyze the error and point of confusion. Examine the root cause of misunderstanding when students articulate an idea that is inaccurate, incomplete, or off track. These in-the-moment occurrences are often called "teachable" moments. They are some of the most crucial learning opportunities in classrooms. Effective teachers capitalize on these moments to fire up understanding and turn mistakes into learning opportunities. This type of error analysis is critical to student learning and has been identified as one of the most effective practices to increase student achievement (Hattie, 2009; Marzano, 2007).

In order for students to learn from mistakes, they must have the opportunity to review their assessments and think through the items missed. Provide opportunities often for students to figure out what they did wrong rather than give them the answers or show them the process. They learn to solve problems, think, and remember the process when correcting their own errors. This self-analysis works best for students who have some basic understanding or comprehension of the simple concepts but are struggling to achieve the more complex ideas.

Students do not learn from their mistakes when they are unable to understand what they did wrong the first time. If students are making mistakes that indicate they do not have a basic understanding of the concept, a different explanation or guided intervention is needed for reteaching. Students grow as learners when they revise their work with new insights. Whether guided by the teacher or found on their own, exciting aha moments occur during effective error review.

If teachers dance around the truth and try to make students feel good even though they have made mistakes, we are doing them a disservice. When students fix their mistakes, they will feel a sense of accomplishment while learning. It isn't always comfortable to hear that you made a mistake, but when specific action helps you understand more, confidence is built. When students receive the message that mistakes are opportunities to learn and with effort, they can achieve more. In the absence of hearing the truth, students rely too heavily on a score to determine their self-worth (Hattie & Timperley, 2007).

Ask yourself, "Do my students view mistakes as a place to begin analyzing their understanding and planning what they need to learn? When they have misconceptions, do my students attempt to figure out what they do not understand?" If not, students will see mistakes as penalties. Teach them to embrace mistakes to improve.

Turning Mistakes Into Learning Opportunities

To ignite the fire of understanding, mistakes must become learning opportunities that are addressed the moment they occur. When students understand and see mistakes as learning experiences, they are more likely to engage.

Consider the following steps to turn mistakes into learning opportunities.

- Determine the learning goals of the assignment, test, quiz, or activity.
- Clarify the learning goals of the assignment by identifying which item accompanies each learning goal.
- Plan time for students to address their mistakes and reflect and analyze what is wrong with the error. Have students ask themselves:
    - "What mistakes did I make?"
    - "What is wrong?"
    - "How can I fix the mistake?"
    - "What resources do I need? My textbook? Other students? A website? A teacher explanation?"
    - "What will I do differently next time?"
- Provide a structure to help students analyze their mistakes.
    - Mark how many items were wrong at the top of the page, but do not indicate which problems were wrong. Have students work with a partner or a small group to figure out errors and how to correct each one.
    - Have students individually analyze their mistakes and turn in a summary of their errors and what they now understand.
    - Alternatively, have students work in groups according to the items marked wrong. This collaboration helps learners meet their individual needs.

When you realize students are lost, confused, misguided, or misunderstood, have a number of strategies ready to address these issues. Consider the following ideas in planning for these moments:

- Ask another student to explain the concept.
- Ask students to turn to a partner and draw a picture or create a symbol to represent the concept.
- Have individuals write key words or concepts to help them understand the concept.
- Have students brainstorm possible ways to answer the question.
- Connect what they do not understand to the big picture. For example, if students are struggling with fractions and identifying the numerator and denominator, use a scenario and image to help them understand. Pie, pizza, and cake are all good analogies for fractions.

Tips and Traps

Timing is key. As soon as you realize students have misunderstood the intended learning, make a plan to address it. Then give students another opportunity to use their new learning in another problem, example, or task. This is an effective way to analyze the impact of the learning activity. When you give students full credit or full points for their new understanding, you honor their new learning and send a message that mistakes are learning opportunities, not penalties.

Remember, grading practices impact the messages we send students about mistakes. Often, when kids make a mistake, we mark it wrong, and they lose points or receive a lower grade. When they fix it later and receive partial or no credit, the message is as follows: "Learn from your mistakes, but you will not receive a higher grade." This may influence a student's motivation to revise or make corrections. While some students inherently want to get the answer right or improve, many stop trying because the grade itself does not reflect any improvement or growth.

In formative assessment practice, some experts recommend not grading assignments that were designed for practice and for learning (Wiliam, 2007; O'Connor, 2002; Stiggins et al., 2005). Sometimes assignments are just valuable learning experiences. If teachers grade these assignments and students later make corrections and demonstrate growth, their grades should reflect the change by giving full credit for improvement.

Instead of going over the process to solve every problem or answer, try providing only the correct answer, so that students can refer to it. Then let students make the corrections and explain their rationale. Provide the time for students to talk with each other about their mistakes.

If teachers find themselves doing more of the explaining than students, learners may not transfer the explanation to their next chance at that type of task or question. Just talking louder and slower doesn't necessarily work (Guskey, 2009).

Putting It Into Practice

To ignite understanding, use active-learning opportunities to engage students in the content. Provide time for students to self-monitor their levels of understanding, prompt for deep thinking, and differentiate mistake analysis.

Teach Self-Monitoring Skills

Students are motivated when they understand their current knowledge level and how it helps them take the next step. This creates a feeling of accomplishment and of making progress. In order to self-monitor, learners must recognize where they are in their understanding and how they feel about it. Consider creating signs for the categories, such as in figure 6.1. Post this continuum of understanding on the wall in your classroom so students can pause and monitor their own understanding.

Prompt for Deep Thinking

Effective teachers use questions and prompts to respond to students on the spot and help them analyze their learning process.

For example, let's say students are assigned five math problems that require the same process or skill. While monitoring, teachers point out which are right and which are wrong. Learners are prompted to explain their thinking process for one of the problems they got correct. Next, students apply the process to the problems they got incorrect. This allows each student a chance to

1	2	3	4	5
I am totally confused!	I understand some of the problem.	I am getting it!	I understand and own my thinking.	I completely understand!
I'm lost. I do not understand.	I do not know what to ask.	I understand enough to ask questions.	I can explain, show, or demonstrate my understanding.	I completely understand, and the knowledge comes naturally to me now. It's automatic.
I feel unmotivated and frustrated.	I am unsure, but I could either give up or keep going.	I am curious and willing to continue learning.	I am motivated and could teach the material to others.	I am comfortable with the material, but I might get bored. I am ready for the next challenge.

Figure 6.1: Self-monitoring continuum of student understanding.

correct mistakes using his or her own thinking instead of the teacher's. Celebrate this accomplishment by having the student be a peer tutor and teach someone else the way to work the problem.

Apply prompting for deep thinking in other areas as well. For example, if students in a writing class are having trouble creating clear topic sentences, ask students to turn to a peer and describe the paragraph in one sentence. Then have students write the shared sentence at the beginning of their first draft of their writing sample. It is rewarding and surprising to see this new topic sentence—a reason to celebrate!

Differentiate Mistake Analysis

Teachers can differentiate mistake analysis to review students' mistakes on an assessment. Here we use a science assessment as an example. The assessment measured students' understanding of data, specifically the following learning goals:

- Students can identify responding and manipulated variables.
- Students can read graphs, specifically identifying the variables and the meaning.
- Students can evaluate graphs by explaining which graph is best to use in various situations.

After reviewing the student results from the assessment, it was clear that certain items on the test were associated with student understanding or lack of understanding on these three goals. As a result, teachers asked students to identify the items they got wrong and work in groups to help each other analyze their mistakes and describe what to do differently next time. Figure 6.2 (page 176) is a template students can use to first individually record their mistakes, do some initial brainstorming to analyze them, and then work in groups to discuss and learn more.

Strategy 22: Provide Descriptive Feedback

Effective feedback affirms learning that has occurred and requires students to take specific action to move their learning forward. Ineffective feedback is a sea of red marks that overwhelm students and cause them to shut down. Too much of the feedback teachers offer students stops at identifying the mistake. The power of feedback lies in what students do with the information

Review Your Scientific Process Assessment

Name: _____

Directions: In the first column, write the number of the question you got wrong. Use a separate row for each item. Then, in the second column, explain why you answered the question the way you did. Go back and look at how you answered the question to explain it. Third, in your groups, find and discuss the right answer. Finally, in the fourth column, explain how you could fix your answer to make it right.

Item You Missed	Why Did You Answer the Question This Way?	What Is the Right Answer?	Explain Your Answer

Figure 6.2: Sample worksheet for group collaboration.

(Hattie & Timperley, 2007; Hattie, 2009; Reeves, 2007). If feedback does not give students direction, they cannot use it to improve. Survey and assess to find out what students know to identify the next steps.

There are many types of feedback. In general, *evaluative* feedback quantifies learning and makes a judgment on the value of the work. *Descriptive* feedback describes learning, or what students know. In addition, descriptive feedback offers an actionable step that will produce more understanding or increased achievement. This actionable step is one of the things that makes descriptive feedback different than praising with specific comments, which we'll discuss in the next strategy (strategy 23, page 180). Descriptive feedback to ensure learning is also focused on comments that relate to students' performance or proficiency on the learning goal, rather than other factors, such as behavior or timeliness.

Feedback must be immediate and specific to work effectively. Specific feedback describes where more improvement is needed, or how to correct errors or revise work.

Descriptive feedback can be offered by a teacher, by another student, or through the learner's self-reflection process. While time consuming, teacher feedback honors the work students are producing and sends a message that the work is important. Growth occurs when students act on the feedback, make the revision, or try another problem. This is a valuable return on the investment of teacher time. It is important to note that students do not always jump at the opportunity to revise their work. However, it is in the revision process that students grow. Teachers sometimes expect students to transfer the insight from a comment to a future assignment. Often, it doesn't happen.

As a result, teachers are frustrated because they feel students are making the same mistake over and over again, and their effort to provide descriptive feedback is not working. Focus descriptive feedback comments on the learning goal—offer only a few comments, and require students to make revisions before moving to the next assignment. This reduces the teacher's workload because students are doing more with less. Consequently, students learn more because they are revising their work (Hattie & Timperley, 2007).

Teach and model how to use descriptive feedback. When the learning goal is clear and the students learn the appropriate terms and phrases to use, they can begin to offer feedback to each other. Ultimately, students self-assess and use the elements of quality feedback to reflect on their own work and independently make plans to improve.

However the feedback is received, it must result in action to increase learning. As Nicole (Vagle, 2009, p. 208) notes:

> When we offer feedback for the purpose of increasing learning, we must *inspire* and *require* action. Students must very clearly understand what the intended learning looks like, and they must identify the very next step in their learning. If students understand what to do, they can be *inspired* to take that next step. If these next steps are *required*—and teachers provide the time, structure, and support for students to act on the feedback—increased learning will follow (Hattie & Timperley, 2007).

Characteristics of Descriptive Feedback

Source: Adapted from Vagle, 2009, pp. 208–210.

The qualities of descriptive feedback became even clearer to Nicole after an interaction with her daughter, Maya, when she was in second grade. On Wednesday of each week, students in Maya's classroom received an object and were asked to create something and write about it using details. They brought the "imagination creation" and description back to school on Friday to share it with their peers. Maya brought her writing home on Monday, and usually the feedback the teacher provided was "Super Job." After Maya had been doing these imagination creations for about two months, Nicole looked at her writing more closely and was struck by a few things. While she included some specific details, she also had spaces and capital letters in the middle of words that made it more difficult to understand. As a former English teacher and her mother, Nicole decided to ask her about it. Maya's response was laced with exasperation as she exclaimed, "Mom, it doesn't matter! Miss Johnson puts 'Super Job' on it anyway."

The qualities of descriptive feedback that promote learning and not just compliance or efforts toward a better grade are as follows.

➤ **Descriptive feedback describes learning; it doesn't quantify or evaluate it.**
Grades, percentages, smiley faces, and nonspecific criticism ("Try harder," "Try again," "Missing") do not describe learning but quantify it. Ruth Butler (1988) studied the impact of giving grades on learning. Students were given a book with a range of activities on a certain topic. The work was collected and graded. Then students were randomly divided into three groups that were each given a different type of feedback: marks/grades only, feedback comments only, or marks/grades and comments. A few weeks later, students were given a similar set of tasks and told they would receive the same type of feedback. Students receiving marks/grades only and both marks/grades and comments made no progress in achievement, but students receiving only comments gained an average of 30

percent. Anne Davies (2007a, 2007b) suggests that the common practice of giving students comments and grades/marks simultaneously could be slightly modified so that students would receive only comments to begin with, and the grade/mark would be delayed a few days, giving students time to act on the feedback in order to improve their work.

➤ **Descriptive feedback describes strengths in terms of the learning criteria** (Hattie & Timperley, 2007; Marzano, 2007; Reeves, 2007). In reflecting on her feedback practices as a teacher, Nicole recalls writing "Excellent" or "Creative" on papers many times. While offered with the best intention, the message was general and not focused on the learning criteria that would help students identify their strengths. *She* knew what was excellent and why, but did her students?

➤ **Descriptive feedback provides next steps for specific action** (Davies, 2007a, 2007b; Wiliam, 2007). Comments such as "Check your work," "Explain," or "Many fragments" identify the beginning of the next step, but more detailed and active statements give students clear ideas about how to confidently make progress toward the intended learning:

  ➤ "In the analysis section of your lab report, explain how the results in your data table support your hypothesis."

  ➤ "Find and fix three sentence fragments."

  ➤ "Use two words from our math word wall to describe how you came to the answer to problem #3."

➤ **Descriptive feedback is focused and manageable.** Teachers should identify manageable chunks to target so that students see possibility and have hope of being able to learn and actually accomplish the next step in their learning (Stiggins et al., 2005).

➤ **Descriptive feedback is timely** (Reeves, 2007). When feedback is provided after the grade has been given, the motivation to learn from this feedback is drastically reduced. Students see the grade or mark as an ending, not as part of a cyclical process designed to improve learning (Hattie & Timperley, 2007). In addition, if too much time passes between the assessment and the feedback, students may be in a different spot on the learning journey, making the feedback inaccurate and confusing.

In general, effective descriptive feedback does the following:

  ➤ Helps students understand and articulate more deeply the intended learning (where am I going?)

  ➤ Provides students with opportunities to determine where they are and their very next step (where am I now?)

  ➤ Helps students understand and plan the steps toward achieving the intended learning (how can I close the gap?)

Teachers need to provide specific feedback often. Students learn the characteristics of descriptive feedback and can practice providing that kind of feedback to their peers. Furthermore, students learn how to self-assess. They become effective and skillful at identifying individual strengths and weaknesses in their own work.

A Protocol for Giving Feedback

Teachers should take three steps to plan for descriptive feedback in their classrooms. Using these three steps, teachers will ensure learning and motivate students to engage.

1 Choose the formative assessment on which you want to focus.

2 Plan descriptive feedback. Consider the following questions:

- How will students identify strengths? What tells them what they know? (For example, will you use comments or models of strong and weak work, or have students identify their own strengths and the evidence of quality?)

- How will students identify their next steps? What tells them what they don't understand?

3 Consider how students will respond.

- Will students self-assess? What will they be required to do?

- We know that most learning occurs when students understand where they are and what they need to do next. Knowing that, how will students actively respond to their understanding or misunderstanding?

- Will students have to work with a partner to identify and set goals for their next steps? To fix mistakes?

- How will students analyze their mistakes to determine what they did incorrectly and how to fix it?

Tips and Traps

When using rubrics, underline statements that describe what students did well, and circle phrases directing them to their next step. This saves the teacher time in writing comments. Direct the students to interpret circled phrases as what they need to do to improve their work.

Be specific, and do not dance around the truth. When something is wrong, it is wrong. Tell students or let them discover their errors. Students should understand the part that is not right. Misleading them with a false sense of success may help in the moment, but is more detrimental in the long run. Students know when their work is not the best. Giving them half-truths or praise in order to build their confidence has the opposite effect. While it isn't always easy to hear what needs improvement, feedback tells students what they need to fix and gives them a concrete action for improving. In the end, this builds confidence as students begin to see progress and believe success is possible.

Putting It Into Practice

Conferences and rubrics are effective practices that ensure learning and provide models for effective feedback.

Hold Student Conferences

Student conferences are great opportunities to provide descriptive feedback. Use appropriate lead-ins or questions to help gain deeper understanding of what they already know, and correct mistakes or identify the next steps in their learning. Here are some examples of effective prompts and questions to use:

- "Tell me more."

- "Explain this part."

- "Give me an example."

➤ "How can you use this information?"

➤ "How can you relate to this solution or dilemma?"

➤ "What do you know that is similar to this?"

Create Rubrics

Create rubrics that describe what students know at each level. Then teach students to read the rubrics; they should know that their score describes what they know—their strengths—and the next level identifies their next steps—areas to grow. For example, review the rubric in table 6.3, which describes levels of proficiency of the discussion leader for a book-club activity.

Table 6.3: Book-Club Rubric for Effective Questions of a Discussion Leader

1 Recall	2 Comprehension	3 Analysis	4 Connections
Questions cause students to answer yes or no. Questions cause students to talk about events or stories not related to the text.	Questions cause students to identify facts, characters, or events directly from the story. Students talk about what happened in the text.	Questions cause students to discuss what the story means or the significance of events. Students predict what will happen next or evaluate what would have happened if something different had occurred in the story.	Questions cause students to make connections to what is happening today in the school, community, or world. Students talk about the themes in the text and how it influences them or the world today.

Strategy 23: Praise and Inspire With Specific Comments

Mike Schmoker (2006) reminds us, "Meaningful recognition and specific praise does not cost anything. It is one of the most valuable ways to increase levels of meaningful recognition for learners" (p. 147). Positive words are affirmations that show students that teachers care and notice. Learners will work harder to avoid disappointing teachers when they know they take their learning seriously. When using praise to motivate and engage students or to build confidence, be intentional about the words used: "Encouraging words from a teacher [should focus] on the task, process, product, or behavior" (Barkley, 2007, p. 92). If you say you are proud of a student, identify the particular behavior or action you observed that makes you proud (Denton, 2007). Positive comments that are descriptive are intrinsic rewards that have motivational benefits to students. Research shows that students "rewarded with verbal praise or positive feedback showed greater intrinsic motivation and spent more time on a task once the reward was withdrawn than non-rewarded subjects" (Hattie, 2009, p. 175). So praise with specific comments not only increases student confidence and self-efficacy, it can also lead to more appropriate behavior in the classroom.

Remember that the reactions teachers have to students' learning, misunderstanding, disruptive behavior, attitudes, success, excitement, or feelings send messages to students about their own self-worth, capabilities, and roles in the learning community. When students take a little longer on an assignment, and the extra time is met with ridicule or an unspoken "hurry up," students feel inadequate, and their beliefs in their own abilities sink. When a teacher responds with words that reassure students that learning happens on all kinds of timelines, however, hope and self-efficacy are built. Praise improvement, quality, and effort—not the speed of learning.

Giving the Right Kind of Praise

Begin with a praise phrase, and then follow it up with a specific comment that describes the desired action, behavior, or words, for example, "Excellent work! Your illustration clearly shows how you solved the problem." Descriptive praise is effective because it doesn't leave students wondering why they were praised—they know exactly why, and they begin to connect their efforts with progress. When they make that connection, they begin to believe that learning is possible. For students who have never experienced this feeling of progress, the new sensation of pride and hope motivates them to keep trying. The specific description of what was done well also helps students understand what is expected in their behavior and in their learning. Both the clarity in knowing what we are learning and feeling a sense of progress and self-efficacy are associated with increased engagement and achievement (Hattie, 2009). In the absence of the description, by contrast, students begin to assign the positive or negative feedback to their own feelings of self-worth or self-esteem (Hattie & Timperley, 2007). Figure 6.3 shows the praise-phrase process.

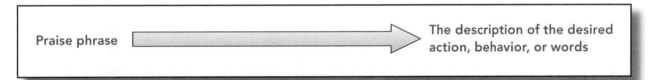

Figure 6.3: Praise-phrase process.

Example praise phrases include:

- "Keep on going! You have the problem correct so far."
- "Great thinking! You explained that part well."
- "I am proud of you because you shared the materials with the group."

Specific praise can be used to build personal relationships with students, too. Make each learner feel important as an individual. Students can tell if you like them or not. Like and honor each student, even when you do not approve of his or her actions.

- Verbally recognize students with genuine praise or a comment about a favorite shirt, a cool new haircut, a groovy backpack, or other things that will make him or her think, smile, and know that you cared enough to comment. This is a great door-greeter comment. However, be careful that your comments on a visible quality of one student do not make another student feel unimportant.

- Comment on a great attitude, mood, smile, or other positive feelings and emotions. Returning a smile for a smile shows teachers notice and welcome positive, happy learners.

- Notice kind deeds, such as helping a peer, celebrating a peer response or action, and showing nice manners. Acknowledge that respect for others deserves recognition. Good deeds are contagious, not only when modeled by the teacher, but when modeled by other students. Call attention to them!

Tips and Traps

Sometimes it is hard to find something to praise. In these instances, it is easy to stretch the truth, but it is more important to avoid giving false or empty praise. Praise that is empty or lacks genuine spirit will do more harm than good as it affirms low expectations and sabotages confidence. Give appropriate, balanced praise that identifies which parts are right and which are wrong.

Some students do not know how to accept positive praise and feedback. "Problem" students are used to receiving only negative feedback. Offer positive and genuine caring and praise. Stay neutral—all have talents, and all can learn. Make it a point to constantly show you care. Positive approval, expressed verbally or nonverbally, goes a long way. Catch learners being engaged, completing tasks, or just in passing.

Teach students to give specific praise when giving feedback. Praise the specific action; instead of saying, "Good job," say, "You did a great job explaining each step in the process. Now I understand why you placed that reason under the causes instead of the effects on the graphic organizer." Actively listen to establish open communication. This allows learners to answer a question and defend it. At first it may appear not to be correct, but their explanation can offer another plausible way to solve the problem.

Be as fair and positive about enforcing the rules when things go wrong as you are about giving praise when things go right. Don't take students' rude comments or disrespectful behavior personally. Be consistent in your responses to undesired behaviors and your enforcement of the rules. Sometimes accepting and other times rejecting a behavior will send mixed messages about expectations and weaken the effectiveness of the praise.

Putting It Into Practice

Teachers can ensure learning and praise and inspire students by writing positive notes, showing what went right, and having brag time.

Write Positive Notes

Build the "I believe in me" and "I can succeed" feelings in students. If a student does well on a test, for example, write a note to the student telling him or her that the hard work studying really paid off. Some other examples of notes teachers can write to students are:

- "Your comment in class sparked some good discussion."
- "I noticed how much you worked to listen to your friends today."
- "Thanks for showing the new student how to play that game."
- "Your paper really showed creative thinking."

Show What Went Right

Struggling students need positive contact more than ever. Find ways to turn problems into opportunities to show care and help students learn. If a student does not do well on a spelling test, for example, you could consider doing the following:

- Review the spelling test, and identify any words the student did know. Identify his strengths and help him see that even though he didn't do as well as he hoped, he did know some words.
- Talk about the words he didn't know. Consider the following questions: What went wrong? Did he know them and then forget? Did he get confused? Did the words sound unfamiliar?

➤ Then discuss concrete ways he could work on those words. Make a plan and follow through.

Set a time to retest on the words on which he worked. If there was improvement, replace the grade with the evidence that he now knows the words, and celebrate his hard work through specific praise. Show students that the effort they put in makes a difference.

Have Brag Time

Create time to praise and celebrate through specific observable comments. Let students know what is working, and that you noticed it is working.

Make the whole class feel success by using praise statements like:

➤ "I was so proud of the way you entered class, got in your seats quickly, and went to work on the bell-ringer assignment."

➤ "All of you worked well together, honored each other's comments, and stayed on task during group time yesterday. Stand up and give yourself the Three Yes cheer to celebrate!" (On three, everyone in the class rises and shouts, "Yes!" three times in a row.)

Sample praise to give to a small group or partners includes:

➤ "Yesterday I noticed that you each added your initials to one entry on the graphic organizer. That shows me you worked together, and you each contributed a part."

➤ "First, tell your partner what he or she did well during the activity. Then, brainstorm what you need to do next, and decide who will do which part. This way, both of you will be able to begin thinking about your future contributions."

Be sure that individual comments are distributed to all students over the course of time. Praising a group of students more often may lead to more disengagement from those students who do not get acknowledged. Praise for individual success could be shared in a reflection circle:

➤ "Samantha, your writing contained juicy words like *melodious* and *gripping*."

➤ "Rhys, the sculpture you created has a beautiful symmetrical feel."

➤ "Travis, your perseverance in solving that problem was spectacular. This really demonstrates that learning happens when we stick with something!"

Students can also self-reflect or praise others in a reflection circle:

➤ Each student could write a personal highlight about what he or she learned on a sticky note or a small piece of paper. Alternatively, students can also write one thing they appreciate about a member of the class. This would need to be organized so all members receive one positive comment.

➤ Have students write a response to the statement, "I was successful today when I . . ."

➤ Each member then reads his or her personal reflection piece aloud to the circle.

Strategy 24: Get Students Involved

A comedian elicited quite a laugh during his act when he described an interaction he had at the bookstore (Harker, 2008). He said, "I asked the saleswoman, 'Where's the self-help section?' She said if she told me, it would defeat the purpose."

All joking aside, many students get so dependent on being told what to do that they do not become self-directed learners. The role a teacher plays in empowering students can be a bit tricky—teachers must balance finding independence among students, teaching them how to be independent, and modeling it for them. Allowing students to flounder alone through the material is not the answer and does not create successful, independent learners; only those with support at home or who already understand school succeed in that model. True student involvement requires that reflection become an ongoing and frequent part of students' classroom experience, carefully modeled and structured in the beginning so students learn what it looks like and how it benefits their learning. Then, through repeated experience, students begin to internalize these reflective practices; once they know what to do, teachers can loosen the structure.

During a visit to an English classroom, we observed high school students texting on their phones, doing their nails, whispering to friends, and reading personal novels while the teacher was "leading" the class in reading from a textbook. While the room was quiet, the on-task behavior rate was probably about 50 percent. However, the minute the teacher shut the book and put her notes up on a monitor in front of the class, students stopped what they were doing and began copying the notes into their notebooks. This task created engagement. The notes were basically a summary of the story just read, but the act was familiar to students because someone was telling them what to do, and they felt confident that they could write these notes down. Perhaps one of the reasons students did not listen or stay on task during the story was that they knew the notes were coming. It was not essential to really know the story from the text. While engagement is the goal, mindless copying of notes is not. Turn an activity like this into a beneficial and meaningful experience where students are actively involved by implementing any of the following techniques and suggestions:

- Provide probing questions as lead-ins to each segment of the text.
- Select the sections that are important and read those aloud.
- Design stopping points along the way to reflect on the meaning of the text and take guided notes.
- Assign a partner for each student to discuss important details between the passages.

Student involvement cannot be arbitrary. It should be purposeful and designed to help students understand why they are learning what is being addressed, how to self-assess what they need to do next, what helps them learn, and what actions they can take. Student involvement must set out to make students partners in their learning who own and believe in their success.

To understand certain concepts and information, students need to work through and discover, solve, and unlock the puzzle on their own. *Self-regulated learning* is another term used to describe student ownership of their learning. Schunk and Zimmerman (2007) describe it as "an approach to a learning task involving forethought, performance control, and self-reflection" (p. 8). Self-regulation is important for students to become independent and lifelong learners. The term *lifelong learner* has become common in mission statements and purpose statements; it is a promise made by many schools. But what does becoming a lifelong learner really mean? If students can gain a sense of what it is to be a learner—if they know how to reflect on their own learning and take steps to push forward—then that skill will help students find success in every aspect of life.

Royce Sadler (1989) focused student involvement on three key questions that should drive students owning their own learning: Where am I going? Where am I now? How can I close the gap? Hattie (2009) also contributes to thinking about lifelong learning and student involvement:

Students need to be involved in determining their own success criteria, setting higher expectations, and being open to experiences relating to differing ways of knowing and problem-solving. This then leads to their development of beliefs and reputations as a learner and engaging in self-assessing, self-evaluating, self-monitoring, self-learning. (p. 37)

Consider some of the common practices teachers employ on a daily basis. Table 6.4 compares and contrasts characteristics of ineffective and effective student involvement.

Table 6.4: Characteristics of Ineffective and Effective Student Involvement

Ineffective Student Involvement	Effective Student Involvement
Most assignments are worksheets.	The teacher uses a variety of activities and assignments in instruction and assessment.
Students always work alone during independent work time.	Classroom structure varies. Sometimes learners work alone, other times with partners or small groups.
Assignments are often used as busywork.	Assignments are based on assessment data and clearly aligned to the learning goals and standards.
Students sit in their seats to complete assignments, and silence is expected most of the time. Students usually work quietly with little chance to ask questions or resolve concerns.	Learning can be noisy. Students sometimes sit quietly, but frequently talk, ask questions, experiment, and work at stations, in small groups, at centers, or other places, depending on their needs.
The teacher works with a small group or conferences with an individual for a long period of time. Students sit at their desks and do not disturb the teacher.	The teacher circulates the room asking processing questions, probing for explanations, and resolving misunderstandings. Students post questions, ask each other, and lean on other materials in the classroom to answer their questions.
Emphasis is on finishing work on time and receiving the grade.	Emphasis is on learning more, so the students and teacher work to take the time needed to understand the most essential concepts.
A peer often checks the paper so the answer can't be changed after it is graded. Scores are recorded. When learners view their papers, they look at the grade more than analyzing and correcting mistakes.	Often learners check and correct their answers after completing an assignment to get immediate feedback. Students consistently review mistakes and reflect on how to fix them.
The teacher grades and returns the finished work. Many mistakes are discussed, but the grade is the important part of the feedback. Students do not go back and fix their mistakes or revise their work.	When the teacher gives back an assessment, students examine their mistakes, revise their work, and turn their assignments back in. Grades reflect the revised work and are not averaged between the two or three chances.

A Protocol to Get Students Involved in Their Learning

Plan and execute instruction and assessment to help students answer the following three questions (Sadler, 1989; Hattie & Timperley, 2007; Stiggins et al., 2005):

1 Where am I going?

- Clearly define the learning goal or objective.

- Give students an opportunity to talk about their interpretations of the learning goal.

- Show examples of what the learning goal looks like and what it does not look like in terms of student work.

2 Where am I now?

- Help students identify what they know through their assessment information, mistakes, and rubric scores.

- Show them what they need to do next, or help them identify it.

- Provide descriptive feedback (see strategy 22, page 175).

3 How can I close the gap?

- Guide students to design a plan based on their self-assessment.

- Plan and structure class time and work to help students execute their plans.

Intentionally plan motivating, student-focused learning opportunities. Table 6.5 illustrates activities to use in planning. In these activities, learners can work alone or with others. The teacher determines a flexible time frame based on student understanding: the time frame can vary, for example one class period, a week, or during the entire unit of study. Assignments are based on assessment data. Some are completed by the entire class, others by a small group of students, and some by just one learner; assignments address a specific strength or weakness.

Table 6.5: Student-Focused Activities

Stations or Centers	The teacher designates areas for students to work on specific needs.
Agenda Folder	Each student has a special folder with independent assignments for a day, week, or unit. These assignments are developed to meet students' differentiated needs.
Computer Lab	The teacher uses a program to teach a specific skill or research task. Students work independently to create or experience something.
Board Work	The teacher posts a daily assignment.
Choice Board	The teacher creates a list of two or more assignments, and each student selects one to complete.
Cooperative Learning	Students complete a cooperative learning assignment. Each group member has a designated role, and the group comes to consensus.
Small Groups	Partners or small groups work together to complete the designated assignment. Students share, brainstorm, or tutor each other.

After presenting clear directions and moving the learners to their starting points, the teacher might be seen working with a small group for instruction or intervention, conferencing with a learner, or walking around among the students while they are working. This is an excellent time to use probing questions or statements to assess progress and assist with individual needs. To use this strategy effectively, the teacher should work first with students who struggle; they often need a re-explanation or more direct instruction (Hattie & Timperley, 2007; Hattie, 2009), so beginning with this group of students is important in making this strategy successful.

Tips and Traps

Spend time up front teaching students how to be involved—how to identify quality work, how to revise to make work better, how to self-assess, and how to effectively choose a way to learn more. The time spent teaching these skills will ultimately save time as students will be able to learn more independently in the future.

Model the thinking or brainstorming you are requesting of students. Model this metacognitive process to make students feel more confident. Include the time it takes to meaningfully respond. Being involved in learning is not always easy for students, and they do not always get excited about it the first time around. Once they see its value and experience success, it will be much easier for them, and they will ask for the opportunity to get involved.

Give students permission to explore their own ideas. Initially, they will want teacher direction and approval, so encourage them to try their own ideas and then self-reflect to see if their plans worked. If it did, they can keep using the strategy; if not, they should try something different. Teach students to try something out, self-assess, and then make plans accordingly. These are critical skills.

Asking students to self-assess without providing some way for them to identify their strengths and weaknesses with accuracy can lead to frustration for everyone. If the self-reflection is too general, it won't help the students take their next step. Students will see the process as not worth their time, and, in turn, they will not take it seriously the next time.

Student-involved activities must follow the same guidelines as regular activities. They must address the standards, directions must be clear, and materials and supporting resources must be available. Schedule the activity in the appropriate place in the lesson, at a point when students will have enough background experience or information to execute it successfully.

Putting It Into Practice

An easy way to ensure learning and get students involved is to invite their feedback and use it to adjust instruction, policies, and consequences. You can also use reflection activities after assessments to ensure learning.

Solicit Student Feedback on Instruction, Policies, and Consequences

Invite learners to step up and speak out! Collect students' opinions, observations, and perceptions; they give great insight about how to revise the class instruction, policies, or even consequences in order to create a positive place to learn. For example, check in with students informally after a new activity. Intentionally ask for their feedback on the structure of the class, what is helping them learn, and what is getting in the way of their learning so that you make modifications if necessary. Ask for their evaluations of the class at the end of your time together, use their comments as a way to reflect on your teaching and instructional practice, and take steps to become an even more effective teacher in the future.

Consider asking the following questions at the appropriate times:

- "What part of the classroom works and does not work for you?"
- "What frustrates you?"
- "What part is not clear?"
- "What do you need to make the class more productive?"
- "What suggestions do you have to make this work?"
- "What are your peers doing that displeases, frustrates, or bothers you?"
- "What am I doing that frustrates, angers, or bothers you?"
- "What do you expect of this classroom situation and me?"

- ➤ "What is your role?"

- ➤ "What do you think will help this situation? What can I do? What are you going to do?"

- ➤ "What goals do you have for yourself? What will you need to do to obtain this goal?"

Use a Reflection Activity After Assessments

In this example, students are deeply involved in learning from their assessment information. Reflections after assessments require students to tease out what they already know and what they do not know. The activity Mixed Up-Sticky Notes engages students and ensures learning (A. Smith, personal communication, July 6, 2010). After a short assessment, give students a blank piece of paper with four sticky notes labeled A, B, C, and D. Write varying combinations of correct and incorrect responses to the assessment questions on three sticky notes. On the remaining sticky note, write only the correct answers. Then break students into groups, and challenge them to figure out which sticky note contains the correct answers. First, students have to figure out the correct answers, and then apply the knowledge accordingly. This activity can also be used after multiple short assessments in which the correct answers to the tests are provided on sticky notes, and students have to match the sticky note with the right assessment. Learners will have a lot of fun and learn more through discussion with peers!

Strategy 25: Respond With Targeted Interventions

When a learner does not have the background or struggles to understand the information being taught, timely and targeted interventions can ensure learning. Students who need reteaching on a certain skill, standard, or concept benefit from immediate response to their misunderstanding.

Based on formative assessment data, determine the learners who need more support and in what areas. Then meet with the individual or a small group of individuals who have a common weakness.

Every barrier to grasping a concept needs to be eliminated. Identify the most crucial concepts that are not being learned, and intervene with quality activities. These interventions can be implemented as part of instruction—quality interventions are not an addition to what occurs in the classroom but rather an integrated part of the process of learning, instructing, and assessing. If student time at literacy stations and math centers is a regular part of the school day, for example, use assessment information to drive what happens at the stations during that time. Use your already-structured schedule to incorporate timely interventions! In the secondary classroom, the assessment during instruction can lead to interventions the next day. In this way, lesson planning is driven by the assessments already planned. Always remember to:

- ➤ Focus the intervention on the mistakes or misunderstandings from the assessment.

- ➤ Organize students according to the learning they need to work on.

Tips and Traps

Use your existing assessments as intervention tools. If students made mistakes, have them go back, analyze, and fix their mistakes. Offer students descriptive feedback, and provide students time to act on that feedback. Assist in a small-group, teacher-directed activity. Make sure to allow for the learners to have some student-engagement time. Students need to think through the process and claim ownership. Other strategies in this chapter provide guidance on what to do during the interventions.

Remember to move students in *and* out of interventions as needed. Keeping students in an intervention group after they have mastered the learning damages their motivation and bores them. Once students understand the material, they need to move out and work on the grade-level assignment that addresses the current concept, skill, or standard.

Putting It Into Practice

Interventions must always be based on what we know about student learning. When individual teachers or teams use assessment data to plan interventions, they are taking steps forward to ensure learning. Use elements of formative assessment, in which teachers respond to students' learning needs, to form intervention plans. In this section, we show how teachers can create intervention plans for elementary reading, middle school science, and high school English to help identify students in need of intervention.

Use Assessment Data for Elementary Reading

In an elementary reading class, students took an assessment on using evidence from the text to make judgments and inferences about setting, characters, and events. Prior to this assessment, the teacher described what judgments and inferences were and gave a few examples outside of the text. Then students individually created their own judgments and inferences for the text.

Following the assessment, the teacher grouped students into three different categories and had them work in groups to understand what they did wrong on their assessment and what they will do differently next time. Table 6.6 (page 190) is a sample teacher intervention plan.

Use Assessment Data for Middle School Science

In an eighth-grade science class, students were studying chemical equations. The teacher decided to formatively assess students on the following learning targets in order to adjust instruction for the next two days:

- I can understand the relationship between the different types of atoms and bonds.
- I can balance chemical equations.
- I know the laws of conservation of matter and energy.
- I can identify different chemical reactions.

After administering the assessment and analyzing the data, students were placed in one of two groups: those who struggled with balancing chemical equations and those who understood how to balance chemical equations. These groups targeted a need for strategic interventions for the learning and understanding of these items. Table 6.7 (page 190) is a sample intervention plan for this scenario.

Use Assessment Data for High School English

Table 6.8 (page 191) shows an intervention plan for a high school English course in which students took a short formative quiz after reading a newspaper article. The individual teacher reviewed the formative assessment results and planned to have students work in three groups.

Table 6.6: Elementary Reading Intervention Plan for a Targeted Learning Goal

Learning Target/Objective: I can make judgments and inferences about setting, characters, and events and support them with evidence from the text.

Students Who Struggle With Simple Ideas	Students Who Need Practice With Complex Ideas	Students Who Need Enrichment
Rita Dexter Xiao-Hong Eric	Kate Jorge Ira Pablo	Dwight Talbot Francois Lee
Targeted Interventions		
These students missed the boat entirely. They need more intensive direct instruction. I will work with this group of students after making sure the other two groups know what to do. I will have each student look at his or her answers to the questions they got wrong to talk through different answers and discuss why each would be a judgment or not. Then I will ask students to choose one judgment, search for evidence that would support it, and collaborate to write a response. I will ask them to: • Identify what makes a good response • Look back at their responses, determine the correct answers, and make revisions while I help individual students at the same time • Form pairs and work to make a sample response better • Take home a sample response and work to improve it (Have them make a revision plan before they leave.)	These students made a judgment about the event, but struggled to support it with evidence from the text. As a result, I will have these students do the following in pairs: • Exchange papers and review each other's judgments and try to find evidence to support them using the text • Exchange papers to revise their answers to include evidence from the text • Make new judgments and find support from the text	These students understood and performed well on making judgments and inferences about events. As a result, I will have these students work together to do one or more of the following: • Write a different ending to the story • Become a news team from the local paper and write a front-page story. • Draw and write a paragraph describing a personal experience in which the student stood up for something he or she really believed in. Ask them to describe their actions and the outcome.

Table 6.7: Eighth-Grade Science Intervention Plan for a Targeted Learning Goal

Learning Target/Objective: I can understand the relationship between the different types of atoms and bonds. I can balance chemical equations. I know the laws of conservation of matter and energy. I can identify different chemical reactions.

Students Who Struggle With Balancing Chemical Equations	Students Who Clearly Understand Balancing Chemical Equations
Joshua Zeke Lily Emma	Amanda Chloe Sam Jose

Students Who Struggle With Balancing Chemical Equations	Students Who Clearly Understand Balancing Chemical Equations
Targeted Interventions	
These students need intervention. They will focus on reading and using the periodic table and identifying each element's atomic number, protons, and neutrons. I will have students: • Play cards to practice reading and using the periodic table • Analyze their mistakes in balancing chemical equations on the assessment and explain what they did wrong and what to do differently next time • Take another test to reassess on balancing chemical equations	These students are proficient and need enrichment. They will compare and contrast balancing a chemical equation (science) with solving an equation (math). I will have students: • Solve three math equations and balance three chemical equations • Write the steps involved in solving and balancing • Complete a Venn diagram comparing and contrasting solving and balancing • Produce something for other students to use to practice or understand each of these concepts

Table 6.8: High School Language Arts Intervention Plan for a Targeted Learning Goal

Learning Target/Objective: I can critically evaluate nonfiction text and can state the argument presented and explain how it is effective or not so effective.

Students Who Struggle With Simple Ideas	Students Who Need Practice With Complex Ideas	Students Who Need Enrichment
Gary Jade Joao Ian	Patrick Martin Shelley Sean	Alejandro Kyle Ava Mary
Targeted Interventions		
These students did not identify the main argument and supporting details. I will provide samples of the arguments they picked and work with students to have them: • Discuss the evidence of each argument • Discuss why the real argument makes the most sense • Discuss strategies to tease out the argument • Read another short paragraph I will model an effective evaluation and have students: • Describe what they saw me doing • Analyze an article on their own	These students identified the claim accurately, but need help in supporting why it is an effective or ineffective argument. I will group students and have them: • Decide the claim of the article • List the evidence that makes them think this • List the parts of the argument that are convincing • List the parts of the argument that are weak	These students effectively identified the argument and evaluated its effectiveness. I will group students and have them: • Write the opposite argument I will model an example or two and have students: • Create a game to identify the argument in a series of short scenarios • Write an editorial for a newspaper and really send it (after revisions and editing)

Chapter 6 Campfire Talk

This chapter described strategies to ensure learning. Consider your own understanding, perceptions, and experiences about what works to ensure that students really learn. Reflect on the following questions.

1 Which steps in planning for learning do you need to become more productive? What do you need to do to improve this area?

2 Do you assess before, during, and after the learning? Which part needs to be more productive, and how will you improve it?

3 Do you use the data effectively?

4 Based on the data, are you planning quality, motivating activities in which students learn what they need to learn? How can you make that process more efficient?

5 When do your students become bored? Unchallenged? Unproductive? Lost? How can you use what they are learning to make them excited, motivated, and on-task learners?

Discuss the following questions and activities in your professional learning community, department, grade-level team, or a staff meeting.

6 Compile a list of informal and formal formative assessment tools. Distribute or post the list for everyone to refer to for new ideas during individual planning.

7 Have members of the collaborative group share a strategy they have used in the past to ensure learning. Then have each teacher plan to try something new before the next meeting. Reflect on how the new strategy worked.

8 Use the Plan for Student Motivation reproducible to discover, diagnose, and plan to address the needs of individual unmotivated students when ensuring learning.

Plan for Student Motivation

Strategy	Name the Unmotivated Student(s) in Need of the Strategy	Identify the Wrapper the Student Is Wearing	List Observable Evidence, Behavior, Habits, or Traits	Develop an Action to Address the Need	Assess and Reflect on Implementation	Additional Comments
19. Use Assessment Before, During, and After Learning (page 164)						
20. Ignite Thinking With Probing Questions (page 168)						
21. Fire Up Understanding (page 172)						
22. Provide Descriptive Feedback (page 175)						

Strategy	Name the Unmotivated Student(s) in Need of the Strategy	Identify the Wrapper the Student Is Wearing	List Observable Evidence, Behavior, Habits, or Traits	Develop an Action to Address the Need	Assess and Reflect on Implementation	Additional Comments
23. Praise and Inspire With Specific Comments (page 180)						
24. Get Students Involved (page 183)						
25. Respond With Targeted Interventions (page 188)						

Intervention Plan for a Targeted Learning Goal

Decide on a learning target for an upcoming assessment. Identify students who struggled, need practice, or need enrichment. Plan targeted interventions for these students.

Learning Target/Objective:

Students Who Struggle	Students Who Need Practice	Students Who Need Enrichment

Targeted Interventions

Keeping the Flame Burning!

A motivating teacher is like a roaring fire that lights the exciting, challenging, and mysterious path for learners. This type of teacher is a gift to students. Being or becoming a motivating teacher takes intention and commitment. Inspiring motivation in students can be tremendously successful when the school community fosters a shared culture and intentionally improves the support system at the classroom, building, and community levels. This means the roles of collaborative teacher teams, administrators, and parents and families are significant in creating a learning culture that is motivating and engaging for all students. A supportive school and community culture embraces and problem solves together to work to engage all students. When the system is working well with clear communication in place, there are many possibilities for teachers and students in increasing engagement.

Here we draw on the previous chapters and move the discussion to larger school and community roles in motivational practice. After summarizing the teacher role in motivation and the classroom characteristics that distinguish a prosperous culture, we move on to outline roles of school staff, administrators, community, and parents and the significant influence these stakeholders can have on student motivation. Finally, this chapter provides possible solutions to some of the most common motivational issues.

Teacher Role

Lighting the fire of engagement for students who are unmotivated to learn or participate is powerful, exhausting, and exciting work. As we have seen in previous chapters, teachers who create an environment where all students are engaged, motivated, and learning focus on the following five core areas:

1. Building a positive classroom learning community

2. Describing and planning learning with students

3. Making learning an adventure while infusing humor, fun, wonder, interest, and passion into the lessons

4. Offering students choices and allowing them to have some control over their learning and their school experience

5. Ensuring students learn by making them revise their work, fix their mistakes, and self-assess

There are many recipes for creating a classroom that invites learning and engagement. The right combination of actions, words, strategies, and structure is specific to context and the strengths and personality of the teacher. Table 7.1 lists some teacher actions that affect motivation for better or for worse.

Table 7.1: Teacher Actions That Affect Motivation

Practices and Characteristics of Ineffective Teachers	Practices and Characteristics of Effective Teachers
Puts a cap on student potential	Always looks for a new, innovative way to teach information
Fails to plan	Preassesses learners to find out what they know
Gives easy-to-use, boring assignments like worksheets and textbook questions	Plans strategically from preassessment data to meet diverse student needs
Uses mostly teacher-directed teaching	Creates assignments around student needs and interests that best teach the standards, using the appropriate content and resources
Uses the same lessons and instructional strategies repeatedly	
Teaches above or below the learners' levels	Strategically plans student-directed assignments and opportunities for students to take control of their learning
Believes "I taught you that, so you should know it"	
Threatens students	Listens, observes, and talks with students, then acts accordingly with respect
Blames parents and previous teachers for students not having the background and foundation needed to learn the grade-level information	Knows the standards and content to be taught
	Plans using a variety of resources and techniques to reach them all
Does not earn the students' respect	Uses lots of tricks, hooks, and gimmicks that excite learners to want to learn
Does not like the students	
Does not teach the grade-level standards, content, and skills in innovative ways with rigor	Moves around the classroom among the students while teaching, assisting, observing, and facilitating
Constantly gives the same lesson to everyone	Greets the students at the door each day; calls them by name
Sits to teach	Surveys students to get to know them
Doesn't get to know students and doesn't let students get to know him or her	Allows mistakes to be learning experiences; guides students through processes with confidence and patience
Is not forgiving and has little patience	Has the attitude that it is never too late to learn and all students can learn; learns to find any way possible to reach all students
Feels depressed at the end of the day; dreads going to school	
Shows a negative attitude	
Often isolates him- or herself, and when around others, gripes constantly	Focuses on the things that went right each day and why and how they worked; reflects on what went wrong to learn how to move forward
Focuses on a lack of time versus effectively using the time he or she has	Shows passion and loves to teach and see the lightbulb turn on when a student succeeds or learns something new
	Has respect for others; is positive and upbeat; offers praise; laughs often

As you experiment with different ways of motivating and engaging students, keep in mind the evidence of success. Table 7.2 describes what a classroom might look, feel, act, and sound like when the fire of engagement is lit.

Table 7.2: A Motivating, Engaging Classroom

What Do You See?	How Do Students Feel?	What Are You Doing?	What Are Students Doing?
Movement	Excited	Planning	Problem solving
Respect	Respected	Presenting lecturettes with a strong knowledge base	Processing
Work at stations and centers	Challenged	Using a variety of strategies	Questioning
Flexible grouping	Stimulated	Assessing before, during, and after learning	Discussing
Project work	Enthusiastic	Using assessment data to drive instruction	Sharing
Students working together and alone	Content	Using flexible grouping	Cooperating
Students on task and engaged	Accepted	Using movement to monitor and engage students	Collaborating
Accessible materials	Energetic	Sharing the responsibility with students	Being engaged
Effective use of materials and resources (such as gadgets, computers, manipulatives)	Safe	Providing choices	Planning
A variety of strategies and activities	Positive	Providing many opportunities for students to talk about their learning	Producing
Students' work displayed	Upbeat	Using appropriate materials and resources effectively	Learning
	Cooperative	Learning individual strengths and weaknesses	Showing evidence of learning
	Confident		Thinking
	Hopeful		Discussing, asking questions, and posing solutions to problems
			Making links and connections to their learning
			Being metacognitive, reflecting on their learning, and setting goals for their next steps

While classroom teachers deal with motivation issues daily, they have people they can turn to for more support. The stakeholders in a school support system include school support staff, administrators, teachers, parents and families, businesses, and the community. Working together, this support system strives to intentionally foster a culture where students are vital, contributing members of the school community.

School Staff Role

Teachers can tap other adults in the building to support motivation in the classroom. Engaging all adults in the work of creating a motivational climate can have a positive effect on the classroom and the school. Ask for the whole staff to come together and strategize how to make the school environment a supporting, motivating culture. Who are the adults with whom students engage over the course of a day? During meetings with staff, including noncertified personnel, discuss ways to address specific problems of the unmotivated students. Observe students. Who are the adults they gravitate to in the building? Those key people may be hall monitors, lunch staff, bus drivers, administrative assistants, or custodians. In any case, checking in with school staff both individually and collectively can help solve individual or group motivational issues. Use the Three-Step Protocol for Motivating Students found in chapter 1 (page 20) as a way to guide your interventions. Develop a positive learning environment in the entire school as well as in the classroom.

Administrator Role

Attitudes and work ethics are contagious. When a motivated administrator intentionally plans, supports, and models the kind of culture that provides successful learning environments, the lead firelighter has arrived! As a teacher, engage administrators in these conversations and discuss success stories, challenges, and strategies that have potential to improve not only the classroom culture but also the school culture. An individual teacher can make a big difference by raising these issues, experimenting with strategies in the classroom, and suggesting ways for the school to support and encourage this type of active engagement desired for and by students. A motivating school community welcomes all students and staff and capitalizes on their strengths and talents. Table 7.3 describes some of the actions successful administrators take.

Table 7.3: Administrator Actions That Affect Motivation

Practices and Characteristics of Ineffective Administrators	Practices and Characteristics of Effective Administrators
Stays in the office or away from the campus; does not mingle; is not visible; does not know or attempt to know students' names	Is constantly seen throughout the school; knows the names of staff and students
Visits classrooms for formal observations only	Is in and out of classrooms constantly; students and teachers are used to visits
Talks negatively about the faculty and students	Shows professionalism and respects confidentiality; talks in positive terms
Has favorites; in meetings, calls on the same people all the time	Is fair
Main objective: being the boss; managing behavior, building, and tasks	Main objective: being committed to serving as a devoted leader for the faculty, students, and community
Not accessible; difficult to approach	Has an open-door policy; welcomes office visits
Is authoritarian; makes final decisions with no input from others	Listens and is open to opinions of others; makes decisions after considering all points of view and input
Blames others for school problems	Assigns committees to help solve school problems
Makes plans on behalf of teachers without input	Allows staff to have input into school procedures, socials, meetings, and professional development
Does not attend professional development with faculty	Attends professional development with faculty so they learn and grow together
Lectures staff and students about the things wrong, such as low test scores or discipline problems	Provides ways to improve instruction, academic rigor, and achievement while celebrating successes
Is negative; does not smile or laugh; seems not to enjoy life or the job	Is positive and has passion about the school's success and the role as administrator
	Has a welcoming, warm manner; smiles

Community Role

Forge partnerships with local community businesses, organizations, and government. In collaboration with the community, teachers and administrators can offer students opportunities to organize, lead, and participate in special projects that contribute to community and business interests. A community is a potentially strong ally in providing relevance and challenge in the curriculum. Tap these resources to spice up classroom activities and projects. Use the community resources as a way to build or strengthen a positive reputation for the school.

- Send school news, art, and student work to local newspapers or television stations to publicize success and acknowledge students.

- Lead or participate in projects that address needs or problems of local organizations, businesses, or schools, such as recycling, beautifying an indoor or outdoor location, volunteering, and doing service projects. When students find a project of interest, teachers can use it as a privilege to motivate students to engage themselves in the classroom.

Parent Role

Building positive relationships with parents and families is a key factor in engaging a learner and igniting excitement about school. Analyze students' home environments and family members' attitudes about school through home visits or school conferences. When a parent displays a bad attitude toward school, do not take it personally. The parent could have had a bad experience in school as a student or bad experiences with other school personnel regarding his or her own child. Perhaps the school has communicated primarily negative aspects about the child. This can cause resentment to build, and then, no matter who contacts the parent with a school-related issue, it becomes a negative, resistant situation. That type of attitude does not change easily; the relationship must be nurtured over a period of time. Once parents believe the school is providing the quality education their child deserves and treating their child fairly, they start to build a more positive attitude and support the school faculty. Then the home situation motivates the student to cooperate, and, more importantly, thrive in school.

Parent support is helpful and rewarding for all. Make phone calls to make contact. Do not only call when there is a problem; share the accomplishments and good qualities of a child. If the student shares a project with the class or works cooperatively with a group, for example, let the parent know, or allow the child to make the call. Celebrate success!

Talk positively about the school in public places. If you see a parent in public, be friendly and gracious. Discuss topics other than school-related problems; these issues are too private to be talked about in public places.

Troubleshooting Common Issues

Common questions arise about classroom motivation issues, problems, and concerns. Difficult motivational situations can sap a teacher's energy and weigh heavy on his or her mind. While we've offered suggestions for dealing with this behavior, always remember that the reasons students are unmotivated vary, based on a host of factors. When educators identify the root cause of the behavior, they can form a plan to address not only the behavior, but also the underlying cause of it. With this information in hand, the plan has greater potential to create an intrinsic desire to learn and act. That kind of deep change transforms behavior for the long term. Consider these sample statements from students regarding their motivation:

- "Writing this paper will give me practice in becoming a better writer, something I want to do when I leave school. So I'll write this paper and hand it in."

- "The last time I handed in a paper, I got it back with an F and red writing all over it. I am not a good writer, so I won't do this assignment."

- "If I walk quietly through the hall, I'll get to have a pizza party on Friday."

- "If I walk quietly through the hall, my teacher will be happy, and the classroom will be a place that is happy."

- "If I walk through the hall quietly, I won't get a check by my name."

- "If I walk through the hall quietly, I won't have any fun today. I have to be quiet in class, in the hall, during lunch, and even sometimes during games in gym. I need to have a little fun, so if I skip a bit and hum a tune, I'll have a little fun."

While some students will walk quietly down the hall because they want pizza, others could care less and just want a peaceful, happy classroom. When teachers know their students well, they have greater potential of creating the conditions for learners to intrinsically desire to engage in the classroom in meaningful and positive ways. With this knowledge in hand, the best plan to address common motivational issues becomes clearer.

The following questions cover common motivational issues. Use these answers to begin your own discussion and self-reflection to begin to ignite the fire of engagement for all learners.

What Do You Do When a Learner Is Unmotivated to Perform, Participate, or Complete an Assignment?

If this behavior happens regularly, remember being unmotivated is a learned behavior or action so ingrained that learners unconsciously respond or do not respond out of habit; this may take some perseverance to fix. First, conference one on one with the student, and listen to what the student says. Probe and *listen* for the reasons the learner gives. Allow the student time to voice his or her thoughts, and empower the learner by asking when he or she could get the assignment done. Negotiate until the plan is created and agreed upon by both of you. What is your purpose for the assignment? Is it to hold students accountable for turning things in? Is it to help them practice what they do not understand? Before determining the course of action, take into account the original purpose of the assignment. Students may not turn it in because they feel it is a waste of their time. Negotiating isn't as effective in this case. If a student didn't understand the directions or doesn't know where to start, the conversation should explore how to help the student understand better. Negotiation is important but not as important as getting students the help they need. After giving support, the teacher may not need to negotiate a date, just set one after more instruction has taken place.

Teachers must plan and work strategically to make lessons meaningful and come alive so that students do learn. Teachers must accept that learning is more than students choosing and wanting to be in school. Students may be present physically, but the information and the activity must capture them emotionally and mentally for the learning experience to be purposeful. Students need to be excited about what is happening and wait with eager anticipation to see what is going to happen next. Then they will stay tuned in and learn.

Many learners have embraced the wrong attitude about homework assignments. The attitude of some students (and some family members) is that most homework is a burden and a time waster; it creates negative and resistant emotions from the students and the parents. Some students decide not to do assignments, have someone else do the assignments for them, or do them with less than their best work.

Make sure the student fully understands the assignment and is capable of doing the assignment alone. Not all learners have assistance at home, and for those who do, it is sometimes difficult to know if completed work represents the students' understanding or that of the parents. Students who do not have the help or support at home are truly left to their own devices. Penalizing them for not having that support at home is disheartening. Give clear directions, and provide any materials and resources needed to complete the assignment. Differentiate homework assignments so that all learners can have an experience that meets their areas of need.

Design homework assignments to be fun, exciting, and stimulating. Try one of the following simple motivating, problem-solving assignments to enhance the classroom learning at home:

- Watch a television show, and write down a connection to the lesson.
- Make a collage representing an aspect of the targeted learning objective. (For example, ask learners to search magazines or newspapers to find shapes they are learning about.)
- Go on a scavenger hunt in texts, notes, or around the house, and find items related to the topic.
- Make up a two-line rap to learn a vocabulary term and its meaning.
- Interview a family member or friend about the topic or learning objective. For example, a grandfather might recall what it was like to live through an event the class is studying in history. Perhaps a mother might explain how she learned to calculate percentages.

At the beginning of class, have students share their findings or products with a partner as a bell-ringer activity to engage students while you take care of any logistics such as attendance or make-up work. This type of assignment motivates students, and doesn't produce more papers for teachers to grade!

The many assignments given during class and for homework must be challenging, meaningful, and obtainable for a student to spend time completing them. Use table 7.4 to analyze your assignments. Determine whether your assignments are a valuable use of time or a potential cause of disengagement; adjust them accordingly.

Table 7.4: Characteristics of Ineffective and Effective Assignments

Assignments That Students Do Not Complete	Assignments That Students Do Complete
Students don't know how to do the work or need assistance to do the work.	Students know how to do the work, can complete it independently, and feel a sense of pride and accomplishment upon completion.
Purpose is unclear.	Purpose is clear to students.
Directions are unclear.	Students are able to follow directions.
The assignment is too long or has too much to do.	The assignment requires a reasonable amount of work; students learn by doing.
Students find the work: Not interesting Too difficult Too easy Not relevant Not important The same old thing Boring A waste of time	Students find the work: Challenging Novel, interesting, and enjoyable Important Relevant Just the right amount A quality use of time

What Do You Do When a Student Settles for Minimum Competency?

Some students seem to be satisfied with just getting by. It is up to the teacher to set learning expectations, however. If you feel that a particular student needs to take more steps forward, you must make that expectation clear.

Grades can inadvertently reinforce a student's decision to stop trying and settle for what he or she has already achieved. Once we have graded something and students see a percentage or a grade, they often feel the assignment is final—even when you know they are capable of making better grades. The education world seems to accept and be satisfied with minimum competency: passing is enough. Capable learners do not have to work as hard as struggling learners, and for them it is easier to settle for a passing grade or meet standards than it is to work hard. When teachers evaluate work by checking it off or assigning a grade, while knowing a student can go further, they contribute to this problem. Consider not grading student work until it is at the level of quality you expect.

Create assignments that require improvement. Assess background knowledge to find out what the student knows. Use the data from the assessment to determine what the student needs to learn next, and then design a differentiated, challenging assignment that makes the student think, problem solve, and learn more. This also helps a bored student find excitement and perhaps some motivation.

Check in with the student's family. Parents may be able to offer more information that will lead to the cause of this unmotivated behavior. Parents may also be able to provide support and encouragement at home.

Even though it takes time to plan stimulating activities that meet individual needs and tap individual interests, it is worth the effort. Create mysteries to entice students to come to class anxiously anticipating what learning or activity will be next. Don't cap any student's potential; keep stoking the flame of engagement so that it continues to burn.

How Do You Get Students to Participate in Discussions?

Provide think time before the discussion. Often students need to get prepared before taking a risk in front of others. Think time not only allows learners to pull thoughts and questions together and organize them before speaking in a group, but also builds anticipation of what is going to be discussed.

Share the topic and discussion questions pertaining to the topic as an introduction to this thinking time. During this time, move among the students and probe for responses. With your affirmation, learners will be more likely to offer their thoughts in the group.

Another way to get unmotivated students answering questions is to use partner discussion time. Remember, when partners answer questions, half of the class is giving the answer instead of just one student in the whole group. Another way to motivate a learner to answer is to put the discussion in the form of a game and vary how you call on students and how they can respond. Try the following suggestions to engage nonparticipants:

- When you call on a student, allow him or her to answer or pass. When a student passes, he or she can call on the next person to answer. If a learner passes more than twice, ask the student to offer a question he or she is wondering or confused about. This parameter does not put the student on the spot, which has potential to further disengage him or her, but it does require participation. Questions are great contributions to discussion as they signal to others that it is OK not to know. In fact, students learn when they identify questions and struggle with the concepts.

- When a student answers, allow him or her to call on the next person.
- Pull names out of a hat, box, or bag to make who answers the luck of the draw.
- Let students call on each other.
- Form groups and let the spokesperson answer for the group.
- Jot down the answer to the question and place it in a secret place in the classroom; ask students to run around and take a peek.
- Celebrate valuable input with affirmations, claps, or some other marking of success.
- Use clickers, whiteboards, or response cards to get every learner responsible for revealing the answer to the question. Ask the students how and why they know their answers are correct.
- Assign the nonparticipant a role, such as captain of a team. This responsibility builds trust and shows that he or she is a valued member of the class community.

Prior to the discussion, ask students to write down two comments and a question they plan to offer the group. Some students will be more secure in offering their ideas.

Some students will not answer because of the many put-downs they have experienced from adults. When a student gives an answer or expresses his or her point of view in the classroom, be sure to acknowledge the response. Avoid degrading or dismissing students' perceptions.

How Do You Get Students to Complete Ungraded Assignments?

Most teachers spend hours grading papers. Some of this is necessary if the paper is a graded assessment or a summative assessment to evaluate the learning students have achieved. Formative assessment, by design, supports learning and helps teachers understand what learners know and do not know so they can learn more. If we don't grade an assignment, there must be another, more important reason for students to complete it. If students are unclear about what to do or why they are doing an assignment, there is a good possibility they will not do it. However, just because we do grade something does not mean the grade always goes in the gradebook.

When a paper is returned, students first look for the grade. The teacher did all that work, and the only value students perceive lies in the grade. In order for this thinking to shift, students need to see their assignments tied explicitly to their learning. Try the following:

- Put learning objectives on the assignment.
- Ask students to self-assess and identify their strengths and what they need to work on.
- Require them to work on it either in the class activity or on their own time.
- When students show growth and learn more about a concept, provide a grade, and give them full credit for their learning.
- Use the assignment in a class activity. For example, have students analyze their mistakes in small groups and report to the class how they will respond differently next

time. Learners can share their answers to questions and then collectively come up with another answer that synthesizes and deepens the answer they individually thought.

- Provide time for students to score their own assignments as soon as they complete them.

- Call on students to share one of their answers and their problem-solving process. This creates buy-in from learners because they know if they do not do the work, their peers will know it—and most kids do not want to be embarrassed in front of their peers. Students also get instant feedback about what is right and wrong and hear others explain their answers; everyone starts to understand the inside thinking and problem-solving process. Remember to give students another opportunity to demonstrate their learning.

When students start to see the fruits of their labor—the work invested in these formative assignments—learning increases, better grades follow, and the individual score won't be their focus anymore.

In-class assessment activities are a better use of the teacher's time than grading busywork, because students are responsible for the work. To be effective and get student buy-in, the ungraded activity must meet the student's personal learning needs. Though teachers often expect students to complete an assignment just because they have been told to do it, communicating clear reasons for completing the work and showing how it is tied to learning will better develop a sense of intrinsic desire and accomplishment.

What Do You Say When a Student Asks, "Why Do We Have to Learn This?"

This is a great opportunity to reiterate to students why this information is so important to learn. Each piece of learning has a purpose, and students need to know it. Explain the purpose of the lesson and what standards will be learned. Do not get impatient when learners ask this more than once. Perhaps they are testing to see if a teacher is really serious about this assignment or learning. A solid purpose for the assignment and the learning objective is needed.

Another effective strategy to address this question is to turn it back on the students. Ask individuals, pairs, or small groups to brainstorm all the possible ways the intended learning could be used or applied in the future. Tap learners' insights to strengthen the learning community. By flipping the question to the class, teachers signal that they value and trust the contributions of students. Each individual needs to have a personal, compelling reason to know the information or experience the assignment in order to engage. When learners realize and see the importance and connection in the concepts, they become more willing to do the assigned task. In particular, if there is a direct way students will use the information in the future, be sure to explain that to them. Be proactive. Ask students to reflect on this question and their comments at the end or the beginning of a lesson to see if they can draw the relationship between an activity or assignment and learning goal. If not, then they are going to need another explanation.

If there is not a good response to this question, it may be that this particular assignment or task is not as essential as it initially seemed when planned. A teacher has the opportunity and responsibility to reflect and adjust accordingly. If it appears the assignment is not as essential, consider moving on to deeper and more relevant tasks. If the assignment is relevant, consistently refer back to the message and the relevance. It is the glue that holds the lesson together and makes the information or concepts stick for students.

What Do You Do About the Student Who Is Constantly Talking With Peers Instead of Listening?

Sometimes, visiting with friends is more important to students than the instructional activity or learning at hand. Many students are driven by a strong need to connect interpersonally and belong or fit in. These learners are happy when given assignments such as working with a partner or small group, assisting a peer, distributing papers, or leading a team during a task. In addition, many interpersonal learners thrive on feedback and specific praise from others. Offer them a blend of opportunities that allows time to work alone and time to work with others.

Don't assume that students who are talking are necessarily off task. Find out what they are discussing. Often teachers will discover these students are on target. Rather than take instructional time to address off-task behavior, consider this kind of talk as a signal that you need to stop talking and provide time for students to process in partners or small groups.

If off-task talking persists, then the obvious thing to do is to separate the students. However, do this only after reflecting on the structure of the classroom and the amount of time you are allocating for students to talk and connect with their learning rather than listen to an adult talk.

Some students continue to talk no matter where they sit. If they have preferred seating locations, bribery is an alternative: "As long as you stay on task, you can remain sitting here. This means that you are talking during designated times for sharing and discussion and not while I am talking." Make sure the learner knows that the teacher realizes he or she often has something to say that is beneficial for the whole class to hear. Encourage the student to talk appropriately: "Instead of talking with just your neighbor, raise your hand and share your input with everyone."

Communicate to students that there should be no talking when a student is speaking to the whole class. Respect must be given to any student who is contributing, and everyone in the room should be a quality listener. Stop and wait. Ask the student to repeat the comment. Ask another student to summarize what his or her classmate just said. Use tricks such as these to keep the focus on the value of the ideas that classmates contribute versus trying to control behavior, which can sometimes feel like herding cats.

Adults need to model this attentive listening at all times. It is not right for teachers to require students to be active listeners but to use the time when a student is talking to prepare materials or gather their thoughts about the next activities. Teachers must show students they are listening to them, too.

How Do You Motivate Students Who Are Difficult to Like?

Some students are more likeable than others, and students can tell whether we like them or not. While some student behavior can be difficult to manage, it only gets worse when students know that we do not like them. How do we avoid making students feel like we don't like them?

Get to know the students who cause you the most difficulty, and find the good in them. Find out their likes and their talents, and plan ways to provide assignments that address their way of learning. Be friendly with a warm smile, handshake, high five, or a thumbs-up for accomplishments. Call them by name to say hello. Check in with them when you notice them upset, happy, or frustrated. Do these things to let them know you genuinely care. Show each student with sincerity that you are glad he or she is a member of your classroom.

Most importantly, always address what students do wrong, or their specific behavior, when employing discipline procedures. Never address a student's personal characteristics or label him or her "problematic" or "bad"—keep your comments focused on the student's *actions*.

What Do You Do When a Student Avoids In-Class Work?

Not only do some students refuse to do the assignment after being given the instructions and told that it is time to work, they seem not to care if they are punished! A power struggle can easily emerge, and students often end up winning the battle and having more fun getting in trouble than learning.

Suppose a student puts his head on the desk, or even dozes. He gets a great, refreshing daydream or nap! Sleeping can simply indicate that a student did not get enough rest the night before or had a big lunch. If this is the case, the learner needs to move, get a drink of water, or do some other action to be re-energized and motivated.

However, this refusal can also be a sign of learning issues. If the student does not understand and does not know how to move forward, his or her inaction might be caused by overwhelming feelings. This student needs the task broken down into manageable chunks. Try giving students one step to complete. Go back and check in, and address issues that may have emerged. Then provide the next step. When students experience success, they will be more willing to take risks and try tasks on their own. Other students may refuse because they find a task boring or irrelevant. Depending on the situation, ask the learners to design their own assignment that they might find more interesting. The only rule is that it must address the same topic or learning objective.

Suppose another student refuses to work and is sent to the assistant principal's office. The hall gives her a much-needed stretch and change of scenery. She sees other friends out in the hall and waves excitedly to friends in the other classrooms. When she gets to the office, she visits with the other students while waiting to see the assistant principal. When she finally faces the administrator, she gets a tongue-lashing and then heads back to class, and along the way has another adventure in the hall! On reentering the classroom, she gets to disrupt the class once again and interfere with learning and teaching. As she walks back to her desk, the activity she wanted to avoid is complete, and the class is moving on. She's feeling quite satisfied that she went on a more exciting journey than remaining in class, and given the effect, will probably try this tactic again. As each student and situation is different, pay close attention to the effect the response has on a learner's behavior. If the desired result is achieved, the tactic worked. If not, try something different.

A failing grade rarely motivates a student to do the activity. She needs a better reason to engage. If she's already failing, another low grade will just be a reminder of her lack of success. And, it will deepen the hole she is probably already in in terms of her grades. With a deep hole, students may see little hope of recovering and won't try because they don't think it will do any good.

If at all possible, do not add to the power struggle by giving in to a tantrum and sending the student to the office. Do not give in to the student's whining and fussing. Show that you cannot be manipulated. Avoid taking this defiance personally. More than likely, refusal is not about you or an attempt to disrespect you. Consider the underlying cause and redirect as often as possible.

What Do You Do When the Learner Is Too Engaged and Won't Begin the Next Task?

Is there such a thing as too much engagement? Suppose a teacher has instructed students to finish up their work and move to the next task, but one student is so deeply involved that he keeps working or won't leave his station. This is difficult, because we value engagement. But this has potential to disrupt the whole class.

Consider the following strategies to proactively avoid this problem:

- Build in "Time's nearly up!" signals, or use timers with a warning bell so that students know, for example, that in five minutes it will be time to move. This helps them start mentally preparing to stop before you ask.

- Have students work in teams that compete in a race to see who can move to the next place or get ready to begin the next task first. This adds team pressure to move on so they can win or not be last.

- Enforce time limits regularly and with all students. If teachers sometimes give in and sometimes do not, learners get confused. The learner will think, "The last time I got away with it, so maybe this time I will, too." Students are motivated to push us to the limit, so nip these kinds of problems in the bud. In addition, whoever disobeys the rule should receive the same consequence. If a plan is announced, follow through with its promise, just as students are expected to do.

- Remember that adult reactions send messages to students about what's important. If teachers engage in a power struggle, the student behavior is going to continue or escalate.

To address this problem on a long-term basis with a child who struggles to manage time, consider the following:

- Use an agenda or planner to track independent assignments. Give the student a folder with assignments for a certain amount of time (a day, a week, or a whole unit). Providing this big-picture plan for the learner may help him or her expect to transition and plan accordingly. This way, the student knows the deadline to have *all* the work completed. More interesting or difficult assignments take longer, while others that are easy or not as interesting take less time. This puts the responsibility of managing time on the learner instead of on the teacher. The teacher must explicitly relay these expectations and parameters to the learner. Consider including a checklist of tasks in the packet so that students can check off each completed activity and quickly see how many remain. Tracking one's progress can be very motivational as progress is made!

- Ask the student what kind of movement, picture, or gesture you can show or perform to send the message it is time to stop and do something different. This nonverbal expression is sometimes a nice way to avoid multiple incessant verbal reminders, which usually end up escalating the frustration level.

Personal Performance and Implementation of the Motivational Strategies

Use table 7.5 (see page 214 for a reproducible version) to self-assess how well you keep the fire of engagement burning by implementing motivating strategies. You can revisit the self-assessment to check your progress all year.

Check the boxes according to the following characteristics:

- The fire is not yet lit—The wood is in place. I am considering and planning my next steps and just beginning to learn what the strategies are. I have not implemented any of them yet.

- The fire is lit—I am just beginning to implement the strategies and/or reflect on how some of the familiar strategies could be used more intentionally.

- The fire is burning—I have implemented many strategies and am seeing some results.

- The fire is roaring—I have implemented strategies intentionally, and I'm seeing results!

Table 7.5: Personal Performance and Implementation of Motivational Strategies

Strategy	The Fire Is Not Yet Lit	The Fire Is Lit	The Fire Is Burning	The Fire Is Roaring	Additional Notes
1. Know your students' interests, personalities, and beliefs (page 24).					
2. Discover how your students learn best (page 30).					
3. Be culturally responsive (page 38).					
4. Build relationships with and among students (page 43).					
5. Set clear rules and expectations (page 48).					
6. Clarify learning (page 71).					
7. Drive instruction with assessments (page 76).					
8. Provide challenging learning opportunities (page 86).					
9. Make connections (page 90).					
10. Co-create criteria and activities (page 94).					
11. Use irresistible hooks and clever closures (page 104).					
12. Get plugged in (page 110).					
13. Play games to learn, review, and remember (page 115).					
14. Spice it up (page 119).					
15. Create optimism and celebrate! (page 123).					
16. Provide quality choices (page 134).					
17. Set a goal, make a deal (page 138).					
18. Use the arts (page 145).					
19. Use assessment before, during, and after learning (page 164).					
20. Ignite thinking with probing questions (page 168).					
21. Fire up understanding (page 172).					
22. Provide descriptive feedback (page 175).					
23. Praise and inspire with specific comments (page 180).					
24. Get students involved (page 183).					
25. Respond with targeted interventions (page 188).					

Final Thoughts

> The greater the obstacle, the more glory in overcoming it.
>
> —Molière

Teachers encourage or discourage students' engagement through words, silence, actions, or even a glance. A teacher's practices and policies send messages to students about the definition of a successful learner. In many of today's schools, a successful student is one who can pass tests and make good grades. This is a misleading message that may cause some students who feel they are not good test takers to lose confidence and find it difficult to learn. Others find this focus on grades and testing monotonous and boring. And yet, in any case, these learners can be incredible problem solvers! Unfortunately, they often feel defeated and not smart in the classroom. No wonder they decide not to participate. On the other hand, many students engage for the sole purpose of getting the high test score and good grade and use little or nothing of what they learn.

Effective teachers identify and celebrate their students' diverse talents, interests, and learning styles. Motivating teachers help students see connections between what they like and understand and new information being taught. They teach students to take more responsibility for their own learning by involving them in assessing their progress and showing them how to recognize and reuse strategies that lead to success.

Teachers with the capacity to motivate learners:

- Are prepared with a strong knowledge base
- Enjoy coming to work
- Have a sense of humor
- Plan effectively
- Use novelty
- Use innovative strategies based on students' interests and learning needs
- Work as part of a collaborative team that supports student learning
- Are willing to share and accept ideas during brainstorming
- Expect students to learn
- Honor differences, and see them as strengths rather than deficits
- Ensure that the physical, mental, social, and emotional needs of students are met
- Use assessment data, both formal and informal, to guide teaching
- Become emotionally vested in the students' lives
- Use specific praise and feedback, and avoid put-downs

Teachers have tremendous power and control in what they do and say to motivate students to learn. We hope the ideas in this book spark inspiration and possibility so that teachers believe they can inspire and motivate students; it is all about finding the right fuel to ignite and keep the fire of engagement burning.

Chapter 7 Campfire Talk

This chapter summarized the ways that teachers can keep the flame of engagement burning and provided solutions for some common motivational problems. Consider your own understanding, perceptions, and experiences about what works to ensure that students really learn. Discuss the following questions and activities in your professional learning community, department, grade-level team, or a staff meeting with colleagues.

1 Consider observing each other's classrooms and providing feedback, using the following questions. Provide specific examples and suggestions for improvement.

- What is the teacher's definition of a successful learner? How was that apparent in the class?

- What actions did the teacher take when students were clearly unmotivated? How did student motivation change as a result?

- How did the teacher redirect unmotivated students to participate? Was this successful or not?

- How did the teacher connect classroom activities to the interests and needs of the learners?

- What innovative ideas were used to hold the students' attention?

- What enticing learning strategies did the instructor teach or model?

- What learning strategies did students use on their own? Were students involved in their learning? In what ways?

- How would you characterize students' overall approach to and attitude about the classroom experience?

- What amount of time was used for teacher-directed instruction? Student-directed instruction?

- Overall, what is working?

- Overall, what is not working?

- What are some suggestions and tips for improvement?

2 Form groups among your school staff to discuss schoolwide strategies to promote motivation. These can be listed and published in school handbooks and displayed on walls in teacher workrooms. Some may be made into posters for hallways and other displays.

3 Gather a group of students that represents the student body to brainstorm ways the school could motivate and support students.

4 Target individual concerns by having each team member share his or her biggest struggle to meet the individual motivational needs of students. Discuss the different questions or concerns, and collaborate on solutions and interventions.

5 Use the Questions Reflection reproducible (page 216) to reflect on the common questions about student misbehavior discussed in this chapter, and consider which of the twenty-five strategies in *Motivating Students* to use.

Personal Performance and Implementation of Motivational Strategies

Check the boxes according to the following characteristics:

- The fire is not yet lit—The wood is in place. I am considering and planning my next steps and just beginning to learn what the strategies are. I have not implemented any of them yet.
- The fire is lit—I am just beginning to implement the strategies and/or reflect on how some of the familiar strategies could be used more intentionally.
- The fire is burning—I have implemented many strategies and am seeing some results.
- The fire is roaring—I have implemented strategies intentionally, and I'm seeing results!

Strategy	The Fire Is Not Yet Lit	The Fire Is Lit	The Fire Is Burning	The Fire Is Roaring	Additional Notes
1. Know your students' interests, personalities, and beliefs (page 24).					
2. Discover how your students learn best (page 30).					
3. Be culturally responsive (page 38).					
4. Build relationships with and among students (page 43).					
5. Set clear rules and expectations (page 48).					
6. Clarify learning (page 71).					
7. Drive instruction with assessments (page 76).					
8. Provide challenging learning opportunities (page 86).					
9. Make connections (page 90).					
10. Co-create criteria and activities (page 94).					
11. Use irresistible hooks and clever closures (page 104).					

page 1 of 2

Strategy	The Fire Is Not Yet Lit	The Fire Is Lit	The Fire Is Burning	The Fire Is Roaring	Additional Notes
12. Get plugged in (page 110).					
13. Play games to learn, review, and remember (page 115).					
14. Spice it up (page 119).					
15. Create optimism and celebrate! (page 123).					
16. Provide quality choices (page 134).					
17. Set a goal, make a deal (page 138).					
18. Use the arts (page 145).					
19. Use assessment before, during, and after learning (page 164).					
20. Ignite thinking with probing questions (page 168).					
21. Fire up understanding (page 172).					
22. Provide descriptive feedback (page 175).					
23. Praise and inspire with specific comments (page 180).					
24. Get students involved (page 183).					
25. Respond with targeted interventions (page 188).					

Questions Reflection

Reflect on the common questions about student misbehavior, and consider which of the twenty-five strategies in *Motivating Students* to use.

Question	Reflections From the Text	New Ideas, Interventions, and Solutions
1. What do you do when a learner is unmotivated to perform, participate, or complete an assignment?		
2. What do you do when a student settles for minimum competency?		
3. How do you get students to participate in discussions?		
4. How do you get students to complete ungraded assignments?		
5. What do you say when a student asks, "Why do we have to learn this?"		
6. What do you do about the student who is constantly talking with peers instead of listening?		
7. How do you motivate students who are difficult to like?		
8. What do you do when a student avoids in-class work?		
9. What do you do when the learner is too engaged and won't begin the next task?		

References and Resources

Ainsworth, L. (2003a). *Power standards: Identifying the standards that matter most.* Englewood, CO: Advanced Learning Press.

Ainsworth, L. (2003b). *Unwrapping standards: A simple process to make standards manageable.* Englewood, CO: Advanced Learning Press.

Ainsworth, L., & Viegut, D. (2006). *Common formative assessments: How to connect standards-based instruction and assessment.* Thousand Oaks, CA: Corwin Press.

Allensworth, E., Correa, M., & Ponisciak, S. (2008). *From high school to the future: ACT preparation—too much, too late.* Chicago: Consortium on Chicago School Research.

Ames, C., & Archer, J. (1988). Achievement goals in the classroom: Students' learning strategies and motivation processes. *Journal of Educational Psychology, 80*(3), 260–267.

Apter, M. J. (2001). *Motivational styles in everyday life: A guide to reversal theory.* Washington, DC: American Psychological Association.

Barker, K., Dowson, M., & McInerney, D. M. (2002). Performance approach, performance avoidance and depth of information processing: A fresh look at relations between students' academic motivation and cognition. *Educational Psychology, 22,* 571–589.

Barkley, S. G. (2007). *Tapping student effort: Increasing student achievement.* Cadiz, KY: Performance Learning Systems.

Barton, A. C., Tan, E., & Rivet, A. (2008). Creating hybrid spaces for engaging school science among urban middle school girls. *American Educational Research Journal, 45*(1), 68–103.

Becker, B. E., & Luthar, S. S. (2002). Social-emotional factors affecting achievement outcomes among disadvantaged students: Closing the achievement gap. *Educational Psychologist, 37,* 197–214.

Black, P., Harrison, C., Lee, C., Marshall, B., & Wiliam, D. (2003). *Assessment for learning: Putting it into practice.* London: Open University.

Black, P. J., & Wiliam, D. (1998). Inside the black box: Raising standards through classroom assessment. *Phi Delta Kappan, 80*(2), 139–148.

Block, P. (2003). *The answer to how is yes: Acting on what matters.* San Francisco: Berrett-Koehler.

BrainyMedia. (2010). *BrainyQuote.* Accessed at www.brainyquote.com/quotes/topics/topic_war.html on October 19, 2010.

Brophy, J. (2004). *Motivating students to learn* (2nd ed.). Mahwah, NJ: Erlbaum.

Brophy, J. (2005). Goal theorists should move on from performance goals. *Educational Psychologist, 40,* 167–176.

Brophy, J. (2010). Cultivating student appreciation of the value of learning. In R. Marzano (Ed.), *On excellence in teaching* (pp. 301–317). Bloomington, IN: Solution Tree Press.

Burke, K. (2010). *Balanced assessment: From formative to summative.* Bloomington, IN: Solution Tree Press.

Butler, R. (1988). Enhancing and undermining intrinsic motivation: The effects of task-involving and ego-involving evaluation on interest and performance. *British Journal of Educational Psychology, 78*(3), 210–216.

Carini, R. M., Kuh, G. D., & Klein, S. P. (2006). Student engagement and student learning: Testing the linkages. *Research in Higher Education, 47*(1), 1–32.

Carle, E. (1969). *A very hungry caterpillar.* New York: Philomel Books.

Chadwick, B. (1999, July 19–23). Consensus building institute at Eden Prairie Schools, MN.

Chapman, C., & King, R. (2005). *Differentiated assessment strategies: One tool doesn't fit all.* Thousand Oaks, CA: Corwin Press.

Chapman, C., & King, R. (2009a). *Differentiated instructional management: Work smarter, not harder!* Thousand Oaks, CA: Corwin Press.

Chapman, C., & King, R. (2009b). *Differentiated instructional strategies for reading in the content areas* (2nd ed.). Thousand Oaks, CA: Corwin Press.

Chapman, C., & King, R. (2009c). *Test success in the brain-compatible classroom.* Thousand Oaks, CA: Corwin Press.

Cherubini, G., Zambelli, F., & Boscolo, P. (2002). Student motivation: An experience of in-service education as a context for professional development of teachers. *Teaching and Teacher Education, 18,* 273–288.

Clarke, S. (2005). *Formative assessment in action: Weaving the elements together.* London: Hodder Arnold.

Conrad, F. (1992). *The arts in education and a meta-analysis.* Unpublished doctoral dissertation, Purdue University, West Lafayette.

Covington, M. N. (2002). Rewards and intrinsic motivation: A needs-based developmental perspective. In F. Pajares & T. Urdan (Eds.), *Academic motivation of adolescents* (pp. 169–192). Greenwich, CT: Information Age.

Crooks, T. J. (1988). The impact of classroom evaluation practices on students. *Review of Educational Research, 58*(4), 438–481.

Davies, A. (2007a). Involving students in the classroom assessment process. In D. Reeves (Ed.), *Ahead of the curve: The power of assessment to transform teaching and learning* (pp. 31–58). Bloomington, IN: Solution Tree Press.

Davies, A. (2007b). *Making classroom assessment work* (2nd ed.). Courtenay, British Columbia, Canada: Connections.

Denton, P. (2007). *The power of words: Teacher language that helps children learn.* Greenfield, MA: Northeast Foundation for Children.

Dodge, D. T., & Colker, L. J. (2001). *The creative curriculum for early childhood.* Washington, DC: Teaching Strategies.

Dörnyei, Z. (2001). *Teaching and researching motivation.* New York: Longman.

Dowson, M., & McInerney, D. M. (2003). What do students say about their motivational goals? Towards a more complex and dynamic perspective on student motivation. *Contemporary Educational Psychology, 28,* 91–113.

DuFour, R., Eaker, R., & DuFour, R. (Eds.). (2005). *On common ground: The power of professional learning communities.* Bloomington, IN: Solution Tree Press.

Dunn, R., Griggs, S. A., Olson, J., Beasley, M., & Gorman, B. S. (1995). A meta-analytic validation of the Dunn and Dunn model of learning-style preferences. *Journal of Educational Research, 88*(6), 353–362.

Dweck, C. S. (1999). *Self-theories: Their role in motivation, personality, and development.* Philadelphia: Psychology Press.

Dweck, C. S. (2006). *Mindset: The new psychology of success.* New York: Random House.

Elliot, A. J., & Thrash, T. M. (2004). The intergenerational transmission of fear of failure. *Personality and Social Psychology Bulletin, 30,* 957–971.

Ferriter, W. M., & Garry, A. (2010). *Teaching the iGeneration: Five easy ways to introduce essential skills with web 2.0 tools.* Bloomington, IN: Solution Tree Press.

Fisher, D., & Frey, N. (2007). *Checking for understanding: Formative assessment techniques for your classroom.* Alexandria, VA: Association for Supervision and Curriculum Development.

Foster, M. (1997). *Black teachers on teaching.* New York: New Press.

Frey, N., Fisher, D., & Everlove, S. (2009). *Productive group work: How to engage students, build teamwork, and promote understanding.* Alexandria, VA: Association for Supervision and Curriculum Development.

Furr, C., & Skinner, E. (2003). Sense of relatedness as a factor in children's academic engagement and performance. *Journal of Educational Psychology, 95,* 148–162.

Gareis, C. R., & Grant, L. W. (2008). *Teacher-made assessments: How to connect curriculum, instruction, and student learning.* Larchmont, NY: Eye on Education.

Garmston, R., & Wellman, B. (1999). *The adaptive school: A sourcebook for developing collaborative groups.* Norwood, MA: Christopher-Gordon.

Gay, G. (2002). Preparing for culturally responsive teaching. *Journal of Teacher Education, 53,* 106–116.

Glasser, W. (1999). *Choice theory: A new psychology of personal freedom.* New York: HarperCollins.

Green, J., Martin, A. J., & Marsh, H. W. (2007). Motivation and engagement in English, mathematics and science high school subjects: Towards an understanding of multidimensional domain specificity. *Learning and Individual Differences, 17,* 269–279.

Guskey, T. (2004). Are zeros your ultimate weapon? *Education Digest: Essential Readings Condensed for Quick Review, 70*(3), 31–35.

Guskey, T. (2009). Using assessments to improve teaching and learning. In D. Reeves (Ed.), *Ahead of the curve: The power of assessment to transform teaching and learning* (pp. 15–29). Bloomington, IN: Solution Tree Press.

Guskey, T. R., & Bailey, J. M. (2001). *Developing grading and reporting systems for student learning.* Thousand Oaks, CA: Corwin Press.

Hareli, S., & Weiner, B. (2000). Accounts for success as determinants of perceived arrogance and modesty. *Motivation and Emotion, 24,* 215–236.

Hareli, S., & Weiner, B. (2002). Social emotions and personality inferences: A scaffold for a new direction in the study of achievement motivation. *Educational Psychologist, 37,* 183–193.

Harker, L. (2008). *Laughter is an instant vacation: Humorous quotes on life.* Naperville, IL: Simple Truths.

Hattie, J. (2009). *Visible learning: A synthesis of over 800 meta-analyses relating to student achievement.* New York: Routledge.

Hattie, J., & Timperley, H. (2007). The power of feedback. *Review of Educational Research, 77*(1), 81–112.

Hoaglin, R. (1999). *Motivation and learning.* Unpublished action research project, Stoughton High School, Stoughton, Wisconsin.

Illinois State Board of Education. (2007). *Illinois assessment frameworks.* Accessed at www.isbe.state.il.us/assessment/iafindex.htm on October 4, 2009.

Inman, E. (2010, October 20). Study says genetic marker not predictor of heart disease. *The Stanford Daily.* Accessed at www.stanforddaily.com/2010/10/20/heart on October 20, 2010.

Jensen, E. (2001). *Arts with the brain in mind.* Alexandria, VA: Association for Supervision and Curriculum Development.

Jensen, E., & Nickelsen, L. (2008). *Deeper learning & powerful strategies for in-depth and longer-lasting learning.* Thousand Oaks, CA: Corwin Press.

Kardash, C. A. M., & Wright, L. (1987). Does creative drama benefit elementary students: A meta-analysis. *Youth Theater Journal, 1*(3), 11–18.

Kidder, T. (2010). *Quotations about teachers.* Accessed at www.quotegarden.com/teachers.html on September 27, 2010.

Kleinfeld, J. (1975). Effective teachers of Eskimo and Indian students. *School Review, 83*(2), 301–344.

Ladson-Billings, G. (1995). But that's just good teaching! The case for culturally relevant pedagogy. *Theory into Practice, 34,* 159–165.

Lambert, L. (2003). *Leadership capacity for lasting school improvement.* Alexandria, VA: Association for Supervision and Curriculum Development.

Linnenbrink, E. A., & Pintrich, P. R. (2003). Achievement goals and intentional conceptual change. In G. M. Sinatra & P. R. Pintrich (Eds.), *Intentional conceptual change* (pp. 347–374). Mahwah, NJ: Erlbaum.

Ma, X. (1999). A meta-analysis of the relationship between anxiety toward mathematics and achievement in mathematics. *Journal for Research in Mathematics Education, 30*(5), 520–541.

Martin, A. J. (2002). Motivation and academic resilience: Developing a model of student enhancement. *Australian Journal of Education, 46,* 34–49.

Martin, A. J. (2003). Boys and motivation: Contrasts and comparisons with girls' approaches to school work. *Australian Educational Research, 30,* 43–65.

Martin, A. J. (2005). Exploring the effects of a youth enrichment program on academic motivation and engagement. *Social Psychology of Education, 8,* 179–206.

Martin, A. J. (2006). Personal bests (PBs): A proposed multidimensional model and empirical analysis. *British Journal of Educational Psychology, 76,* 803–825.

Martin, A. J. (2007). Examining a multidimensional model of student motivation and engagement using a construct validation approach. *British Journal of Educational Psychology, 77,* 413–440.

Martin, A. J. (2008a). Enhancing student motivation and engagement: The effects of a multidimensional intervention. *Contemporary Educational Psychology, 33,* 239–269.

Martin, A. J. (2008b). Motivation and engagement in music and sport: Testing a multidimensional framework in diverse performance settings. *Journal of Personality, 76,* 135–170.

Martin, A. J. (2009). Age appropriateness and motivation, engagement and performance in high school: Effects of age-within-cohort, grade retention, and delayed school entry. *Journal of Educational Psychology, 101,* 101–114.

Martin, A. J., & Dowson, M. (2009). Interpersonal relationships, motivation, engagement, and achievement: Yields for theory, current issues, and educational practice. *Review of Educational Research, 79,* 327–365.

Martin, A. J., & Marsh, H. W. (2003). Fear of failure: Friend or foe? *Australian Psychologist, 38,* 31–38.

Martin, A. J., & Marsh, H. W. (2008). Academic buoyancy: Towards an understanding of students' everyday academic resilience. *Journal of School Psychology, 46,* 53–83.

Martin, A. J., Marsh, H. W., & Debus, R. L. (2001). Self-handicapping and defensive pessimism: Exploring a model of self-protection from a longitudinal perspective. *Journal of Educational Psychology, 93,* 87–102.

Marzano, R. J. (2003). *What works in schools: Translating research into action.* Alexandria, VA: Association for Supervision and Curriculum Development.

Marzano, R. J. (2006). *Classroom assessment and grading that work.* Alexandria, VA: Association for Supervision and Curriculum Development.

Marzano, R. J. (2007). *The art and science of teaching: A comprehensive framework for effective instruction.* Alexandria, VA: Association for Supervision and Curriculum Development.

Marzano, R. J. (2010). Using games to enhance student achievement. *Educational Leadership, 67*(5), 71–72.

Marzano, R. J., & Kendall, J. S. (2007). *The new taxonomy of educational objectives* (2nd ed.). Thousand Oaks, CA: Corwin Press.

Maslow, A. (1968). *Toward a psychology of being.* Princeton, NJ: Van Nostrand.

McTighe, J. (2010). Understanding by design and instruction. In R. Marzano (Ed.), *On excellence in teaching* (pp. 271–300). Bloomington, IN: Solution Tree Press.

Mendler, A. N. (2000). *Motivating students who don't care: Successful techniques for educators.* Bloomington, IN: Solution Tree Press.

Meyer, D. K., & Turner, J. C. (2002). Discovering emotion in classroom motivation research. *Educational Psychologist, 37*, 107–114.

New Horizons for Learning. (2002). *Assessment terminology: A glossary of useful terms.* Accessed at www .newhorizons.org/strategies/assess/terminology.htm on June 24, 2010.

Newmann, F. L., King, M. B., & Carmichael, D. (2007). *Authentic instruction and assessment: Common standards for rigor and relevance in teaching academic subjects.* Des Moines: Iowa Department of Education.

Nicholls, J. G., Cheung, P. C., Lauer, J., & Patashnick, M. (1989). Individual differences in academic motivation: Perceived ability, goals, beliefs, and values. *Learning and Individual Differences, 1*, 63–84.

O'Connor, K. (2002). *How to grade for learning: Linking grades to standards* (2nd ed.). Arlington Heights, IL: Skylight Press.

Ormiston, M. (2011). *Creating a digital-rich classroom: Teaching and learning in a web 2.0 world.* Bloomington, IN: Solution Tree Press.

Pajares, F. (2005). Self-efficacy beliefs in academic settings. *Review of Educational Research, 66*(4), 543–578.

Pearson Assessment Training Institute. (2010). *Getting started with classroom assessment for student learning: A one-day workshop.* Portland, OR: Author.

Pianta, R. C., Nimetz, S. L., & Bennett, E. (1997). Mother-child relationships, teacher-child relationships, and school outcomes in preschool and kindergarten. *Early Childhood Research Quarterly, 12*, 263–280.

Pink, D. H. (2009). *Drive: The surprising truth about what motivates us.* New York: Riverhead.

Pintrich, P. R. (2003). A motivational science perspective on the role of student motivation in learning and teaching contexts. *Journal of Educational Psychology, 95*, 667–686.

Popham, W. J. (2001). *The truth about testing: An educator's call to action.* Alexandria, VA: Association for Supervision and Curriculum Development.

Reeves, D. (2001). *Making standards work: How to implement standards-based assessment in the classroom, school and district* (3rd ed.). Englewood, CO: Advanced Learning Press.

Reeves, D. (Ed.). (2007). *Ahead of the curve: The power of assessment to transform teaching and learning.* Bloomington, IN: Solution Tree Press.

Reeves, J., Deci, E. L., & Ryan, R. M. (2004). Self-determination theory: A dialectical framework for understanding sociocultural influences on student motivation. In D. McInerney & S. Van Etten (Eds.), *Big theories revisited* (pp. 31–60). Greenwich, CT: Information Age.

Rideout, V. J., Foehr, U. G., & Roberts, D. F. (2010). *Generation M2: Media in the lives of 8- to 18-year-olds.* Menlo Park, CA: Henry J. Kaiser Family Foundation.

Robinson, J. (2008, October 13). *Classroom 2.0: The power of Nintendo DS* [Blog post]. Accessed at http:// thepegeek.com/2008/10/13/another-utter-mobile-post-2 on September 24, 2010.

Rubie-Davies, C. M. (2007). Classroom practices: Exploring high- and low-expectation teachers. *British Journal of Educational Psychology, 77*, 289–306.

Rubie-Davies, C. M., Hattie, J. A. C., & Hamilton, R. (2006). Expecting the best for students: Teacher expectations and academic outcomes. *British Journal of Educational Psychology, 77*, 429–444.

Ryan, R. M., & Deci, E. L. (2000). Self-determination theory and the facilitation of intrinsic motivation, social development, and well-being. *American Psychologist, 55*, 68–78.

Sadler, D. R. (1989). Formative assessment: Revisiting the territory. *Assessment in Education, 5*(1), 77–84.

Saphier, J. (2005). Masters of motivation. In R. DuFour, R. Eaker, & R. DuFour (Eds.), *On common ground: The power of professional learning communities* (pp. 85–114). Bloomington, IN: Solution Tree Press.

Schmoker, M. (2006). *Results now: How we can achieve unprecedented improvements in teaching and learning.* Alexandria, VA: Association for Supervision and Curriculum Development.

Schunk, D. H, & Miller, S. D. (2002). Self-efficacy and adolescents' motivation. In F. Pajares & T. Urdan (Eds.), *Academic motivation of adolescents* (pp. 29–52). Greenwich, CT: Information Age.

Schunk, D. H., & Zimmerman, B. J. (2007). Influencing children's self-efficacy and self-regulation of reading and writing through modeling. *Reading and Writing Quarterly, 23*(1), 7–25.

Schwartz, M., Sadler, P., Sonnert, G., & Tai, R. (2008, December). Depth versus breadth: How content coverage in high school science courses relates to later success in college science coursework. *Science Education,* 1–29.

Scieszka, J., & Smith, L. (1995). *Math curse.* New York: Viking.

Scieszka, J., & Smith, L. (2004). *Science verse.* New York: Viking.

Simple Truths. (2008). *Laughter is an instant vacation.* Naperville, IL: Author.

Sizer, T. (1984, 2004). *Horace's compromise: The dilemma of the American high school.* Boston: Houghton Mifflin.

Sousa, D. (2006). *How the brain learns.* Thousand Oaks, CA: Corwin Press.

Stiggins, R. J., Arter, J., Chappuis, J., & Chappuis, S. (2005). *Classroom assessment* for *student learning: Doing it right—using it well.* Portland, OR: ETS Assessment Training Institute.

Strong, R., Silver, H., & Perini, M. (2001). *Teaching what matters most: Standards and strategies for raising student achievement.* Alexandria, VA: Association for Supervision and Curriculum Development.

Study Island. (2010). *Illinois standards-based ISAT preparation.* Accessed at www.studyisland.com /demoAsk.cfm?myState=IL on June 24, 2010.

Tang, G., & Briggs, H. (2001). *The grapes of math.* New York: Scholastic Books.

Thompson, M., & Wiliam, D. (2007, April 9–13). *Tight but loose: A conceptual framework for scaling up school reforms.* Paper presented at the annual conference of the American Educational Research Association, Chicago, IL.

Vagle, N. (2009). Inspiring and requiring learning. In T. Guskey (Ed.), *The teacher as assessment leader* (pp. 85–114). Bloomington, IN: Solution Tree Press.

Weiner, B. (1994). Integrating social and personal theories of achievement striving. *Review of Educational Research, 64,* 557–573.

Weinstein, R. S. (2002). *Reaching higher: The power of expectations in schooling.* Cambridge, MA: Harvard University Press.

Wentzel, K. R. (1999). Social-motivational processes and interpersonal relationships: Implications for understanding motivation at school. *Journal of Educational Psychology, 91,* 76–97.

Whitaker, T. (2003). *What great teachers do differently.* Larchmont, NY: Eye on Education.

Wigfield, A., & Tonks, S. (2002). Adolescents' expectancies for success and achievement task values during the middle and high school years. In F. Pajares & T. Urdan (Eds.), *Academic motivation of adolescents* (pp. 53–82). Greenwich, CT: Information Age.

Wiggins, G., & McTighe, J. (1998). *Understanding by design.* Alexandria, VA: Association for Supervision and Curriculum Development.

Wiliam, D. (2007). Keeping learning on track: Classroom assessment and the regulation of learning. In F. K. Lester Jr. (Ed.), *Second handbook of mathematics teaching and learning* (pp. 1053–1098). Greenwich, CT: Information Age.

Willis, J. (2008). *Research-based strategies to ignite student learning.* Alexandria, VA: Association for Supervision and Curriculum Development.

Wolfe, P. (2001). *Brain matters: Translating research into classroom practice.* Alexandria, VA: Association for Supervision and Curriculum Development.

Yount, W. (2009, September 4). *Mrs. Yount's class news* [Weblog]. Accessed at http://blog.oconee .k12.ga.us/wyount/page/2 on June 24, 2010.

Zimmerman, B. (2008). Investigating self-regulation and motivation: Historical background, methodological developments, and future prospects. *American Educational Research Journal, 45*(1), 166–183.

Index

You've Got to Reach Them to Teach Them
Mary Kim Schreck
Navigate the hot topic of student engagement with a true expert. Become empowered to demand an authentic joy for learning in your classroom. Real-life notes from the field, detailed discussions, practical strategies, and space for reflection complete this essential guide to student engagement.
BKF404

Motivating Students Who Don't Care
Allen N. Mendler
Spark enthusiasm in your classroom. Proven strategies and five effective processes (emphasizing effort, creating hope, respecting power, building relationships, and expressing enthusiasm) empower you to reawaken motivation in students who aren't prepared, don't care, and won't work.
BKF360

Enriched Learning Projects
James Bellanca
Foreword by Bob Pearlman
Translate standards-based content into enriched learning projects that build 21st century skills. A valuable tool for teachers, this book helps develop critical thinking and creative skills, highlights useful e-tools, and presents a variety of research-based instructional strategies.
BKF296

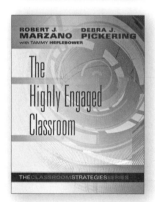

The Highly Engaged Classroom
Robert J. Marzano and Debra J. Pickering
With Tammy Heflebower
Gain in-depth understanding of how to generate high levels of student attention and engagement. Using the suggestions in this book, every teacher can create a classroom environment where engagement is the norm, not the exception.
BKL005

Solution Tree | Press

a division of
Solution Tree

Visit solution-tree.com or call 800.733.6786 to order.